Air Fryer Cookbook

365 Days of Quick & Effortless Air Fryer Recipes
for Beginners and Advanced Users

By Jason Muniz

Table of Contents

VEGAN

Air Grilled Tofu

(**Ready in about** 15 minutes | **Servings** 3)

Ingredients

8 ounces firm tofu, pressed and cut into bite-sized cubes
1 tablespoon tamari sauce
1/2 teaspoon onion powder
1 teaspoon peanut oil
1/2 teaspoon garlic powder

Directions

Toss the tofu cubes in a bowl with the tamari sauce, peanut oil, garlic powder, and onion powder.

Cook your tofu for about 13 minutes in a preheated Air Fryer at 380 degrees F, shaking the basket once or twice to ensure even browning.

Good appetite!

Per serving: 112 Calories; 6.6g Fat; 3.6g Carbs; 12.1g Protein;

Golden Beet Salad with Tahini Sauce

(**Ready in about** 40 minutes | **Servings** 2)

Ingredients

2 golden beets
Sea salt and ground black pepper, to taste
2 tablespoons soy sauce
1/2 jalapeno pepper, chopped
1 clove garlic, pressed
1 tablespoon sesame oil
2 tablespoons tahini
2 cups baby spinach
1 tablespoon white vinegar
1/4 teaspoon ground cumin

Directions

Toss the golden beets with sesame oil. Cook the golden beets in the preheated Air Fryer at 400 degrees F for 40 minutes, turning them over once or twice to ensure even cooking.

Let your beets cool completely and then, slice them with a sharp knife. Place

the beets in a salad bowl and add in salt, pepper and baby spinach.

In a small mixing dish, whisk the remaining Ingredients until well combined.

Spoon the sauce over your beets, toss to combine and serve immediately. Bon appétit!

Per serving: 253 Calories; 18.1g Fat; 19.1g Carbs; 6.4g Protein; 10.1

Easy Roasted Fennel

(**Ready in about** 25 minutes | **Servings** 3)

Ingredients

1 pound fennel bulbs, sliced
1 tablespoon olive oil
1/2 teaspoon dried marjoram
1/2 teaspoon dried basil
1/4 cup vegan mayonnaise
Sea salt and ground black pepper, to taste

Directions

Toss the fennel slices with the olive oil and spices and transfer them to the Air Fryer cooking basket.

Roast the fennel at 370 degrees F for about 20 minutes, shaking the basket once or twice to promote even cooking.

Serve the fennel slice with mayonnaise and enjoy!

Per serving: 158 Calories; 11.2g Fat; 13.1g Carbs; 3.4g Protein

Asian-Style Brussels Sprouts

(**Ready in about** 20 minutes | **Servings** 3)

Ingredients

1 pound Brussels sprouts, trimmed and halved
1 tablespoon agave syrup
1 teaspoon rice vinegar
1 clove garlic, minced
1 tablespoon sesame seeds, toasted
2 tablespoons Shoyu sauce
1 teaspoon coconut oil
1/2 teaspoon Gochujang paste
2 scallion stalks, chopped

Directions

Toss the Brussels sprouts with coconut oil, Shoyu sauce, agave syrup, rice vinegar, Gochujang paste and garlic.

Cook the Brussels sprouts in the preheated Air Fryer at 380 degrees F for 15 minutes, shaking the basket halfway through the cooking time.

Place the roasted Brussels sprouts on a serving platter and garnish with scallions and sesame seeds. Serve immediately!

Per serving: 124 Calories; 3.6g Fat; 21.1g Carbs; 5.9g Protein;

Korean-Style Broccoli

(**Ready in about** 12 minutes | **Servings** 2)

Ingredients

1/2 pound broccoli florets
1/4 teaspoon coriander seeds
1/2 teaspoon garlic powder
1 tablespoon brown sugar
1 tablespoon sesame oil

1 tablespoon soy sauce
1/2 teaspoon gochukaru
(Korean red chili powder)
Sea salt and ground black
pepper, to taste

Directions

Toss the broccoli florets with the other Ingredients until well coated.

Air fry your broccoli at 390 degrees F for about 10 minutes, shaking the basket halfway through the cooking time.

Serve with your favorite vegan dip. Enjoy!

Per serving: 141 Calories; 8.6g Fat; 14.2g Carbs; 3.9g Protein;

Cauliflower Oatmeal Fritters

(**Ready in about** 20 minutes | **Servings** 3)

Ingredients

1/2 pound cauliflower florets
1 cup rolled oats
2 tablespoons sunflower
seeds
1 glove garlic, chopped
Kosher salt and freshly
ground black pepper, to taste
1 tablespoon canola oil

1 tablespoons flaxseed meal
1 small yellow onion
4 tablespoons pumpkin seeds
butter
1/2 teaspoon smoked paprika
2 tablespoons hemp hearts

Directions

In a food processor or blender, combine all of the ingredients and blend until well combined. After that, form the mixture into small patties and place them in the Air Fryer cooking basket.

Cook the cauliflower patties for 16 minutes in a preheated Air Fryer at 375°F, shaking the basket halfway through to ensure even browning. Good appetite!

Per serving: 408 Calories; 18.3g Fat; 45.5g Carbs; 16.1g Protein;

Louisiana-Style Eggplant Cutlets

(**Ready in about** 45 minutes | **Servings** 3)

Ingredients

1 pound eggplant, cut
lengthwise into
1 cup fresh bread crumbs
1/2-inch thick slices
Sea salt and ground black
pepper, to taste 1 cup tomato
sauce

1/4 cup almond milk
1/4 cup plain flour
1 teaspoon Cajun seasoning
mix
1 teaspoon brown mustard
1/2 teaspoon chili powder

Directions

Toss your eggplant with 1 teaspoon of salt and leave it for 30 minutes; drain and rinse the eggplant and set it aside.

In a shallow bowl, mix the flour with almond milk until well combined. In a separate bowl, mix the breadcrumbs with Cajun seasoning mix, salt and black pepper.

Dip your eggplant in the flour mixture, then, coat each slice with the breadcrumb mixture, pressing to adhere.

Cook the breaded eggplant at 400 degrees F for 10 minutes, flipping them halfway through the cooking time to ensure even browning.

In the meantime, mix the remaining Ingredients for the sauce. Divide the tomato mixture between eggplant cutlets and continue to cook for another 5 minutes or until thoroughly cooked.

Transfer the warm eggplant cutlets to a wire rack to stay crispy. Bon appétit!

Per serving: 214 Calories; 1.3g Fat; 43g Carbs; 6.1g Protein;

Fried Green Beans

(**Ready in about** 10 minutes | **Servings** 2)

Ingredients

1/2 pound green beans,
cleaned and trimmed
1 tspn extra-virgin olive oil
1/2 teaspoon shallot powder
1/4 teaspoon cumin powder
1/2 teaspoon cayenne pepper
1 tablespoon soy sauce

1/2 teaspoon onion powder
1/2 teaspoon garlic powder
1/4 cup pecans,chopped
Himalayan salt and freshly
ground black pepper, to taste
1 tablespoon lime juice

Directions

Toss the green beans with olive oil, spices and lime juice.

Cook the green beans in your Air Fryer at 400 degrees F for 5 minutes, shaking the basket halfway through the cooking time to promote even cooking.

Toss the green beans with soy sauce and serve garnished with chopped pecans. Bon appétit!

Per serving: 162 Calories; 11.3g Fat; 13g Carbs; 4.1g Protein;

Famous Everything Bagel Kale Chips

(**Ready in about** 12 minutes | **Servings** 1)

Ingredients

2 cups loosely packed kale leaves, stems removed

Coarse salt and ground black pepper, to taste

1 teaspoon sesame seeds, lightly toasted

1 tablespoon nutritional yeast flakes

1/2 teaspoon poppy seeds, lightly toasted

1 teaspoon olive oil

1/4 teaspoon garlic powder

Directions

Toss the kale leaves with olive oil, nutritional yeast, salt and black pepper.

Cook your kale at 250 degrees F for 12 minutes, shaking the basket every 4 minutes to promote even cooking.

Place the kale leaves on a platter and sprinkle evenly with sesame seeds, poppy seeds and garlic powder while still hot. Enjoy!

Per serving: 134 Calories; 7.3g Fat; 12.1g Carbs; 7.5g Protein;

Portobello Mushroom Schnitzel

(**Ready in about** 10 minutes | **Servings** 2)

Ingredients

7 ounces Portobello mushrooms

1/3 cup beer

1/2 teaspoon porcini powder

1/2 teaspoon dried basil

1/4 cup chickpea flour

ground black pepper, to taste

Kosher salt

1/4 cup plain flour

1/2 teaspoon garlic powder

1 cup breadcrumbs

1/4 teaspoon dried oregano

1/4 teaspoon ground cumin

1/4 teaspoon ground bay leaf

1/2 teaspoon shallot powder

Directions

Set aside the Portobello mushrooms after patting them dry.

Then, in a rimmed plate, combine the flour and beer thoroughly. In a separate bowl, combine the breadcrumbs and spices.

Dip the mushrooms in the flour mixture, then in the breadcrumb mixture.

Cook the breaded mushrooms for 6 to 7 minutes in a preheated Air Fryer at 380 degrees F, flipping halfway through the cooking time. Consume while warm.

Per serving: 156 Calories; 1.4g Fat; 27.1g Carbs; 7.2g Protein;

Baby Potatoes with Garlic-Rosemary Sauce

(**Ready in about** 50 minutes | **Servings** 3)

Ingredients

1 pound baby potatoes, scrubbed

1 tablespoon fresh rosemary leaves, chopped

Salt and freshly ground black pepper

1/2 garlic bulb, slice the top 1/4-inch off the garlic head

1/2 cup white wine

1 tablespoon olive oil

1 teaspoon sherry vinegar

Directions

Brush the baby potatoes with olive oil and transfer them to the air Fryer cooking basket. Cook the baby potatoes at 400 degrees F for 12 minutes, shaking the basket halfway through the cooking time.

Place the garlic bulb into the center of a piece of aluminum foil. Drizzle the garlic bulb with a nonstick cooking spray and wrap tightly in foil.

Cook the garlic at 390 degrees F for about 25 minutes or until the cloves are tender.

Let it cool for about 10 minutes; remove the cloves by squeezing them out of the skins; mash the garlic and add it to a saucepan.

Stir the remaining Ingredients into the saucepan and let it simmer for 10 to 15 minutes until the sauce has reduced by half. Spoon the sauce over the baby potatoes and serve warm. Bon appétit!

Per serving: 166 Calories; 4.6g Fat; 28.1g Carbs; 3.5g Protein;

Authentic Platanos Maduros

(**Ready in about** 15 minutes | **Servings** 2)

Ingredients

1 very ripe, sweet plantain

1 teaspoon coconut oil, melted

1 teaspoon Caribbean Sorrel Rum Spice Mix

Directions

Cut your plantain into slices.

Toss your plantain with Caribbean Sorrel Rum Spice Mix and coconut oil.

Cook your plantain in the preheated Air Fryer at 400 degrees F for 10 minutes, shaking the cooking basket halfway through the cooking time.

Serve immediately and enjoy!

Per serving: 129 Calories; 2.5g Fat; 28.2g Carbs; 1.1g Protein;

Quinoa-Stuffed Winter Squash

(**Ready in about** 30 minutes | **Servings** 2)

Ingredients

1/2 cup quinoa
1 teaspoon sesame oil
1 clove garlic, pressed
1 tablespoon fresh parsley, roughly chopped
1 cup loosely mixed greens, torn into small pieces
1 small winter squash, halved lengthwise, seeds removed
Sea salt and ground black pepper, to taste

Directions

Rinse your quinoa, drain it and transfer to a pot with 1 cup of lightly salted water; bring to a boil.

Turn the heat to a simmer and continue to cook, covered, for about 10 minutes; add in the mixed greens and continue to cook for 5 minutes longer.

Stir in the sesame oil and garlic and stir to combine. Divide the quinoa mixture between the winter squash halves and sprinkle it with the salt and pepper.

Cook your squash in the preheated Air Fryer at 400 degrees F for about 12 minutes.

Place the stuffed squash on individual plates, garnish with fresh parsley and serve. Bon appétit!

Per serving: 279 Calories; 5.1g Fat; 53.1g Carbs; 8.7g Protein;

Italian-Style Tomato Cutlets

(**Ready in about** 10 minutes | **Servings** 2)

Ingredients

1 beefsteak tomato – sliced into halves
1/2 cup breadcrumbs
1/2 cup almond milk
1/2 cup all-purpose flour
1 teaspoon Italian seasoning mix

Directions

Pat the beefsteak tomato dry and set it aside.

In a shallow bowl, mix the all-purpose flour with almond milk. In another bowl, mix breadcrumbs with Italian seasoning mix.

Dip the beefsteak tomatoes in the flour mixture; then, coat the beefsteak tomatoes with the breadcrumb mixture, pressing to adhere to both sides.

Cook your tomatoes at 360 degrees F for about 5 minutes; turn them over and cook on the other side for 5 minutes longer. Serve at room temperature and enjoy!

Per serving: 181 Calories; 2.6g Fat; 32.2g Carbs; 6.1g Protein;

Paprika Squash Fries

(**Ready in about** 15 minutes | **Servings** 3)

Ingredients

1/4 cup rice milk
2 tablespoons nutritional yeast
1/4 teaspoon shallot powder
1/2 teaspoon paprika
1 pound butternut squash, peeled and into sticks
1/4 cup almond flour
Sea salt and ground black pepper, to taste
1/2 teaspoon garlic powder
1 cup tortilla chips, crushed

Directions

Combine the milk flour, nutritional yeast, and spices in a mixing bowl. Place the crushed tortilla chips in a separate shallow bowl.

Dip the butternut squash sticks into the batter, then roll them in the crushed tortilla chips until thoroughly coated.

Place the squash pieces in the cooking basket of the Air Fryer. Cook the squash fries for about 12 minutes at 400 degrees F, shaking the basket once or twice. Good appetite!

Per serving: 202 Calories; 5.8g Fat; 30.2g Carbs; 8.1g Protein;

Green Potato Croquettes

(**Ready in about** 45 minutes | **Servings** 2)

Ingredients

1/2 pound cup russet potatoes
1 cups loosely packed mixed greens, torn into pieces
1/4 teaspoon red pepper flakes, crushed
1/2 teaspoon garlic, pressed
1 teaspoon olive oil
Sea salt and ground black pepper, to taste
2 tablespoons oat milk

Directions

Cook your potatoes for about 30 minutes until they are fork-tender; peel the potatoes and add them to a mixing bowl.

Mash your potatoes and stir in the remaining Ingredients.

Shape the mixture into bite-sized balls and place them in the cooking basket; sprits the balls with a nonstick cooking oil.

Cook the croquettes at 390 degrees F for about 13 minutes, shaking the cooking basket halfway through the cooking time.

Serve with tomato ketchup if desired. Bon appétit!

Per serving: 137 Calories; 2.9g Fat; 25.2g Carbs; 4.1g Protein;

Old-Fashioned Potato Wedges

(**Ready in about** 15 minutes | **Servings** 2)

Ingredients

2 medium potatoes, scrubbed and cut into wedges
1 teaspoon shallot powder
1/4 teaspoon cayenne pepper
1 teaspoon garlic powder
1 teaspoon olive oil
Kosher salt and ground black pepper, to season

Directions

Toss the potato wedges with olive oil and spices and transfer them to the Air Fryer cooking basket.

Cook the potato wedges at 400 degrees F for 6 minutes; shake the basket and cook for another 6 to 8 minutes.

Serve with your favorite vegan dip. Bon appétit!

Per serving: 184 Calories; 2.4g Fat; 37.2g Carbs; 4.3g Protein;

Easy Homemade Falafel

(**Ready in about** 15 minutes | **Servings** 3)

Ingredients

1 cup dry chickpeas, soaked overnight
2 tablespoons fresh parsley
Sea salt and ground black pepper, to taste
2 tablespoons fresh cilantro
1 small onion, sliced
1/2 teaspoon cayenne pepper
2 cloves garlic
1/2 teaspoon ground cumin

Directions

Drain and rinse your chickpeas and place them in a bowl of a food processor.

Add in the remaining Ingredients and blitz until the Ingredients form a coarse meal. Roll the mixture into small balls with oiled hands.

Cook your falafel in the preheated Air Fryer at 395 degrees F for 5 minutes; turn them over and cook for another 5 to 6 minutes. Bon appétit!

Per serving: 274 Calories; 4.2g Fat; 46.7g Carbs; 14.3g Protein

Italian-Style Pasta Chips

(**Ready in about** 15 minutes | **Servings** 2)

Ingredients

1 cup dry rice pasta
1/2 teaspoon dried oregano
1/2 teaspoon dried basil
Kosher salt and ground black pepper, to taste
1 tablespoon nutritional yeast
1 teaspoon dried parsley flakes
1 teaspoon olive oil

Directions

Cook the pasta according to the manufacturer's instructions. Drain your pasta and toss it with the remaining Ingredients.

Cook the pasta chips at 390 degrees F for about 10 minutes, shaking the cooking basket halfway through the cooking time.

The pasta chips will crisp up as it cools.

Serve with tomato ketchup if desired. Bon appétit!

Per serving: 224 Calories; 3.4g Fat; 43.4g Carbs; 6.1g Protein;

Shawarma Roasted Chickpeas

(**Ready in about** 20 minutes | **Servings** 2)

Ingredients

8 ounces canned chickpeas
1/4 teaspoon turmeric powder
1/2 teaspoon ground coriander
1/4 teaspoon ground ginger
1/4 teaspoon allspice
1/4 teaspoon cinnamon
1/4 teaspoon smoked paprika
Coarse sea salt and freshly ground black pepper, to taste

Directions

Rinse the chickpeas under cold running water and pat them dry with kitchen towels.

Place the spices in a plastic bag with the chickpeas and shake until the chickpeas are evenly coated with the spices.

Transfer the spiced chickpeas to the Air Fryer cooking basket after sprinkling them with nonstick cooking oil.

Cook your chickpeas for 13 minutes in a 395°F preheated Air Fryer. Cook for an additional 6 minutes at 350 degrees F in your Air Fryer.

Per serving: 217 Calories; 9.4g Fat; 25.4g Carbs; 8g Protein;

Bell Pepper Fries

(**Ready in about** 15 minutes | **Servings** 2)

Ingredients

1 cup flour
1/2 teaspoon dried marjoram
1/2 teaspoon turmeric
powder
2 large bell peppers

1 cup oat milk
Sea salt and ground black
pepper, to taste
1 cup seasoned breadcrumbs

Directions

In a shallow bowl, thoroughly combine the flour, milk, marjoram, turmeric, salt and black pepper. In another bowl, place seasoned breadcrumbs.

Dip the pepper rings in the flour mixture; then, coat the rings with the seasoned breadcrumbs, pressing to adhere.

Transfer the pepper rings to the Air Fryer cooking basket and spritz them with a nonstick spray.

Cook the pepper rings at 380 degrees F for about 10 minutes, shaking the basket halfway through the cooking time to promote even cooking. Bon appétit!

Per serving: 392 Calories; 5.5g Fat; 71.1g Carbs; 13.4g Protein;

Polish Placki Ziemniaczan

(**Ready in about** 10 minutes | **Servings** 2)

Ingredients

1/2 pound potatoes, peeled
and finely grated
1/2 teaspoon turmeric
powder
2 tablespoons granulated
sugar
2 ounces sour cream

1/4 cup all-purpose flour
2 tablespoons breadcrumbs
Kosher salt and freshly
ground black pepper, to taste
2 tablespoons breadcrumbs

Directions

Place the grated potatoes in a triple layer of cheesecloth; now, twist and squeeze the potatoes until no more liquid comes out of them.

Place the potatoes in a mixing bowl; stir in the onion, flour, turmeric powder, breadcrumbs, salt and black pepper.

Cook them at 380 degrees for about 10 minutes, turning over after 5 minutes. Serve with granulated sugar and sour cream. Enjoy!

Per serving: 262 Calories; 3.7g Fat; 50.1g Carbs; 6.4g Protein;

Favorite Lentil Burgers

(**Ready in about** 15 minutes | **Servings** 3)

Ingredients

1/2 cup wild rice, cooked
1 cup red lentils, cooked
1/2 small onion, quartered
1/4 cup walnuts
Sea salt and ground black
pepper, to taste
1/2 teaspoon cayenne pepper

1/2 small beet, peeled and
quartered
1 garlic clove
2 tablespoons breadcrumbs
1 tablespoon vegan barbecue
sauce

Directions

Pulse all of the ingredients in a food processor until a moldable dough forms.

Form the mixture into equal patties and place them in the Air Fryer cooking basket that has been lightly oiled.

Cook your burgers for about 15 minutes at 380 degrees F, flipping halfway through.

Enjoy! Serve on burger buns.

Per serving: 195 Calories; 4.8g Fat; 31.1g Carbs; 8.9g Protein;

Traditional Indian Pakora

(**Ready in about** 35 minutes | **Servings** 2)

Ingredients

1 large zucchini, grated
2 scallion stalks, chopped
1/2 teaspoon paprika
14 teaspoon ginger-garlic
paste

1/2 teaspoon baking powder
1/4 teaspoon curry powder
1/2 cup besan flour
Sea salt and ground black
pepper, to taste
1 teaspoon olive oil

Directions

Sprinkle the salt over the grated zucchini and leave it for 20 minutes. Then, squeeze the zucchini and drain off the excess liquid.

Mix the grated zucchini with the flour, baking powder, scallions, paprika, curry powder and ginger-garlic paste. Salt and pepper to taste.

Shape the mixture into patties and transfer them to the Air Fryer cooking basket. Brush the zucchini patties with 1 teaspoon of olive oil.

Cook the pakora at 380 degrees F for about 12 minutes, flipping them halfway through the cooking time.

Serve on dinner rolls and enjoy!

Per serving: 175 Calories; 4.4g Fat; 24.6g Carbs; 9.5g Protein;

The Best Crispy Tofu

(**Ready in about** 55 minutes | **Servings** 4)

Ingredients

16 ounces firm tofu, pressed and cubed
1 teaspoon cider vinegar
5 tablespoons cornstarch
1/2 teaspoon shallot powder
1/2 teaspoon porcini powder
1 teaspoon garlic powder
1 tablespoon tamari sauce
1 tablespoon vegan oyster
1 teaspoon pure maple syrup
1 teaspoon sriracha
1 tablespoon sesame oil

Directions

Toss the tofu with the oyster sauce, tamari sauce, vinegar, maple syrup, sriracha, shallot powder, porcini powder, garlic powder, and sesame oil. Let it marinate for 30 minutes.

Toss the marinated tofu with the cornstarch.

Cook at 360 degrees F for 10 minutes; turn them over and cook for 12 minutes more. Bon appétit!

Per serving: 245 Calories; 13.3g Fat; 16.7g Carbs; 18.2g Protein;

Crunchy Eggplant Rounds

(**Ready in about** 45 minutes | **Servings** 4)

Ingredients

1 (1-pound) eggplant, sliced
1/2 cup flax meal
Coarse sea salt and ground black pepper, to taste
1 cup cornbread crumbs, crushed
1/2 cup rice flour
1/2 cup vegan parmesan
1 cup water
1 teaspoon paprika

Directions

Toss the eggplant with 1 tablespoon of salt and let it stand for 30 minutes. Drain and rinse well.

Mix the flax meal, rice flour, salt, black pepper, and paprika in a bowl. Then, pour in the water and whisk to combine well.

In another shallow bowl, mix the cornbread crumbs and vegan parmesan.

Dip the eggplant slices in the flour mixture, then in the crumb mixture; press to coat on all sides. Transfer to the lightly greased Air Fryer basket.

Cook at 370 degrees F for 6 minutes. Turn each slice over and cook an additional 5 minutes.

Serve garnished with spicy ketchup if desired. Bon appétit!

Per serving: 327 Calories; 8.5g Fat; 51.9g Carbs; 12.5g Protein

Classic Vegan Chili

(**Ready in about** 40 minutes | **Servings** 3)

Ingredients

1 tablespoon olive oil
2 red bell peppers, seeded and chopped
1 red chili pepper, seeded and minced
1 teaspoon ground cumin
1/2 teaspoon mustard seeds
1/2 teaspoon celery seeds
1 cup vegetable broth
1 bay leaf
1 teaspoon cider vinegar
1/2 yellow onion, chopped
Sea salt and ground black pepper, to taste
2 garlic cloves, minced
1 teaspoon cayenne pepper
1 teaspoon Mexican oregano
1 can (28-ounces) diced tomatoes with juice
1 (15-ounce) can black beans, rinsed and drained
1 avocado, sliced

Directions

Begin by preheating your Air Fryer to 365°F.

In a baking pan, heat the olive oil until it begins to sizzle. Then, in the baking pan, sauté the onion, garlic, and peppers. 4 to 6 minutes in a preheated oven

Now, combine the salt, black pepper, cumin, cayenne pepper, oregano, mustard seeds, celery seeds, tomatoes, and broth in a mixing bowl. Cook, stirring every 4 minutes, for 20 minutes.

Stir in the canned beans, bay leaf, and cider vinegar; cook for another 8 minutes, stirring halfway through.

Serve in individual bowls with avocado slices on top. Enjoy!

Per serving: 335 Calories; 17.6g Fat; 37.3g Carbs; 11.5g Protein;

Cinnamon Pear Chips

(**Ready in about** 25 minutes | **Servings** 1)

Ingredients

1 medium pear, cored and thinly sliced
2 tablespoons cinnamon & sugar mixture

Directions

Toss the pear slices with the cinnamon & sugar mixture. Transfer them to the lightly greased Air Fryer basket.

Bake in the preheated Air Fryer at 380 degrees F for 8 minutes, turning them over halfway through the cooking time.

Transfer to wire rack to cool. Bon appétit!

Per serving: 133 Calories; 0.2g Fat; 35g Carbs; 0.6g Protein;

Dad's Roasted Pepper Salad

(**Ready in about** 25 minutes + chilling time | **Servings** 4)

Ingredients

2 yellow bell peppers
1 Serrano pepper
2 tablespoons cider vinegar
2 red bell peppers
Sea salt, to taste
1 teaspoon cayenne pepper
1/4 cup loosely packed fresh
Italian parsley leaves, roughly
chopped

2 green bell peppers
4 tablespoons olive oil
2 garlic cloves, peeled and
pressed
1/2 teaspoon mixed
peppercorns, freshly crushed
1/2 cup pine nuts

Directions

Start by preheating your Air Fryer to 400 degrees F. Brush the Air Fryer basket lightly with cooking oil.

Then, roast the peppers for 5 minutes. Give the peppers a half turn; place them back in the cooking basket and roast for another 5 minutes.

Turn them one more time and roast until the skin is charred and soft or 5 more minutes. Peel the peppers and let them cool to room temperature. In a small mixing dish, whisk the olive oil, vinegar, garlic, cayenne pepper, salt, and crushed peppercorns. Dress the salad and set aside.

Add the pine nuts to the cooking basket. Roast at 360 degrees F for 4 minutes; give the nuts a good toss. Put the cooking basket back again and roast for a further 3 to 4 minutes. Scatter the toasted nuts over the peppers and garnish with parsley. Bon appétit!

Per serving: 296 Calories; 25.6g Fat; 15.6g Carbs; 4.6g Protein

Swiss Chard and Potato Fritters

(**Ready in about** 35 minutes | **Servings** 4)

Ingredients

8 baby potatoes
1 garlic clove, pressed
1 cup Swiss chard, torn into
small pieces
1 tablespoon flax seed,
soaked in
1 cup vegan cheese, shredded

2 tablespoons olive oil
1/2 cup leeks, chopped
Sea salt and ground black
pepper, to your liking
1/4 cup chickpea flour
3 tablespoon water (vegan
egg)

Directions

Begin by preheating your Air Fryer to 400°F.

Drizzle the potatoes with olive oil. Cook the potatoes in the Air Fryer basket for about 15 minutes, shaking the basket occasionally.

Crush the potatoes lightly to split them; mash the potatoes with the remaining ingredients.

Make patties out of the potato mixture.

Bake for 14 minutes in a preheated Air Fryer at 380 degrees F, flipping halfway through the cooking time. Good appetite!

Per serving: 492 Calories; 18.5g Fat; 66.7g Carbs; 16.9g Protein

Easy Granola with Raisins and Nuts

(**Ready in about** 40 minutes | **Servings** 8)

Ingredients

1 cups rolled oats
1/3 cup almonds chopped
1/4 cup whole wheat pastry
flour
1/2 teaspoon cinnamon
1/3 cup coconut oil, melted
1/2 teaspoon coconut extract
1/2 teaspoon vanilla extract

1/2 cup walnuts, chopped
1/4 cup raisins
1/4 teaspoon nutmeg,
preferably freshly grated
1/2 teaspoon salt
1/3 cup agave nectar

Directions

Thoroughly combine all Ingredients. Then, spread the mixture onto the Air Fryer trays. Spritz with cooking spray.

Bake at 230 degrees F for 25 minutes; rotate the trays and bake 10 to 15 minutes more.

This granola can be stored in an airtight container for up to 2 weeks. Enjoy!

Per serving: 222 Calories; 14g Fat; 29.9g Carbs; 5.3g Protein;

Indian Plantain Chips (Kerala Neenthram)

(**Ready in about** 30 minutes | **Servings** 2)

Ingredients

1 pound plantain, thinly sliced
1 tablespoon turmeric

2 tablespoons coconut oil

Directions

Fill a large enough cup with water and add the turmeric to the water.

Soak the plantain slices in the turmeric water for 15 minutes. Brush with coconut oil and transfer to the Air Fryer basket.

Cook in the preheated Air Fryer at 400 degrees F for 10 minutes, shaking the cooking basket halfway through the cooking time.

Serve at room temperature. Enjoy!

Per serving: 263 Calories; 9.4g Fat; 49.2g Carbs; 1.5g Protein;

Aromatic Baked Potatoes with Chives

(**Ready in about** 45 minutes | **Servings** 2)

Ingredients

4 medium baking potatoes, peeled
1/4 teaspoon smoked paprika
1 tablespoon sea salt
2 tablespoons chives, chopped

1/4 teaspoon red pepper flakes
2 garlic cloves, minced
2 tablespoons olive oil

Directions

Toss the potatoes with the olive oil, seasoning, and garlic.

Place them in the Air Fryer basket. Cook in the preheated Air Fryer at 400 degrees F for 40 minutes or until fork tender.

Garnish with fresh chopped chives. Bon appétit!

Per serving: 434 Calories; 14.1g Fat; 69g Carbs; 8.2g Protein;

Classic Baked Banana

(**Ready in about** 20 minutes | **Servings** 2)

Ingredients

2 just-ripe bananas
1/4 teaspoon grated nutmeg
1/2 teaspoon ground cinnamon
A pinch of salt

2 teaspoons lime juice
2 tablespoons honey

Directions

Toss the banana with all Ingredients until well coated. Transfer your bananas to the parchment-lined cooking basket.

Bake in the preheated Air Fryer at 370 degrees F for 12 minutes, turning them over halfway through the cooking time. Enjoy!

Per serving: 202 Calories; 5.9g Fat; 40.2g Carbs; 1.1g Protein;

Garlic-Roasted Brussels Sprouts with Mustard

(**Ready in about** 20 minutes | **Servings** 3)

Ingredients

1 pound Brussels sprouts, halved
2 garlic cloves, minced
2 tablespoons olive oil

Sea salt and freshly ground black pepper, to taste
1 tablespoon Dijon mustard

Directions

Combine the Brussels sprouts, olive oil, salt, black pepper, and garlic in a mixing bowl.

Cook for 15 minutes at 380°F in a preheated Air Fryer, shaking the basket occasionally.

Enjoy with a dollop of Dijon mustard!

Per serving: 151 Calories; 9.6g Fat; 14.5g Carbs; 5.4g Protein;

Baked Oatmeal with Berries

(**Ready in about** 30 minutes | **Servings** 4)

Ingredients

1 cup fresh strawberries
1/2 cup dried cranberries
A pinch of grated nutmeg
1 ½ cups rolled oats
4 tablespoons agave syrup
1/2 teaspoon vanilla extract

1/2 teaspoon baking powder
A pinch of sea salt
1/2 teaspoon ground cinnamon
1 ½ cups coconut milk

Directions

Spritz a baking pan with cooking spray.

Place 1/2 cup of strawberries on the bottom of the pan; place the cranberries over that.

In a mixing bowl, thoroughly combine the rolled oats, baking powder, salt, nutmeg, cinnamon, vanilla, agave syrup, and milk.

Pour the oatmeal mixtures over the fruits; allow it to soak for 15 minutes. Top with the remaining fruits.

Bake at 330 degrees F for 12 minutes. Serve warm or at room temperature. Enjoy!

Per serving: 387 Calories; 24.1g Fat; 52.5g Carbs; 8.4g Protein;

Green Beans with Oyster Mushrooms

(**Ready in about** 20 minutes | **Servings** 3)

Ingredients

1 tablespoon extra-virgin olive oil
2 cups oyster mushrooms, sliced
Sea salt and ground black pepper, to taste

1/2 cup scallions, chopped
2 garlic cloves, minced
12 ounces fresh green beans, trimmed
1 tablespoon soy sauce

Directions

Start by preheating your Air Fryer to 390 degrees F. Heat the oil and sauté the garlic and scallions until tender and fragrant, about 5 minutes.

Add the remaining Ingredients and stir to combine well.

Increase the temperature to 400 degrees F and cook for a further 5 minutes. Serve warm.

Per serving: 109 Calories; 6.4g Fat; 11.6g Carbs; 3.9g Protein;

Hoisin-Glazed Bok Choy

(**Ready in about** 10 minutes | **Servings** 4)

Ingredients

1 pound baby Bok choy, bottoms removed, leaves separated
½ teaspoon sage
1 tablespoon all-purpose flour
1 teaspoon onion powder
2 garlic cloves, minced
2 tablespoons sesame oil
2 tablespoons hoisin sauce

Directions

Place the Bok choy, garlic, onion powder, and sage in the lightly greased Air Fryer basket.

Cook in the preheated Air Fryer at 350 degrees F for 3 minutes.

In a small mixing dish, whisk the hoisin sauce, sesame oil, and flour. Drizzle the sauce over the Bok choy. Cook for a further 3 minutes. Bon appétit!

Per serving: 235 Calories; 11.2g Fat; 6g Carbs; 25.7g Protein;

Herb Roasted Potatoes and Peppers

(**Ready in about** 30 minutes | **Servings** 4)

Ingredients

1 pound russet potatoes, cut into 1-inch chunks
1 teaspoon dried rosemary
1 teaspoon dried basil
1 teaspoon dried parsley flakes
1/2 teaspoon smoked paprika
2 bell peppers, seeded and cut into 1-inch chunks
1 teaspoon dried oregano
2 tablespoons olive oil
Sea salt and ground black pepper, to taste

Directions

Toss everything into the Air Fryer basket.

Roast for 15 minutes at 400°F, tossing the basket halfway through. Working in batches is recommended.

Serve immediately and enjoy!

Per serving: 158 Calories; 6.8g Fat; 22.6g Carbs; 1.8g Protein;

Corn on the Cob with Spicy Avocado Spread

(**Ready in about** 15 minutes | **Servings** 4)

Ingredients

4 corn cobs
1 clove garlic, pressed
1 tablespoon fresh lime juice
1/2 teaspoon cayenne pepper
1/2 teaspoon dried dill
1 teaspoon hot sauce
1 tablespoon soy sauce
1 avocado, pitted, peeled and mashed
4 teaspoons nutritional yeast
Sea salt and ground black pepper, to taste
2 heaping tablespoons fresh cilantro leaves, roughly chopped

Directions

Spritz the corn with cooking spray. Cook at 390 degrees F for 6 minutes, turning them over halfway through the cooking time.

In the meantime, mix the avocado, lime juice, soy sauce, nutritional yeast, cayenne pepper, dill, salt, black pepper, and hot sauce.

Spread the avocado mixture all over the corn on the cob. Garnish with fresh cilantro leaves. Bon appétit!

Per serving: 234 Calories; 9.2g Fat; 37.9g Carbs; 7.2g Protein;

Winter Squash and Tomato Bake

(**Ready in about** 30 minutes | **Servings** 4)

Ingredients

Cashew Cream:
1/4 cup lime juice
1 tablespoon tahini
Sea salt, to taste
1/2 cup water Squash:
2 ripe tomatoes, crushed
2 tablespoons olive oil
1 cup vegetable broth
2 tablespoons olive oil
1/2 teaspoon dried basil
2 garlic cloves, minced
1/2 cup sunflower seeds, soaked overnight, rinsed and drained
2 teaspoons nutritional yeast
1 pound winter squash, peeled and sliced
Sea salt and ground black pepper, to taste Sauce:
6 ounces spinach, torn into small pieces
1/2 teaspoon dried rosemary

Directions

Mix the Ingredients for the cashew cream in your food processor until creamy and uniform. Reserve.

Place the squash slices in the lightly greased casserole dish. Add the olive oil, salt, and black pepper.

Mix all the Ingredients for the sauce. Pour the sauce over the vegetables. Bake in the preheated Air Fryer at 390 degrees F for 15 minutes.

Top with the cashew cream and bake an additional 5 minutes or until everything is thoroughly heated.

Transfer to a wire rack to cool slightly before sling and serving.

Per serving: 330 Calories; 25.3g Fat; 23.2g Carbs; 8.5g Protein;

Mashed Potatoes with Roasted Peppers

(**Ready in about** 1 hour | **Servings** 4)

Ingredients

4 potatoes
1 pound bell peppers, seeded and quartered lengthwise
2 Fresno peppers, seeded and halved lengthwise
2 tablespoons cider vinegar
1/2 teaspoon dried dill
1 tablespoon vegan margarine
4 tablespoons olive oil
1 teaspoon garlic powder
4 garlic cloves, pressed
Kosher salt, to taste
1/2 teaspoon freshly ground black pepper

Directions

Place the potatoes in the Air Fryer basket and cook at 400 degrees F for 40 minutes. Discard the skin and mash the potatoes with the vegan margarine and garlic powder.

Then, roast the peppers at 400 degrees F for 5 minutes. Give the peppers a

half turn; place them back in the cooking basket and roast for another 5 minutes.

Turn them one more time and roast until the skin is charred and soft or 5 more minutes. Peel the peppers and let them cool to room temperature.

Toss your peppers with the remaining Ingredients and serve with the mashed potatoes. Bon appétit!

Per serving: 490 Calories; 17g Fat; 79.1g Carbs; 10.5g Protein

Hungarian Mushroom Pilaf

(**Ready in about** 50 minutes | **Servings** 4)

Ingredients

1 ½ cups white rice
1 pound fresh porcini mushrooms, sliced
2 tablespoons olive oil
1 onion, chopped
1/2 teaspoon dried tarragon
3 cups vegetable broth
2 garlic cloves
2 tablespoons olive oil
1 teaspoon dried thyme
1/4 cup dry vermouth
1 teaspoon sweet Hungarian paprika

Directions

Place the rice and broth in a large saucepan, add water; and bring to a boil. Cover, turn the heat down to low, and continue cooking for 16 to 18 minutes more. Set aside for 5 to 10 minutes.

Now, stir the hot cooked rice with the remaining Ingredients in a lightly greased baking dish.

Cook in the preheated Air Fryer at 370 degrees for 20 minutes, checking periodically to ensure even cooking.

Serve in individual bowls. Bon appétit!

Per serving: 566 Calories; 19.1g Fat; 72.8g Carbs; 24.6g Protein;

Rosemary Au Gratin Potatoes

(**Ready in about** 45 minutes | **Servings** 4)

Ingredients

2 pounds potatoes
1/2 cup almonds, soaked overnight
1 cup unsweetened almond milk
2 tablespoons nutritional yeast
Kosher salt and ground black pepper, to taste
1/4 cup sunflower kernels, soaked overnight
1 teaspoon shallot powder
2 fresh garlic cloves, minced
1/2 cup water
1 tablespoon fresh rosemary
1 teaspoon cayenne pepper

Directions

Bring a large pan of water to a boil. Cook the whole potatoes for about 20 minutes. Drain the potatoes and let sit until cool enough to handle.

Peel your potatoes and slice into 1/8-inch rounds.

Add the sunflower kernels, almonds, almond milk, nutritional yeast, shallot powder, and garlic to your food processor; blend until uniform, smooth, and creamy. Add the water and blend for 30 seconds more.

Place 1/2 of the potatoes overlapping in a single layer in the lightly greased casserole dish. Spoon 1/2 of the sauce on top of the potatoes. Repeat the layers, ending with the sauce.

Top with salt, black pepper, cayenne pepper, and fresh rosemary. Bake in the preheated Air Fryer at 325 degrees F for 20 minutes. Serve warm.

Per serving: 386 Calories; 15.7g Fat; 50.5g Carbs; 14.3g Protein;

Kid-Friendly Vegetable Fritters

(**Ready in about** 20 minutes | **Servings** 4)

Ingredients

1 pound broccoli florets
1 yellow onion, finely chopped
1 sweet pepper, seeded and chopped
1 teaspoon turmeric powder
1/2 teaspoon ground cumin
1/2 cup all-purpose flour
1 tablespoon ground flaxseeds
1/2 cup cornmeal
2 garlic cloves, pressed
1 carrot, grated
Salt and ground black pepper, to taste 2 tablespoons olive oil

Directions

Blanch the broccoli in salted boiling water for 3 to 4 minutes, or until al dente. Drain well and place in a mixing bowl with the remaining ingredients; mash the broccoli florets.

Form the mixture into patties and place them in the Air Fryer basket that has been lightly greased.

Cook for 6 minutes at 400 degrees F, turning them over halfway through; work in batches.

Warm with your favourite Vegenaise sauce. Enjoy

Per serving: 299 Calories; 11.3g Fat; 44.1g Carbs; 7.9g Protein;

Onion Rings with Spicy Ketchup

(**Ready in about** 30 minutes | **Servings** 2)

Ingredients

1 onion, sliced into rings
1/2 cup oat milk
1 teaspoon cayenne pepper
1/2 cup cornmeal
4 tablespoons vegan parmesan
1 teaspoon curry powder
1/3 cup all-purpose flour
Salt and ground black pepper, to your liking
1/4 cup spicy ketchup

Directions

Place the onion rings in the bowl with cold water; let them soak approximately 20 minutes; drain the onion rings and pat dry using a kitchen towel.

In a shallow bowl, mix the flour, milk, curry powder, cayenne pepper, salt, and black pepper. Mix to combine well.

Mix the cornmeal and vegan parmesan in another shallow bowl. Dip the onion rings in the flour/milk mixture; then, dredge in the cornmeal mixture.

Spritz the Air Fryer basket with cooking spray; arrange the breaded onion rings in the Air Fryer basket.

Cook in the preheated Air Fryer at 400 degrees F for 4 to 5 minutes, turning them over halfway through the cooking time. Serve with spicy ketchup. Bon appétit!

Per serving: 361 Calories; 4.5g Fat; 67.5g Carbs; 12.1g Protein;

Spicy Roasted Cashew Nuts

(**Ready in about** 20 minutes | **Servings** 4)

Ingredients

1 cup whole cashews
Salt and ground black pepper, to taste
1 teaspoon olive oil
1/2 teaspoon smoked paprika
1/2 teaspoon ancho chili powder

Directions

In a mixing bowl, combine all of the ingredients.

Line the Air Fryer basket with parchment paper. In the basket, arrange the spiced cashews in a single layer.

Roast for 6 to 8 minutes at 350°F, shaking the basket once or twice. Working in batches is recommended. Enjoy!

Per serving: 400 Calories; 35.1g Fat; 19.3g Carbs; 7.7g Protein;

Barbecue Tofu with Green Beans

(**Ready in about** 1 hour | **Servings** 3)

Ingredients

12 ounces super firm tofu, pressed and cubed
1 tablespoon coconut sugar
1 tablespoon mustard
1/2 teaspoon sea salt
1/2 teaspoon freshly grated ginger
2 cloves garlic, minced
1 tablespoon white vinegar
1/4 cup ketchup
1/4 teaspoon ground black pepper
1/4 teaspoon smoked paprika
2 tablespoons olive oil
1 pound green beans

Directions

Toss the tofu with the ketchup, white vinegar, coconut sugar, mustard, black pepper, sea salt, paprika, ginger, garlic, and olive oil. Let it marinate for 30 minutes.

Cook at 360 degrees F for 10 minutes; turn them over and cook for 12 minutes more. Reserve.

Place the green beans in the lightly greased Air Fryer basket. Roast at 400 degrees F for 5 minutes. Bon appétit!

Per serving: 316 Calories; 19.8g Fat; 20.8g Carbs; 20.1g Protein

Cinnamon Sugar Tortilla Chips

(**Ready in about** 20 minutes | **Servings** 4

Ingredients

4 (10-inch) flour tortillas
1 ½ tablespoons ground cinnamon
1/4 cup vegan margarine, melted
1/4 cup caster sugar

Directions

Slice each tortilla into eight slices. Brush the tortilla pieces with the melted margarine.

In a mixing bowl, thoroughly combine the cinnamon and sugar. Toss the cinnamon mixture with the tortillas.

Transfer to the cooking basket and cook at 360 degrees F for 8 minutes or until lightly golden. Work in batches.

They will crisp up as they cool. Serve and enjoy!

Per serving: 270 Calories; 14.1g Fat; 32.7g Carbs; 3.8g Protein

BEEF

Paprika Porterhouse Steak with Cauliflower

(Ready in about 20 minutes | **Servings** 4)

Ingredients

1 pound Porterhouse steak, sliced
Coarse sea salt and ground black pepper, to taste
1/2 teaspoon shallot powder
1 pound cauliflower, torn into florets

1 teaspoon butter, room temperature
1/2 teaspoon porcini powder
1 teaspoon granulated garlic
1 teaspoon smoked paprika

Directions

Brush all sides of the steak with butter and season with all spices. Season the cauliflower to taste with salt and pepper.

Place the steak in the cooking basket and roast for 12 minutes at 400 degrees F, turning halfway through.

Remove the cauliflower from the basket and cook your steak for another 2 to 3 minutes, if necessary.

Garnish the steak with the cauliflower. Consume while warm..

Per serving: 196 Calories; 7.8g Fat; 7.5g Carbs; 25.4g Protein;

Chuck Roast with Sweet 'n' Sticky Sauce

(Ready in about 35 minutes | **Servings** 3)

Ingredients

1 pound chuck roast
2 tablespoons butter softened
1 tablespoon coriander, chopped
1 tablespoon fish sauce
2 tablespoons honey

Sea salt and ground black pepper, to taste
1 tablespoon fresh scallions, chopped
1 teaspoon soy sauce

Directions

Season the chuck roast with salt and pepper; spritz a nonstick cooking oil all over the beef.

Air fry at 400 degrees F for 30 to 35 minutes, flipping the chuck roast halfway through the cooking time.

While the roast is cooking, heat the other Ingredients in a sauté pan over medium-high heat. Bring to a boil and reduce the heat; let it simmer, partially covered, until the sauce has thickened and reduced.

Slice the chuck roast into thick cuts and serve garnished with sweet 'n' sticky sauce. Bon appétit!

Per serving: 325 Calories; 16.8g Fat; 13.7g Carbs; 31.9g Protein;

Italian Sausage Peperonata Pomodoro

(Ready in about 15 minutes | **Servings** 2)

Ingredients

2 bell peppers, sliced
1 chili pepper
2 smoked beef sausages
1 teaspoon Italian spice mix
1 garlic clove, minced

1 yellow onion, sliced
1 teaspoon olive oil
2 medium-sized tomatoes, peeled and crushed

Directions

Spritz the sides and bottom of the cooking basket with a nonstick cooking oil. Add the peppers, onion and sausage to the cooking basket.

Cook at 390 degrees F for 10 minutes, shaking the basket periodically. Reserve.

Heat the olive oil in a medium-sized saucepan over medium-high flame until sizzling; add in the tomatoes and garlic; let it cook for 2 to 3 minutes.

Stir in the peppers, onion and Italian spice mix. Continue to cook for 1 minute longer or until heated through. Fold in the sausages and serve warm. Bon appétit!

Per serving: 473 Calories; 34.6g Fat; 19.3g Carbs; 22.1g Protein;

Flank Steak with Dijon Honey Butter

(Ready in about 15 minutes | **Servings** 3)

Ingredients

1 pound flank steak
1/2 teaspoon olive oil
3 tablespoons butter

Sea salt and red pepper flakes, to taste
1 teaspoon Dijon mustard
1 teaspoon honey

Directions

Brush the flank steak with olive oil and season with salt and pepper.

Cook at 400 degrees F for 6 minutes. Then, turn the steak halfway through the cooking time and continue to cook for a further 6 minutes.

In the meantime, prepare the Dijon honey butter by whisking the remaining Ingredients.

Serve the warm flank steak dolloped with the Dijon honey butter. Bon appétit!

Per serving: 333 Calories; 19.8g Fat; 3.5g Carbs; 32.8g Protein;

Easy Homemade Hamburgers

(**Ready in about** 15 minutes | **Servings** 2)

Ingredients

3/4 pound lean ground chuck
3 tablespoons onion, minced
1 teaspoon garlic, minced
1 teaspoon soy sauce
1/4 teaspoon ground cumin
2 burger buns

Kosher salt and ground black pepper, to taste
1/2 teaspoon smoked paprika
1/2 teaspoon mustard seeds
1/2 teaspoon cayenne pepper

Directions

Thoroughly combine the ground chuck, salt, black pepper, onion, garlic and soy sauce in a mixing dish.

Season with smoked paprika, ground cumin, cayenne pepper and mustard seeds. Mix to combine well.

Shape the mixture into 2 equal patties.

Spritz your patties with a nonstick cooking spray. Air fry your burgers at 380

degrees F for about 11 minutes or to your desired degree of doneness.

Place your burgers on burger buns and serve with favorite toppings. Devour!

Per serving: 433 Calories; 17.4g Fat; 40g Carbs; 39.2g Protein;

Greek-Style Roast Beef

(**Ready in about** 55 minutes | **Servings** 3)

Ingredients

1 clove garlic, halved
1 zucchini, sliced lengthwise
2 teaspoons olive oil
1/2 cup Greek-style yogurt

1 ½ pounds beef eye round roast
1 teaspoon Greek spice mix
Sea salt, to season

Directions

Rub the beef eye round roast with garlic halves.

Brush the beef eye round roast and zucchini with olive oil. Sprinkle with spices and place the beef in the cooking basket.

Roast in your Air Fryer at 400 degrees F for 40 minutes. Turn the beef over.

Add the zucchini to the cooking basket and continue to cook for 12 minutes more or until cooked through. Serve warm, garnished with Greek-style yogurt. Enjoy!

Per serving: 348 Calories; 16.1g Fat; 1.6g Carbs; 49g Protein;

Chuck Roast with Rustic Potatoes

(**Ready in about** 50 minutes | **Servings** 3)

Ingredients

1 tablespoon brown mustard
2 tablespoons BBQ sauce
1 tablespoon Worcester sauce
1 ½ pounds chuck roast
Coarse sea salt and ground black pepper, to taste
1 teaspoon granulated garlic
1 teaspoon dried marjoram

2 tablespoons tomato paste, preferably homemade
1 pound medium-sized russet potatoes, quartered
1 teaspoon shallot powder
1/2 teaspoon cayenne pepper

Directions

In a small bowl, combine the mustard, tomato paste, BBQ sauce, and Worcester sauce. This mixture should be rubbed all over the chuck roast.

Place the chuck roast in the Air Fryer cooking basket that has been lightly greased with melted butter and season with salt and pepper.

Air fry for 30 minutes at 400°F; turn over and scatter potato chunks around the beef. Cook for an additional 15 minutes. Check to ensure that the beef is thoroughly cooked.

Seasonings should be tasted and adjusted. Place the meat on a cutting board and set aside. Serve the beef warm, sliced against the grain.

Per serving: 438 Calories; 13.1g Fat; 30.8g Carbs; 50g Protein;

Marinated London Broil

(**Ready in about** 25 minutes+ marinating time | **Servings** 2)

Ingredients

2 tablespoons soy sauce
1 teaspoon mustard
2 tablespoons wine vinegar
1 tablespoon honey
Salt and black pepper, to taste

1 tablespoon olive oil
2 garlic cloves, minced
1 pound London broil
1/2 teaspoon paprika

Directions

In a ceramic dish, mix the soy sauce, garlic, mustard, oil, wine vinegar and honey. Add in the London broil and let it marinate for 2 hours in your refrigerator.

Season the London broil with paprika, salt and pepper.

Cook in the preheated Air Fryer at 400 degrees F for 10 minutes; turn over and continue to cook for a further 10 minutes.

Slice the London broil against the grain and eat warm. Enjoy!

Per serving: 448 Calories; 22.6g Fat; 13.8g Carbs; 48g Protein; 11.7g

Mayo Roasted Sirloin Steak

(**Ready in about** 20 minutes | **Servings** 3)

Ingredients
1 pound sirloin steak, cubed
1/2 cup mayonnaise
1 teaspoon garlic, minced
Kosher salt and ground black pepper, to season

1 tablespoon red wine vinegar
1/2 teaspoon dried basil
1/2 teaspoon cayenne pepper

Directions
Pat dry the sirloin steak with paper towels.

In a small mixing dish, thoroughly combine the remaining Ingredients until everything is well incorporated.

Toss the cubed steak with the mayonnaise mixture and transfer to the Air Fryer cooking basket.

Cook in the preheated Air Fryer at 400 degrees F for 7 minutes. Shake the basket and continue to cook for a further 7 minutes. Bon appétit!

Per serving: 418 Calories; 31.3g Fat; 0.2g Carbs; 30.1g Protein;

Easy Beef Burritos

(**Ready in about** 25 minutes | **Servings** 3)

Ingredients
1 pound rump steak
1/2 teaspoon shallot powder
1/2 teaspoon porcini powder
1/2 teaspoon celery seeds
1 teaspoon piri piri powder
1 teaspoon lard, melted

Sea salt and crushed red pepper, to taste
1/2 teaspoon dried Mexican oregano
3 (approx 7-8" dia) whole-wheat tortillas

Directions
Toss the rump steak with the spices and melted lard.

Cook in your Air Fryer at 390 degrees F for 20 minutes, turning it halfway through the cooking time. Place on a cutting board to cool slightly.

Slice against the grain into thin strips.

Spoon the beef strips onto wheat tortillas; top with your favorite fixings, roll them up and serve. Enjoy!

Per serving: 368 Calories; 13g Fat; 20.2g Carbs; 35.1g Protein;

London Broil with Herb Butter

(**Ready in about** 30 minutes | **Servings** 3)

Ingredients
1 pound London broil Herb butter:
1 teaspoon basil, chopped
1 tablespoon chives, chopped
Coarse sea salt and crushed black peppercorns, to taste

2 tablespoons butter, at room temperature
1 tablespoon cilantro, chopped
1 tablespoon lemon juice

Directions
Pat the London broil dry with paper towels. Mix all Ingredients for the herb butter.

Cook in the preheated Air Fryer at 400 degrees F for 14 minutes; turn over, brush with the herb butter and continue to cook for a further 12 minutes.

Slice the London broil against the grain and serve warm.

Per serving: 378 Calories; 21.3g Fat; 0.4g Carbs; 47g Protein;

BBQ Glazed Beef Riblets

(**Ready in about** 15 minutes + marinating time | **Servings** 3)

Ingredients
1 pound beef riblets
1/4 cup tomato paste
1/4 cup Worcestershire sauce
2 tablespoons hot sauce
2 tablespoons rice vinegar

Sea salt and red pepper, to taste
1 tablespoon oyster sauce
1 tablespoon stone-ground mustard

Directions
Combine all ingredients in a glass dish, cover, and refrigerate for at least 2 hours.

Remove the riblets from the marinade and place them in the Air Fryer cooking basket.

Cook for 12 minutes in a preheated Air Fryer at 360°F, shaking the basket halfway through to ensure even cooking.

In a small skillet over medium heat, heat the reserved marinade; spoon the glaze over the riblets and serve immediately.

Per serving: 258 Calories; 9.5g Fat; 10.4g Carbs; 32.7g Protein

American-Style Roast Beef

(**Ready in about** 30 minutes | **Servings** 3)

Ingredients

1 pound beef eye of round roast
1/4 teaspoon dried bay laurel
1/2 teaspoon cumin powder
1 sprig thyme, crushed
1 teaspoon red pepper flakes
1 teaspoon sesame oil
Sea salt and black pepper, to taste

Directions

Simply toss the beef with the remaining Ingredients; toss until well coated on all sides.

Cook in the preheated Air Fryer at 390 degrees F for 15 to 20 minutes, flipping the meat halfway through to cook on the other side.

Remove from the cooking basket, cover loosely with foil and let rest for 15 minutes before carving and serving. Bon appétit!

Per serving: 294 Calories; 10.9g Fat; 0.3g Carbs; 45.9g Protein

Porterhouse Steak with Tangy Sauce

(**Ready in about** 20 minutes | **Servings** 2)

Ingredients

1/2 pound Porterhouse steak, cut into four thin pieces
1 teaspoon garlic paste
1 teaspoon ginger juice
1 tablespoon soy sauce
1 teaspoon sesame oil
Salt and pepper, to season
1 habanero pepper, minced
2 tablespoons brown sugar
1 tablespoon fish sauce

Directions

Pat the steak dry and generously season it with salt and black pepper.

Cook in the preheated Air Fryer at 400 degrees F for 7 minutes; turn on the other side and cook an additional 7 to 8 minutes.

To make the sauce, heat the remaining Ingredients in a small saucepan over medium-high heat; let it simmer for a few minutes until heated through.

Spoon the sauce over the steak and serve over hot cooked rice or egg noodles. Bon appétit!

Per serving: 309 Calories; 8.1g Fat; 12.3g Carbs; 42.5g Protein

Beef Sausage-Stuffed Zucchini

(**Ready in about** 30 minutes | **Servings** 2)

Ingredients

1/2 pound beef sausage, crumbled
1/4 cup tomato paste
1/2 cup sharp cheddar cheese, grated
1/2 teaspoon garlic, pressed
1/2 cup tortilla chips, crushed
2 small-sized zucchini, halved lengthwise and seeds removed

Directions

In a mixing bowl, thoroughly combine the beef sausage, tortilla chips, garlic and tomato paste. Divide the sausage mixture between the zucchini halves.

Bake in the preheated Air Fryer at 400 degrees F for 20 minutes.

Top with grated cheddar cheese and cook an additional 5 minutes. Enjoy!

Per serving: 435 Calories; 28g Fat; 19.3g Carbs; 26.5g Protein;

Chicago-Style Beef Sandwich

(**Ready in about** 25 minutes | **Servings** 2)

Ingredients

1/2 pound chuck, boneless
1/4 teaspoon ground bay laurel
1/2 teaspoon shallot powder
Kosher salt and ground black pepper, to taste
1 cup pickled vegetables, chopped
1 tablespoon soy sauce
1/2 teaspoon cayenne pepper
1 tablespoon olive oil
1/4 teaspoon porcini powder
2 ciabatta rolls, sliced in half
1/2 teaspoon garlic powder

Directions

Toss the chuck roast with the olive oil, soy sauce, and spices until thoroughly coated.

Cook for 20 minutes in a preheated Air Fryer at 400 degrees F, turning halfway through the cooking time.

Adjust the seasonings and shred the meat with two forks.

Place a generous portion of the meat and pickled vegetables on the bottom halves of the ciabatta rolls. Place the ciabatta roll tops on top of the sandwiches. Serve right away and enjoy!

Per serving: 385 Calories; 17.4g Fat; 28.1g Carbs; 29.8g Protein

Classic Beef Jerky

(**Ready in about** 4 hours 30 minutes | **Servings** 4)

Ingredients

6 ounces top round steak, cut into 1/8-inch thick strips
1/2 tablespoon honey
2 tablespoons Worcestershire sauce
1 teaspoon hot sauce
1 teaspoon onion powder
1/2 teaspoon fresh garlic, crushed
1 teaspoon liquid smoke

Directions

Transfer the strips of steak to a large Ziplock bag; add in the other Ingredients, seal the bag and shake to combine well.

Refrigerate for at least 30 minutes.

Cook in the preheated Air Fryer at 160 degrees F for about 4 hours, until it is dry and firm.

Refrigerate in an airtight container for up to 1 month. Bon appétit!

Per serving: 77 Calories; 2.4g Fat; 4.1g Carbs; 8.9g Protein;

Mediterranean Burgers with Onion Jam

(**Ready in about** 20 minutes | **Servings** 2)

Ingredients

1/2 pound ground chuck
1/2 teaspoon garlic, minced
1 teaspoon brown mustard
2 burger buns
2 ounces Haloumi cheese
1 medium tomato, sliced
2 Romaine lettuce leaves
Onion jam:
Sea salt and ground black pepper, to taste
2 tablespoons scallions, chopped
Kosher salt and ground black pepper, to taste
2 tablespoons butter, at room temperature
2 red onions, sliced
1 cup red wine
2 tablespoons honey
1 tablespoon fresh lemon juice

Directions

Mix the ground chuck, scallions, garlic, mustard, salt and black pepper until well combined; shape the mixture into two equal patties.

Spritz a cooking basket with a nonstick cooking spray. Air fry your burgers at 370 degrees F for about 11 minutes or to your desired degree of doneness.

Meanwhile, make the onion jam. In a small saucepan, melt the butter; once hot, cook the onions for about 4 minutes. Turn the heat to simmer, add salt, black pepper and wine and cook until liquid evaporates.

Stir in the honey and continue to simmer until the onions are a jam-like consistency; afterwards, drizzle with freshly squeezed lemon juice.

Top the bottom halves of the burger buns with the warm beef patty. Top with haloumi cheese, tomato, lettuce and onion jam.

Set the bun tops in place and serve right now. Enjoy!

Per serving: 474 Calories; 26.5g Fat; 32.9g Carbs; 29g Protein

Dad's Meatloaf with a Twist

(**Ready in about** 35 minutes | **Servings** 2)

Ingredients

1 tablespoon olive oil
1 Italian pepper, deveined and chopped
1/2 pound ground beef
1/2 teaspoon liquid smoke
1 tablespoon Dijon mustard
1/2 cup crushed corn flakes
4 tablespoons tomato paste
1/2 teaspoon garlic, minced
1 tablespoon soy sauce
1 onion, chopped
1 Serrano pepper, deveined and chopped
1 teaspoon Italian seasoning mix

Directions

Start by preheating your Air Fryer to 350 degrees F.

In a mixing bowl, thoroughly combine the onion, garlic, peppers, ground beef, soy sauce, mustard and crushed corn flakes. Salt to taste.

Mix until everything is well incorporated and press into a lightly greased meatloaf pan.

Air fry for about 25 minutes. Whisk the tomato paste with the Italian seasoning mix and liquid smoke; spread the mixture over the top of your meatloaf.

Continue to cook for 3 minutes more. Let it rest for 6 minutes before slicing and serving. Bon appétit!

Per serving: 521 Calories; 25.5g Fat; 42.9g Carbs; 32g Protein

Tex-Mex Taco Pizza

(**Ready in about** 20 minutes | **Servings** 1)

Ingredients

1 teaspoon lard, melted
2 tablespoons jarred salsa
4 ounces pizza dough
1/2 teaspoon granulated garlic
2 ounces cheddar cheese grated
4 ounces ground beef sirloin
1/4 teaspoon Mexican oregano
1/2 teaspoon basil
1 plum tomato, sliced

Directions

Melt the lard in a skillet over medium-high heat; once hot, cook the beef until no longer pink, about 5 minutes.

Roll the dough out and transfer it to the Air Fryer cooking basket. Spread the jarred salsa over the dough.

Sprinkle Mexican oregano, basil, garlic and cheese over the salsa. Top with the sautéed beef, then with the sliced tomato.

Bake in your Air Fryer at 375 degrees F for about 11 minutes until the bottom

of crust is lightly browned. Bon appétit!

Per serving: 686 Calories; 27.1g Fat; 72.4g Carbs; 40.2g Protein

Dijon Top Chuck with Herbs

(**Ready in about** 1 hour | **Servings** 3)

Ingredients

1 ½ pounds top chuck	1 tablespoon Dijon mustard
Sea salt and ground black	1 teaspoon dried thyme
pepper, to taste	2 teaspoons olive oil
1/2 teaspoon fennel seeds	1 teaspoon dried marjoram

Directions

Begin by preheating your Air Fryer to 380°F.

In a Ziploc bag, combine all of the ingredients and shake well to combine. Spray the bottom of the Air Fryer basket with cooking spray next.

Cook for 50 minutes, turning every 10 to 15 minutes, with the beef in the cooking basket.

Allow for a 5- to 7-minute rest before slicing and serving. Enjoy!

Per serving: 406 Calories; 24.1g Fat; 0.3g Carbs; 44.1g Protein

Mediterranean-Style Beef Steak and Zucchini

(**Ready in about** 20 minutes | **Servings** 4)

Ingredients

1 ½ pounds beef steak	1 teaspoon dried rosemary
1 teaspoon dried basil	1 teaspoon dried oregano
2 tablespoons extra-virgin	1 pound zucchini
olive oil	
2 tablespoons fresh chives,	
chopped	

Directions

Start by preheating your Air Fryer to 400 degrees F.

Toss the steak and zucchini with the spices and olive oil. Transfer to the cooking basket and cook for 6 minutes.

Now, shale the basket and cook another 6 minutes. Serve immediately garnished with fresh chives. Enjoy!

Per serving: 396 Calories; 20.4g Fat; 3.5g Carbs; 47.8g Protein

Peperonata with Beef Sausage

(**Ready in about** 35 minutes | **Servings** 4)

Ingredients

2 teaspoons canola oil	1 green bell pepper, sliced
1 serrano pepper, sliced	Sea salt and pepper, to taste
1 shallot, sliced	2 bell peppers, sliced
1/2 dried thyme	1 teaspoon dried rosemary
1 teaspoon fennel seeds	1/2 teaspoon mustard seeds
2 pounds thin beef parboiled	
sausage	

Directions

Brush the sides and bottom of the cooking basket with 1 teaspoon of canola oil. Add the peppers and shallot to the cooking basket.

Toss them with the spices and cook at 390 degrees F for 15 minutes, shaking the basket occasionally. Reserve.

Turn the temperature to 380 degrees F

Then, add the remaining 1 teaspoon of oil. Once hot, add the sausage and cook in the preheated Air Frye for 15 minutes, flipping them halfway through the cooking time.

Serve with reserved pepper mixture. Bon appétit!

Per serving: 563 Calories; 41.5g Fat; 10.6g Carbs; 35.6g Protein

New York Strip with Mustard Butter

(**Ready in about** 20 minutes | **Servings** 4)

Ingredients

1 tablespoon peanut oil	2 pounds New York Strip
Sea salt and freshly cracked	1 teaspoon whole-grain
black pepper, to taste	mustard
1/2 stick butter, softened	1 teaspoon cayenne pepper
1/2 teaspoon honey	

Directions

Season the steak with cayenne pepper, salt, and black pepper after rubbing it with peanut oil.

Cook for 7 minutes in a preheated Air Fryer at 400 degrees F, then flip and cook for another 7 minutes.

Meanwhile, whisk together the butter, whole-grain mustard, and honey to make the mustard butter.

Serve the roasted New York Strip with the mustard butter on the side. Good appetite!

Per serving: 459 Calories; 27.4g Fat; 2.5g Carbs; 48.3g Protein

Scotch Fillet with Sweet 'n' Sticky Sauce

(**Ready in about** 40 minutes | **Servings** 4)

Ingredients

2 pounds scotch fillet, sliced into strips
2 tablespoons honey
Sauce:
2 garlic cloves, minced
1/2 cup beef broth
1/2 teaspoon dried dill
2 green onions, chopped
4 tablespoons tortilla chips, crushed
1 tablespoon butter
1/2 teaspoon dried rosemary
1 tablespoons fish sauce

Directions

Start by preheating your Air Fryer to 390 degrees F.

Coat the beef strips with the crushed tortilla chips on all sides. Spritz with cooking spray on all sides and transfer them to the cooking basket.

Cook for 30 minutes, shaking the basket every 10 minutes.

Meanwhile, heat the sauce ingredient in a saucepan over medium-high heat. Bring to a boil and reduce the heat; cook until the sauce has thickened slightly.

Add the steak to the sauce; let it sit approximately 8 minutes. Serve over the hot egg noodles if desired.

Per serving: 556 Calories; 17.9g Fat; 25.8g Carbs; 60g Protein;

Kid-Friendly Mini Meatloaves

(**Ready in about** 30 minutes | **Servings** 4)

Ingredients

2 tablespoons bacon, chopped
1 small-sized onion, chopped
1/2 teaspoon dried mustard seeds
1/2 teaspoon dried marjoram
1/2 cup panko crumbs
1 garlic clove, minced
1 pound ground beef
1/2 teaspoon dried basil
4 tablespoons tomato puree
1 bell pepper, chopped
Salt and black pepper, to taste

Directions

Cook the bacon for 1 to 2 minutes in a nonstick skillet over medium-high heat; add the onion, bell pepper, and garlic and cook for another 3 minutes, or until fragrant.

Turn off the heat. Combine the ground beef, spices, and panko crumbs in a mixing bowl. Stir until everything is well combined. Make four mini meatloaves out of the mixture.

Preheat your Air Fryer to 350 degrees Fahrenheit. Spray the cooking basket with nonstick cooking spray.

Cook the mini meatloaves in the cooking basket for 10 minutes, then turn them over, top with the tomato puree, and cook for another 10 minutes. Good appetite!

Per serving: 451 Calories; 27.6g Fat; 15.3g Carbs; 33.4g Protein

Quick Sausage and Veggie Sandwiches

(**Ready in about** 35 minutes | **Servings** 4)

Ingredients

4 bell peppers
4 medium-sized tomatoes, halved
4 spring onions
1 tablespoon mustard
2 tablespoons canola oil
4 beef sausages
4 hot dog buns

Directions

Start by preheating your Air Fryer to 400 degrees F.

Add the bell peppers to the cooking basket. Drizzle 1 tablespoon of canola oil all over the bell peppers.

Cook for 5 minutes. Turn the temperature down to 350 degrees F. Add the tomatoes and spring onions to the cooking basket and cook an additional 10 minutes.

Reserve your vegetables.

Then, add the sausages to the cooking basket. Drizzle with the remaining tablespoon of canola oil.

Cook in the preheated Air Fryer at 380 degrees F for 15 minutes, flipping them halfway through the cooking time.

Add the sausage to a hot dog bun; top with the air-fried vegetables and mustard; serve.

Per serving: 627 Calories; 41.9g Fat; 41.3g Carbs; 22.2g Protein

Mayonnaise and Rosemary Grilled Steak

(**Ready in about** 20 minutes | **Servings** 4)

Ingredients

1 cup mayonnaise
1 teaspoon smoked paprika
1 ½ pounds short loin steak
1 teaspoon garlic, minced
Sea salt, to taste
1 tablespoon fresh rosemary, finely chopped
2 tablespoons Worcestershire sauce
1/2 teaspoon ground black pepper

Directions

Combine the mayonnaise, rosemary, Worcestershire sauce, salt, pepper, paprika, and garlic; mix to combine well.

Now, brush the mayonnaise mixture over both sides of the steak. Lower the steak onto the grill pan.

Grill in the preheated Air Fryer at 390 degrees F for 8 minutes. Turn the steaks over and grill an additional 7 minutes.

Check for doneness with a meat thermometer. Serve warm and enjoy!

Per serving: 620 Calories; 50g Fat; 2.8g Carbs; 39.7g Protein;

Cheesy Beef Burrito

(**Ready in about** 20 minutes | **Servings** 4)

Ingredients

1 pound rump steak
1/2 teaspoon cayenne pepper
1 teaspoon piri piri powder
Salt and ground black pepper, to taste
1 cup iceberg lettuce, shredded
1 teaspoon garlic powder
1/2 teaspoon onion powder
1 teaspoon Mexican oregano
4 large whole wheat tortillas
1 cup Mexican cheese blend

Directions

Toss the rump steak with the garlic powder, onion powder, cayenne pepper, piri piri powder, Mexican oregano, salt, and black pepper.

Cook in the preheated Air Fryer at 390 degrees F for 10 minutes. Slice against the grain into thin strips. Add the cheese blend and cook for 2 minutes more.

Spoon the beef mixture onto the wheat tortillas; top with lettuce; roll up

burrito-style and serve.

Per serving: 468 Calories; 23.5g Fat; 22.1g Carbs; 42.7g Protein

Tender Marinated Flank Steak

(**Ready in about** 20 minutes + marinating time | **Servings** 4)

Ingredients

1 ½ pounds flank steak
2 tablespoons soy sauce Salt, to taste
1/2 teaspoon red pepper flakes, crushed
1/2 teaspoon dried basil
1/2 cup apple cider vinegar
1/2 teaspoon ground black pepper
1 teaspoon thyme
1/2 cup red wine

Directions

Add all Ingredients to a large ceramic bowl. Cover and let it marinate for 3 hours in your refrigerator.

Transfer the flank steak to the Air Fryer basket that is previously greased with nonstick cooking oil.

Cook in the preheated Air Fryer at 400 degrees F for 12 minutes, flipping over halfway through the cooking time. Bon appétit!

Per serving: 312 Calories; 15.5g Fat; 2.5g Carbs; 36.8g Protein

Homemade Beef Empanadas

(**Ready in about** 35 minutes | **Servings** 5)

Ingredients

1 teaspoon olive oil
1/2 pound ground beef chuck
1/2 cup tomato paste 1/2 cup vegetable broth
10 Goya discs pastry dough
2 egg whites, beaten
1 garlic clove, minced
1/2 teaspoon dried oregano
1/2 onion, chopped
Salt and ground pepper, to taste
1 tablespoon raisins

Directions

Heat the oil in a saucepan over medium-high heat. Once hot, sauté the onion and garlic until tender, about 3 minutes.

Then, add the beef and continue to sauté an additional 4 minutes, crumbling with a fork.

Add the raisins, oregano, tomato paste, vegetable broth, salt, and black pepper. Reduce the heat to low and cook an additional 15 minutes.

Preheat the Air Fryer to 330 degrees F. Brush the Air Fryer basket with cooking oil. Divide the sauce between discs. Fold each of the discs in half and seal the edges. Brush the tops with the beaten eggs.

Bake for 7 to 8 minutes, working with batches. Serve with salsa sauce if desired. Enjoy!

Per serving: 490 Calories; 35.1g Fat; 32g Carbs; 15.1g Protein

Indonesian Beef with Peanut Sauce

(**Ready in about** 25 minutes + marinating time | **Servings** 4)

Ingredients

2 pounds filet mignon, sliced into bite-sized strips
2 tablespoons tamari sauce
1 tablespoon mustard
1 tablespoon honey
2 tablespoons lime juice
1/4 cup peanut butter
2 tablespoons sesame oil
1 tablespoon oyster sauce
1 tablespoon ginger-garlic paste
1 teaspoon chili powder
1 teaspoon red pepper flakes
2 tablespoons water

Directions

In a large ceramic dish, combine the beef strips, oyster sauce, sesame oil, tamari sauce, ginger-garlic paste, mustard, honey, and chilli powder.

Allow it to marinate in the refrigerator for 2 hours, covered.

Cook for 18 minutes in a preheated Air Fryer at 400 degrees F, shaking halfway through. basket on occasion

Combine the peanut butter, lime juice, red pepper flakes, and water in a mixing bowl. Serve the sauce over the air-fried beef strips while they're still warm.

Per serving: 425 Calories; 20.1g Fat; 11.2g Carbs; 50g Protein;

Beef Skewers with Pearl Onions and Eggplant

(**Ready in about** 1 hour 30 minutes | **Servings** 4)

Ingredients
1 ½ pounds beef stew meat cubes
1 tablespoon yellow mustard
1 cup pearl onions
1 medium-sized eggplant,
1 ½-inch cubes Sea salt and ground black pepper, to taste
1/4 cup sour cream
1/4 cup mayonnaise
1 tablespoon Worcestershire sauce

Directions

In a mixing bowl, toss all Ingredients until everything is well coated. Place in your refrigerator, cover, and let it marinate for 1 hour.

Soak wooden skewers in water for 15 minutes

Thread the beef cubes, pearl onions and eggplant onto skewers. Cook in preheated Air Fryer at 395 degrees F for 12 minutes, flipping halfway through the cooking time. Serve warm.

Per serving: 500 Calories; 20.6g Fat; 12.8g Carbs; 63.3g Protein

Sunday Tender Skirt Steak

(**Ready in about** 20 minutes + marinating time | **Servings** 4)

Ingredients
1/3 cup soy sauce
2 tablespoons champagne vinegar
1 teaspoon celery seeds
1 teaspoon paprika
Sea salt and ground black pepper, to taste
4 tablespoon molasses
1 teaspoon porcini powder
2 garlic cloves, minced
1 ½ pounds skirt steak, cut into slices
1 teaspoon shallot powder

Directions

Place the soy sauce, molasses, garlic, vinegar, shallot powder, porcini powder, celery seeds, paprika, and beef in a large resealable plastic bag. Shake well and let it marinate overnight.

Discard the marinade and place the beef in the Air Fryer basket. Season with salt and black pepper to taste.

Cook in the preheated Air Fryer at 400 degrees F for 12 minutes, flipping and basting with the reserved marinade halfway through the cooking time. Bon appétit!

Per serving: 503 Calories; 24.5g Fat; 21.7g Carbs; 46.2g Protein

Beef with Creamed Mushroom Sauce

(**Ready in about** 20 minutes | **Servings** 5)

Ingredients
2 tablespoons butter
Salt and cracked black pepper, to taste
1/2 teaspoon dried rosemary
1 pound Cremini mushrooms, sliced
1 cup sour cream
1/2 teaspoon curry powder
2 pounds sirloin, cut into four pieces
1 teaspoon cayenne pepper
1/4 teaspoon dried thyme
1 teaspoon mustard
1/2 teaspoon dried dill

Directions

Start by preheating your Air Fryer to 396 degrees F. Grease a baking pan with butter.

Add the sirloin, salt, black pepper, cayenne pepper, rosemary, dill, and thyme to the baking pan. Cook for 9 minutes.

Next, stir in the mushrooms, sour cream, mustard, and curry powder. Continue to cook another 5 minutes or until everything is heated through.

Spoon onto individual serving plates. Bon appétit!

Per serving: 349 Calories; 16.2g Fat; 7.4g Carbs; 42.9g Protein

Juicy Strip Steak

(**Ready in about** 30 minutes | **Servings** 4)

Ingredients
1 ½ pounds strip steak, sliced
2 tablespoons honey
2 tablespoons champagne vinegar
1 teaspoon ginger-garlic paste
1/2 teaspoon coriander seeds
1/3 cup Shoyu sauce
1 teaspoon mustard seeds
1 tablespoon cornstarch
1/4 cup chickpea flour

Directions

Start by preheating your Air Fryer to 395 degrees F. Spritz the Air Fryer basket with cooking oil.

Toss the strip steak with chickpea flour. Cook the strip steak for 12 minutes; flip them over and cook an additional 10 minutes.

In the meantime, heat the saucepan over medium-high heat. Add the Shoyu sauce, honey, mustard seeds, champagne vinegar, ginger-garlic paste, and coriander seeds.

Reduce the heat and simmer until the sauce is heated through. Make the slurry by whisking the cornstarch with 1 tablespoon of water.

Now, whisk in the cornstarch slurry and continue to simmer until the sauce has thickened. Spoon the sauce over the steak and serve.

Per serving: 417 Calories; 17.9g Fat; 15.6g Carbs; 49.1g Protein

Birthday Party Cheeseburger Pizza

(**Ready in about** 20 minutes | **Servings** 4)

Ingredients

Nonstick cooking oil
1 pound ground beef
1/2 teaspoon basil
1/2 teaspoon oregano
2 spring onions, chopped
4 burger buns
1/4 cup marinara sauce

Kosher salt and ground black pepper, to taste
1/4 teaspoon red pepper flakes
1 cup mozzarella cheese, shredded

Directions

Start by preheating your Air Fryer to 370 degrees F. Spritz the Air Fryer basket with cooking oil.

Add the ground beef and cook for 10 minutes, crumbling with a spatula. Season with salt, black pepper, oregano, basil, and red peppers.

Spread the marinara pasta on each half of burger bun. Place the spring onions and ground meat mixture on the buns equally.

Set the temperature to 350 degrees F. Place the burger pizza in the Air Fryer basket. Top with mozzarella cheese.

Bake approximately 4 minutes or until cheese is bubbling. Top with another half of burger bun and serve. Bon appétit!

Per serving: 447 Calories; 16.1g Fat; 29.5g Carbs; 44.5g Protein

Filipino Tortang Giniling

(**Ready in about** 20 minutes | **Servings** 3)

Ingredients

1 teaspoon lard
1/2 teaspoon ground bay leaf
1/2 teaspoon ground pepper
Sea salt, to taste
1 tomato, sliced
6 eggs
1/2 cup Colby cheese, shredded

2/3 pound ground beef
1 green bell pepper, seeded and chopped
1 red bell pepper, seeded and chopped
1/3 cup double cream
1/4 teaspoon chili powder

Directions

Melt the lard in a cast-iron skillet over medium-high heat. Add the ground beef and cook for 4 minutes until no longer pink, crumbling with a spatula.

Add the ground beef mixture, along with the spices to the baking pan. Now, add the bell peppers.

In a mixing bowl, whisk the eggs with double cream. Spoon the mixture over the meat and peppers in the pan.

Cook in the preheated Air Fryer at 355 degrees F for 10 minutes.

Top with the cheese and tomato slices. Continue to cook for 5 minutes more or until the eggs are golden and the cheese has melted.

Per serving: 543 Calories; 34.7g Fat; 7.4g Carbs; 48.3g Protein

Pastrami and Cheddar Quiche

(**Ready in about** 20 minutes | **Servings** 2)

Ingredients

4 eggs
2 spring onions, chopped
1/2 cup Cheddar cheese, grated Sea salt, to taste
1 cup pastrami, sliced

1 bell pepper, chopped
1/4 cup Greek-style yogurt
1/4 teaspoon ground black pepper

Directions

Begin by preheating your Air Fryer to 330 degrees F. Spritz the baking pan with cooking oil.

Then, thoroughly combine all of the ingredients and pour the mixture into the prepared baking pan.

Cook for 7 to 9 minutes, or until the eggs are set. Place on a cooling rack for 10 minutes before slicing and serving.

Per serving: 435 Calories; 31.4g Fat; 6.7g Carbs; 30.4g Protein

Roasted Blade Steak with Green Beans

(**Ready in about** 25 minutes | **Servings** 4)

Ingredients

2 garlic cloves, smashed
1 tablespoon Cajun seasoning
1 ½ pounds blade steak
1/2 teaspoon Tabasco pepper sauce

1/2 teaspoon cayenne pepper
2 cups green beans
2 teaspoons sunflower oil
Sea salt and ground black pepper, to taste

Directions

Start by preheating your Air Fryer to 330 degrees F.

Mix the garlic, oil, cayenne pepper, and Cajun seasoning to make a paste. Rub it over both sides of the blade steak.

Cook for 13 minutes in the preheated Air Fryer. Now, flip the steak and cook an additional 8 minutes.

Heat the green beans in a saucepan. Add a few tablespoons of water, Tabasco, salt, and black pepper; heat until it wilts or about 10 minutes.

Serve the roasted blade steak with green beans on the side. Bon appétit!

Per serving: 379 Calories; 18.1g Fat; 5.3g Carbs; 49g Protein;

Indian Beef Samosas

(**Ready in about** 35 minutes | **Servings** 8)

Ingredients

1 tablespoon sesame oil
2 cloves garlic, minced
2 tablespoons green chili peppers, chopped
Salt and ground black pepper, to taste
1 teaspoon coriander
1 (16-ounce) package phyllo dough
4 tablespoons shallots, minced
4 ounces bacon, chopped
1/2 pound ground chuck
1 teaspoon turmeric
1 teaspoon cumin powder
1 cup frozen peas, thawed
1 egg, beaten with
2 tablespoons of water (egg wash)

Directions

Heat the oil in a saucepan over medium-high heat. Once hot, sauté the shallots, garlic, and chili peppers until tender, about 3 minutes.

Then, add the beef and bacon; continue to sauté an additional 4 minutes, crumbling with a fork. Season with the salt, pepper, cumin powder, turmeric, and coriander. Stir in peas.

Then, preheat your Air Fryer to 330 degrees F. Brush the Air Fryer basket with cooking oil.

Place 1 to 2 tablespoons of the mixture onto each phyllo sheet. Fold the sheets into triangles, pressing the edges. Brush the tops with egg wash.

Bake for 7 to 8 minutes, working with batches. Serve with Indian tomato sauce if desired. Enjoy!

Per serving: 266 Calories; 13g Fat; 24.5g Carbs; 12.2g Protein;

Grilled Vienna Sausage with Broccoli

(**Ready in about** 25 minutes | **Servings** 4)

Ingredients

1 pound beef Vienna sausage
1 tablespoon fresh lemon juice
1 pound broccoli
1 teaspoon yellow mustard
1/4 teaspoon black pepper
1/2 cup mayonnaise
1 teaspoon garlic powder

Directions

Start by preheating your Air Fryer to 380 degrees F. Spritz the grill pan with cooking oil.

Cut the sausages into serving sized pieces. Cook the sausages for 15 minutes, shaking the basket occasionally to get all sides browned. Set aside.

In the meantime, whisk the mayonnaise with mustard, lemon juice, garlic powder, and black pepper. Toss the broccoli with the mayo mixture.

Turn up temperature to 400 degrees F. Cook broccoli for 6 minutes, turning halfway through the cooking time.

Serve the sausage with the grilled broccoli on the side. Bon appétit!

Per serving: 477 Calories; 43.2g Fat; 7.3g Carbs; 15.9g Protein

Aromatic T-Bone Steak with Garlic

(**Ready in about** 20 minutes | **Servings** 3)

Ingredients

1 pound T-bone steak
2 tablespoons olive oil
1/4 cup tamari sauce
4 tablespoons tomato paste
1 teaspoon dried rosemary
1/2 teaspoon dried basil
1 teaspoon Sriracha sauce
1/4 cup all-purpose flour
2 teaspoons brown sugar
4 garlic cloves, halved
2 tablespoons white vinegar
2 heaping tablespoons cilantro, chopped

Directions

Rub the garlic halves all over the T-bone steak. Toss the steak with the flour.

Drizzle the oil all over the steak and transfer it to the grill pan; grill the steak in the preheated Air Fryer at 400 degrees F for 10 minutes.

Meanwhile, whisk the tamari sauce, sugar, tomato paste, Sriracha, vinegar, rosemary, and basil. Cook an additional 5 minutes

Serve garnished with fresh cilantro. Bon appétit!

Per serving: 463 Calories; 24.6g Fat; 16.7g Carbs; 44.7g Protein

Sausage Scallion Balls

(**Ready in about** 20 minutes | **Servings** 4)

Ingredients

1 ½ pounds beef sausage meat
1 cup rolled oats
1 teaspoon Worcestershire sauce
1/2 teaspoon granulated garlic
4 teaspoons mustard
4 tablespoons scallions, chopped
1 teaspoon paprika
Flaky sea salt and freshly ground black pepper, to taste
1/2 teaspoon dried oregano
1 teaspoon dried basil
4 pickled cucumbers

Directions

Start by preheating your Air Fryer to 380 degrees F. Spritz the Air Fryer basket with cooking oil.

In a mixing bowl, thoroughly combine the sausage meat, oats, scallions, Worcestershire sauce, salt, black pepper, paprika, garlic, basil, and oregano.

Then, form the mixture into equal sized meatballs using a tablespoon.

Place the meatballs in the Air Fryer basket and cook for 15 minutes, turning halfway through the cooking time.

Serve with mustard and cucumbers. Bon appétit!

Per serving: 560 Calories; 42.2g Fat; 21.5g Carbs; 31.1g Protein

Cube Steak with Cowboy Sauce

(**Ready in about** 20 minutes | **Servings** 4)

Ingredients

1 ½ pounds cube steak Salt, to taste

4 ounces butter

2 tablespoon fresh parsley, finely chopped

1 tablespoon fresh horseradish, grated

1/4 teaspoon ground black pepper, or more to taste

2 garlic cloves, finely chopped

1 teaspoon cayenne pepper

2 scallions, finely chopped

Directions

Season the cube steak with salt and black pepper after patting it dry. Cooking oil should be sprayed into the Air Fryer basket. Place the meat in the basket.

Cook for 14 minutes in a preheated Air Fryer at 400 degrees F.

In the meantime, melt the butter in a skillet over medium heat. Stir in the remaining ingredients and continue to cook until the sauce thickens and reduces slightly.

Serve the warm cube steaks with Cowboy sauce right away.

Per serving: 469 Calories; 30.4g Fat; 0.6g Carbs; 46g Protein

Spicy Short Ribs with Red Wine Sauce

(**Ready in about** 20 minutes + marinating time | **Servings** 4)

Ingredients

1 ½ pounds short ribs

1 lemon, juiced

1 cup red wine

1 teaspoon black pepper

1 teaspoon paprika

1 cup ketchup

1 teaspoon salt

1/2 cup tamari sauce

1 teaspoon fresh ginger, grated

1 teaspoon chipotle chili powder

1 teaspoon garlic powder

1 teaspoon cumin

Directions

In a ceramic bowl, place the beef ribs, wine, tamari sauce, lemon juice, ginger, salt, black pepper, paprika, and chipotle chili powder. Cover and let it marinate for 3 hours in the refrigerator.

Discard the marinade and add the short ribs to the Air Fryer basket. Cook in the preheated Air fry at 380 degrees F for 10 minutes, turning them over halfway through the cooking time.

In the meantime, heat the saucepan over medium heat; add the reserved marinade and stir in the ketchup, garlic powder, and cumin. Cook until the sauce has thickened slightly.

Pour the sauce over the warm ribs and serve immediately. Bon appétit!

Per serving: 505 Calories; 31g Fat; 22.1g Carbs; 35.2g Protein

Beef Schnitzel with Buttermilk Spaetzle

(**Ready in about** 20 minutes | **Servings** 2)

Ingredients

1 egg, beaten

1 teaspoon paprika

1/2 teaspoon coarse sea salt

2 thin-cut minute steaks

Buttermilk Spaetzle:

1/2 cup buttermilk

1/2 teaspoon salt

1/2 teaspoon ground black pepper

1/2 cup tortilla chips, crushed

2 eggs

1 tablespoon ghee, melted

1/2 cup all-purpose flour

Directions

Start by preheating your Air Fryer to 360 degrees F.

In a shallow bowl, whisk the egg with black pepper, paprika, and salt.

Thoroughly combine the ghee with the crushed tortilla chips and coarse sea salt in another shallow bowl.

Using a meat mallet, pound the schnitzel to 1/4-inch thick.

Dip the schnitzel into the egg mixture; then, roll the schnitzel over the crumb mixture until coated on all sides.

Cook for 13 minutes in the preheated Air Fryer.

To make the spaetzle, whisk the eggs, buttermilk, flour, and salt in a bowl. Bring a large saucepan of salted water to a boil.

Push the spaetzle mixture through the holes of a potato ricer into the boiling water; slice them off using a table knife. Work in batches.

When the spaetzle float, take them out with a slotted spoon. Repeat with the rest of the spaetzle mixture.

Serve with warm schnitzel. Enjoy!

Per serving: 522 Calories; 20.7g Fat; 17.1g Carbs; 62.2g Protein

Beef Sausage Goulash

(**Ready in about** 40 minutes | **Servings** 2)

Ingredients
1 tablespoon lard, melted
2 red chilies, finely chopped
1 teaspoon ginger-garlic paste
Sea salt, to taste
4 beef good quality sausages, thinly sliced
2 teaspoons smoked paprika
2 handfuls spring greens, shredded
1 bell pepper, chopped
1/4 teaspoon ground black pepper
1 shallot, chopped
1 cup beef bone broth
1/2 cup tomato puree

Directions
Melt the lard in a Dutch oven over medium-high flame; sauté the shallots and peppers about 4 minutes or until fragrant.

Add the ginger-garlic paste and cook an additional minute. Season with salt

and black pepper and transfer to a lightly greased baking pan.

Then, brown the sausages, stirring occasionally, working in batches. Add to the baking pan.

Add the smoked paprika, broth, and tomato puree. Lower the pan onto the Air Fryer basket. Bake at 325 degrees F for 30 minutes.

Stir in the spring greens and cook for 5 minutes more or until they wilt. Serve over the hot rice if desired. Bon appétit!

Per serving: 565 Calories; 47.1g Fat; 14.3g Carbs; 20.6g Protein

Mom's Toad in the Hole

(**Ready in about** 45 minutes | **Servings** 4)

Ingredients
6 beef sausages
A pinch of salt
2 eggs
1 tablespoon butter, melted
1 cup semi-skimmed milk
1 cup plain flour

Directions
Cook the sausages in the preheated Air Fryer at 380 degrees F for 15 minutes, shaking halfway through the cooking time.

Meanwhile, make up the batter mix.

Tip the flour into a bowl with salt; make a well in the middle and crack the eggs into it. Mix with an electric whisk; now, slowly and gradually pour in the milk, whisking all the time.

Place the sausages in a lightly greased baking pan. Pour the prepared batter over the sausages.

Cook in the preheated Air Fryer at 370 degrees F approximately 25 minutes, until golden and risen. Serve with gravy if desired. Bon appétit!

Per serving: 584 Calories; 40.2g Fat; 29.5g Carbs; 23.4g Protein

Beef Nuggets with Cheesy Mushrooms

(**Ready in about** 25 minutes | **Servings** 4)

Ingredients
2 eggs, beaten
1 cup tortilla chips, crushed
salt and ground black pepper, to taste
1 pound button mushrooms
1 pound cube steak, cut into bite-size pieces
4 tablespoons yogurt
1 teaspoon dry mesquite flavored seasoning mix
Coarse
1/2 teaspoon onion powder
1 cup Swiss cheese, shredded

Directions
In a shallow bowl, whisk together the eggs and yoghurt. Combine the tortilla chips, mesquite seasoning, salt, pepper, and onion powder in a resealable bag.

Dip the steaks in the egg mixture, then place them in the bag and shake to coat on all sides.

Cook for 14 minutes at 400 degrees F, flipping halfway through.time.

Place the mushrooms in the cooking basket that has been lightly oiled. Shredded Swiss cheese on top.

5 minutes in a preheated Air Fryer at 400 degrees F. Serve alongside the beef nuggets. Good appetite!

Per serving: 355 Calories; 15.7g Fat; 13.6g Carbs; 39.8g Protein

POULTRY

Festive Turkey with Chili Mayo

(**Ready in about** 45 minutes | **Servings** 4)

Ingredients

3 teaspoons olive oil
1/2 teaspoon marjoram
Coarse salt and ground black pepper, to taste
1/4 cup mayonnaise
1 tablespoon chili sauce
1 teaspoon basil
1/2 teaspoon garlic powder
1 teaspoon shallot powder
2 pounds turkey breast, boneless Chili mayo:
1/4 cup sour cream
1/2 teaspoon stone-ground mustard

Directions

Start by preheating your Air Fryer to 360 degrees F.

In a mixing bowl, thoroughly combine the olive oil with spices. Rub the turkey breast with the spice mixture until it is well coated on all sides.

Air fry for 40 minutes, turning them over halfway through the cooking time.

Your instant-read thermometer should read 165 degrees.

Meanwhile, mix all of the Ingredients for the chili mayo. Place in your refrigerator until ready to serve.

Place the turkey breast skin-side up on a cutting board and slice it against the grain; serve with chili mayo and enjoy!

Per serving: 409 Calories; 19.2g Fat; 3.4g Carbs; 49.2g Protein

Homemade Chicken Burgers

(**Ready in about** 20 minutes | **Servings** 4)

Ingredients

1 ¼ pounds chicken white meat, ground
1/2 white onion, finely chopped
Sea salt and ground black pepper, to taste
1 ½ cups breadcrumbs
2 small pickles, sliced
1 teaspoon fresh garlic, finely chopped
1 teaspoon paprika
4 burger buns
1/2 cup cornmeal
2 tablespoons ketchup
4 lettuce leaves
1 teaspoon yellow mustard

Directions

Thoroughly combine the chicken, onion, garlic, salt and black pepper in a mixing dish. Form the mixture into 4 equal patties.

In a shallow bowl, mix paprika with cornmeal and breadcrumbs. Dip each patty in this mixture, pressing to coat well on both sides.

Spritz a cooking basket with a nonstick cooking spray. Air fry the burgers at 370 degrees F for about 11 minutes or to your desired degree of doneness.

Place your burgers on burger buns and serve with toppings. Bon appétit!

Per serving: 509 Calories; 9.8g Fat; 34g Carbs; 39.2g Protein;

Italian-Style Turkey Meatballs

(**Ready in about** 20 minutes | **Servings** 5)

Ingredients

1 ½ pounds ground turkey
1/2 cup tortilla chips, crumbled
1 egg, beaten
2 tablespoons Italian parsley, finely chopped
1 teaspoon Italian seasoning mix
1/2 cup parmesan cheese, grated
1 yellow onion, finely chopped
2 cloves garlic, minced
1 tablespoon soy sauce
1 teaspoon olive oil

Directions

Combine all of the ingredients listed above until thoroughly combined. Form the mixture into 10 meatballs.

Spritz a nonstick cooking spray into a cooking basket. Cook at 360°F for about 10 minutes, or until done to your liking. Good appetite!

Per serving: 327 Calories; 18.7g Fat; 6.9g Carbs; 32.2g Protein

Hot Chicken Drumettes with Peppers

(**Ready in about** 45 minutes | **Servings** 3)

Ingredients

1/2 cup all-purpose four
1/2 teaspoon dried basil
1/2 teaspoon dried oregano
1 tablespoon hot sauce
1/4 cup mayonnaise
1/4 cup milk
1 teaspoon shallot powder
1/2 teaspoon smoked paprika
1 teaspoon kosher salt
1 pound chicken drumettes
2 bell peppers, sliced

Directions

In a shallow bowl, mix the flour, salt, shallot powder, basil, oregano and smoked paprika.

In another bowl, mix the hot sauce, mayonnaise and milk.

Dip the chicken drumettes in the flour mixture, then, coat them with the milk mixture; make sure to coat well on all sides.

Cook in the preheated Air Fryer at 380 degrees F for 28 to 30 minutes; turn them over halfway through the cooking time. Reserve chicken drumettes, keeping them warm.

Then, cook the peppers at 400 degrees F for 13 to 15 minutes, shaking the basket once or twice. Eat warm.

Per serving: 397 Calories; 18.8g Fat; 20.6g Carbs; 34.2g Protein

Chicken Nuggets with Turnip Chips

(**Ready in about** 35 minutes | **Servings** 3)

Ingredients

1 egg

1/4 teaspoon Romano cheese, grated

2 teaspoons canola oil

1 medium-sized turnip, trimmed and sliced

1/2 teaspoon garlic powder

1/2 teaspoon cayenne pepper

1 pound chicken breast, cut into slices

1/3 cup panko crumbs

Sea salt and ground black pepper, to taste

Directions

Beat the egg with the cayenne pepper until frothy. In another shallow bowl, mix the panko crumbs with the cheese until well combined.

Dip the chicken slices into the egg mixture; then, coat the chicken slices on all sides with the the panko mixture. Brush with 1 teaspoon of canola oil.

Season with salt and pepper to taste.

Cook in the preheated Air Fryer at 380 degrees F for 12 minutes, shaking the basket halfway through the cooking time; an instant-read thermometer should read 165 degrees F. Reserve, keeping them warm.

Drizzle the turnip slices with the remaining teaspoon of canola oil. Season with garlic powder, salt and pepper to taste.

Cook the turnips slices at 370 degrees F for about 20 minutes. Serve with the warm chicken nuggets. Bon appétit!

Per serving: 361 Calories; 19.1g Fat; 9.6g Carbs; 35g Protein

Thanksgiving Turkey with Gravy

(**Ready in about** 55 minutes | **Servings** 4)

Ingredients

1 ½ pound turkey breast

2 tablespoons butter, at room temperature

Sea salt and ground black pepper, to taste

2 cups vegetable broth

1 tablespoon Dijon mustard

1/2 teaspoon garlic powder

Gravy:

1 teaspoon cayenne pepper

1/4 cup all-purpose flour

Freshly ground black pepper, to taste

Directions

Brush Dijon mustard and butter all over the turkey breast. Season with salt, black pepper, cayenne pepper and garlic powder.

Cook in the preheated Air Fryer at 360 degrees F for about 50 minutes, flipping them halfway through the cooking time. Place the fat drippings from the cooked turkey in a sauté pan. Pour in 1 cup of broth and 1/8 cup of all-purpose flour; continue to cook, whisking continuously, until a smooth paste forms.

Add in the remaining Ingredients and continue to simmer until the gravy has reduced by half. Enjoy!

Per serving: 356 Calories; 18g Fat; 7.8g Carbs; 34.2g Protein

Chicken and Cheese Stuffed Mushrooms

(**Ready in about** 15 minutes | **Servings** 4)

Ingredients

9 medium-sized button mushrooms, cleaned and steams removed

1 teaspoon soy sauce

2 ounces cheddar cheese, grated

1 teaspoon fresh garlic, finely chopped

Sea salt and red pepper, to season

2 ounces goat cheese, room temperature

1/2 pound chicken white meat, ground

2 tablespoons scallions, finely chopped

Directions

Set the mushrooms aside after patting them dry.

In a mixing bowl, thoroughly combine all ingredients except the cheddar cheese. Stir everything together thoroughly before stuffing your mushrooms.

Bake for 5 minutes at 370°F in your Air Fryer. Top with cheddar cheese and continue to cook an additional 3 to 4 minutes or until the cheese melts. Good appetite!

Per serving: 166 Calories; 8.2g Fat; 3.4g Carbs; 19.1g Protein

Tortilla Chip-Crusted Chicken Tenders

(**Ready in about** 15 minutes | **Servings** 3)

Ingredients

1 pound chicken tenders

1/2 teaspoon shallot powder

1/2 teaspoon porcini powder

1/3 cup tortilla chips, crushed

Sea salt and black pepper, to taste

1/2 teaspoon dried rosemary

Directions

Toss the chicken tenders with salt, pepper, shallot powder, porcini powder, dried rosemary and tortilla chips.

Spritz the cooking basket with a nonstick cooking spray. Cook in the preheated Air Fryer at 360 degrees F for 10 minutes, flipping them halfway through the cooking time.

Serve warm with your favorite sauce for dipping. Enjoy!

Per serving: 391 Calories; 25.2g Fat; 9.6g Carbs; 29.2g Protein

Turkey and Bacon Casserole

(**Ready in about** 15 minutes | **Servings** 5)

Ingredients

4 tablespoons bacon bits
1/2 cup sour cream
1 cup milk
1/2 teaspoon smoked paprika
1 cup Colby cheese, shredded
1 pound turkey sausage, chopped
5 eggs
Sea salt and ground black pepper, to your liking

Directions

Add the bacon bits and chopped sausage to a lightly greased baking dish.

In a mixing dish, thoroughly combine the sour cream, milk, eggs, paprika, salt and black pepper.

Pour the mixture into the baking dish.

Cook in your Air Fryer at 310 degrees F for about 10 minutes or until set. Top with Colby cheese and cook an additional 2 minutes or until the cheese is bubbly. Bon appétit!

Per serving: 444 Calories; 27.2g Fat; 17.4g Carbs; 31.2g Protein

Turkey Sausage Breakfast Cups

(**Ready in about** 20 minutes | **Servings** 2)

Ingredients

1 smoked turkey sausage, chopped
4 tablespoons cheddar cheese, shredded
4 tablespoons fresh scallions, chopped
1/2 teaspoon garlic, minced
4 tablespoons cream cheese
4 eggs
1/4 teaspoon mustard seeds
1/4 teaspoon chili powder
Salt and red pepper, to taste

Directions

Divide the sausage into four silicone baking cups.

In a mixing bowl, whisk together the eggs until pale and frothy. Then, add in the remaining ingredients and thoroughly combine.

Fill the cups with the egg mixture.

Cook for 10 to 11 minutes in an Air Fryer at 330°F. Before unmolding, place the cups on wire racks to cool slightly. Enjoy!

Per serving: 619 Calories; 48.2g Fat; 5.9g Carbs; 37.2g Protein

Greek-Style Chicken Salad

(**Ready in about** 20 minutes | **Servings** 2)

Ingredients

1/2 pound chicken breasts, boneless and skinless
2 bell peppers, deveined and chopped
2 tablespoons olives, pitted and sliced
1 cup baby spinach
2 tablespoons Greek-style yogurt 1 teaspoon lime juice
1/4 teaspoon red pepper flakes, crushed
1 Serrano pepper, deveined and chopped
1 red onion, sliced
1 cup arugula
1 cup grape tomatoes, halved
1 cucumber, sliced
1/4 cup mayonnaise
1/4 teaspoon oregano
1/4 teaspoon basil
Sea salt and ground black pepper, to taste

Directions

Spritz the chicken breasts with a nonstick cooking oil.

Cook in the preheated Air Fryer at 380 degrees F for 12 minutes. Transfer to a cutting board to cool slightly before slicing.

Cut the chicken into bite-sized strips and transfer them to a salad bowl.

Toss the chicken with the remaining Ingredients and place in your refrigerator until ready to serve. Enjoy!

Per serving: 391 Calories; 21.3g Fat; 24g Carbs; 28.4g Protein

Authentic Indian Chicken with Raita

(**Ready in about** 15 minutes | **Servings** 2)

Ingredients

2 chicken fillets
2 teaspoons garam masala
1 teaspoon ground turmeric
1/2 cup plain yogurt
1 tablespoon fresh cilantro, coarsely chopped
A pinch of ground cinnamon
Sea salt and ground black pepper, to taste
1 English cucumber, shredded and drained
A pinch of grated nutmeg
1/2 red onion, chopped

Directions

Sprinkle the chicken fillets with salt, pepper, garam masala and ground turmeric until well coated on all sides.

Cook in the preheated Air Fryer at 380 degrees F for 12 minutes, turning them over once or twice.

Meanwhile, make traditional raita by mixing the remaining Ingredients in a bowl. Serve the chicken fillets with the raita sauce on the side. Enjoy!

Per serving: 324 Calories; 15.6g Fat; 10.4g Carbs; 33.8g Protein

Asian-Style Chicken Drumettes

(**Ready in about** 15 minutes + marinating time | **Servings** 3)

Ingredients

1/4 cup soy sauce	1 teaspoon brown mustard
2 tablespoons tomato paste	1 tablespoon brown sugar
2 tablespoons sesame oil	1 teaspoon garlic paste
2 tablespoons rice vinegar	1 pound chicken drumettes

Directions

Place the chicken drumettes and the other Ingredients in a resalable bag; allow it to marinate for 2 hours.

Discard the marinade and transfer the chicken drumettes to the Air Fryer cooking basket.

Cook at 400 degrees F for 12 minutes, shaking the basket halfway through the cooking time to ensure even cooking.

In the meantime, bring the reserved marinade to a boil in a small saucepan. Immediately turn the heat to low and let it simmer until the sauce has reduced by half.

Spoon the sauce over the chicken drumettes and serve immediately.

Per serving: 333 Calories; 17.6g Fat; 10.4g Carbs; 32.8g Protein

Easy Chicken Taquitos

(**Ready in about** 20 minutes | **Servings** 3)

Ingredients

1 pound chicken breast, boneless	Sea salt and ground black pepper, to taste
1/2 teaspoon onion powder	1/2 teaspoon cayenne pepper
1/2 teaspoon garlic powder	1 cup Cotija cheese, shredded
1/2 teaspoon mustard powder	6 corn tortillas

Directions

Salt, black pepper, cayenne pepper, onion powder, garlic powder, and mustard powder season the chicken.

Cook for 12 minutes in a preheated Air Fryer at 380°F; turn the chicken over halfway through the cooking time to ensure even cooking.

Shred the chicken with two forks and place it on a cutting board. Roll up your taquitos and fill them with the chicken and Cotija cheese. Bake the taquitos for 5 to 6 minutes at 390°F; serve immediately.

Per serving: 533 Calories; 27.6g Fat; 24g Carbs; 45g Protein;

Huli-Huli Turkey

(**Ready in about** 35 minutes | **Servings** 2)

Ingredients

2 turkey drumsticks	Sea salt and ground black pepper, to season
1 teaspoon paprika	
1 teaspoon hot sauce	1 teaspoon garlic paste
1 teaspoon olive oil	1/2 teaspoon rosemary
1/2 small pineapple, cut into wedges	2 stalks scallions, sliced
	1 teaspoon coconut oil, melted

Directions

Toss the turkey drumsticks with salt, black pepper, paprika, hot sauce, garlic paste, olive oil and rosemary.

Cook in the preheated Air Fryer at 360 degrees F for 25 minutes. Reserve.

Turn the temperature to 400 degrees F, place pineapple wedges in the cooking basket and brush them with coconut oil.

Cook your pineapple for 8 to 9 minutes. Serve the turkey drumsticks garnished with roasted pineapple and scallions. Enjoy!

Per serving: 533 Calories; 25.3g Fat; 33.4g Carbs; 46.9g Protein

Keto Chicken Quesadillas

(**Ready in about** 25 minutes | **Servings** 2)

Ingredients

1/2 pound chicken breasts, boneless and skinless	3 eggs
	Salt to taste
4 ounces Ricotta cheese	2 tablespoons flaxseed meal
1 teaspoon psyllium husk powder Black pepper, to taste	

Directions

Cook the chicken in the preheated Air Fryer at 380 degrees F for 12 minutes; turn the chicken over halfway through the cooking time. Salt to taste and slice into small strips.

In a mixing bowl, beat the eggs, cheese, flaxseed meal, psyllium husk powder and black pepper. Spoon the mixture into a lightly oiled baking pan.

Bake at 380 degrees F for 9 to 10 minutes.

Spoon the chicken pieces onto your quesadilla and fold in half. Cut your quesadilla into two pieces and serve.

Per serving: 401 Calories; 20.5g Fat; 5.7g Carbs; 48.3g Protein

Garlic Butter Chicken Wings

(**Ready in about** 20 minutes | **Servings** 3)

Ingredients

1 pound chicken wings
1 teaspoon garlic paste
1 lemon, cut into slices
Salt and black pepper, to taste
2 tablespoons butter

Directions

Pat dry the chicken wings with a kitchen towel and season all over with salt and black pepper.

In a bowl, mix together butter and garlic paste. Rub the mixture all over the wings.

Cook in the preheated Air Fryer at 380 degrees F for 18 minutes. Serve garnished with lemon slices. Bon appétit!

Per serving: 270 Calories; 13.1g Fat; 2.9g Carbs; 33.6g Protein

Crispy Chicken Fingers

(**Ready in about** 15 minutes | **Servings** 3)

Ingredients

1 pound chicken tenders
1/2 teaspoon garlic powder
1/2 cup breadcrumbs
Sea salt and ground black pepper, to taste
1 tablespoon olive oil
1/2 teaspoon cayenne pepper
1/4 cup all-purpose flour
1/2 teaspoon onion powder
1 egg

Directions

Pat dry the chicken with kitchen towels and cut into bite-sized pieces.

In a shallow bowl, mix the flour, onion powder, garlic powder, cayenne pepper, salt and black pepper. Dip the chicken pieces in the flour mixture and toss to coat well on all sides.

In the second bowl, place breadcrumbs.

In the third bowl, whisk the egg; now, dip the chicken in the beaten egg. Afterwards, roll each piece of chicken in the breadcrumbs until well coated on all sides.

Spritz the chicken fingers with olive oil. Cook in your Air Fryer at 360 degrees F for 8 to 10 minutes, turning it over halfway through the cooking time.

Serve with your favorite sauce for dipping. Enjoy!

Per serving: 314 Calories; 12.1g Fat; 13.4g Carbs; 35.6g Protein

Chicken Alfredo with Mushrooms

(**Ready in about** 15 minutes | **Servings** 3)

Ingredients

1 pound chicken breasts, boneless
1/2 pound mushrooms, cleaned
1 teaspoon butter, melted
1 medium onion, quartered
Salt and black pepper, to taste
12 ounces Alfredo sauce

Directions

Start by preheating your Air Fryer to 380 degrees F. Then, place the chicken and onion in the cooking basket. Drizzle with melted butter.

Cook in the preheated Air Fryer for 6 minutes. Add in the mushrooms and continue to cook for 5 to 6 minutes more.

Slice the chicken into strips. Chop the mushrooms and onions; stir in the Alfredo sauce. Salt and pepper to taste.

Serve with hot cooked fettuccine. Bon appétit!

Per serving: 334 Calories; 15.1g Fat; 13.4g Carbs; 36g Protein;

Grandma's Chicken with Rosemary and Sweet Potatoes

(**Ready in about** 35 minutes | **Servings** 2)

Ingredients

2 chicken legs, bone-in
2 garlic cloves, minced
1 teaspoon sesame oil
2 sprigs rosemary, leaves picked and crushed
Sea salt and ground black pepper, to taste
1/2 pound sweet potatoes

Directions

Begin by preheating your Air Fryer to 380°F. Rub the chicken legs with the garlic halves.

Drizzle the sesame oil over the chicken legs and sweet potatoes. Season with salt and rosemary. In the cooking basket, combine the chicken and potatoes.

Cook for 30 minutes in a preheated Air Fryer, or until the potatoes are tender. The chicken must be cooked until it reaches an internal temperature of 165 degrees F.

Serve the chicken legs with the sweet potatoes on the side. Good appetite

Per serving: 604 Calories; 36.1g Fat; 23.4g Carbs; 44.5g Protein

Pretzel Crusted Chicken with Spicy Mustard Sauce

(**Ready in about** 20 minutes | **Servings** 6)

Ingredients

1 eggs
1/2 cup crushed pretzels
2 tablespoons olive oil
1 teaspoon shallot powder
1 teaspoon paprika
1/2 cup vegetable broth
1 tablespoon cornstarch
3 tablespoons tomato paste
1 teaspoon yellow mustard
garlic cloves, chopped

1 ½ pound chicken breasts, boneless, skinless, cut into bite-sized chunks
Sea salt and ground black pepper, to taste
3 tablespoons Worcestershire sauce
1 tablespoon apple cider vinegar
1 jalapeno pepper, minced

Directions

Start by preheating your Air Fryer to 390 degrees F.

In a mixing dish, whisk the eggs until frothy; toss the chicken chunks into the whisked eggs and coat well.

In another dish, combine the crushed pretzels with shallot powder, paprika, salt and pepper. Then, lay the chicken chunks in the pretzel mixture; turn it over until well coated.

Place the chicken pieces in the air fryer basket. Cook the chicken for 12 minutes, shaking the basket halfway through.

Meanwhile, whisk the vegetable broth with cornstarch, Worcestershire sauce, tomato paste, and apple cider vinegar.

Preheat a cast-iron skillet over medium flame. Heat the olive oil and sauté the garlic with jalapeno pepper for 30 to 40 seconds, stirring frequently.

Add the cornstarch mixture and let it simmer until the sauce has thickened a little. Now, add the air-fried chicken and mustard; let it simmer for 2 minutes more or until heated through.

Serve immediately and enjoy!

Per serving: 357 Calories; 17.6g Fat; 20.3g Carbs; 28.1g Protein

Chinese-Style Sticky Turkey Thighs

(**Ready in about** 35 minutes | **Servings** 6)

Ingredients

1 tablespoon sesame oil
2 pounds turkey thighs
1 teaspoon pink Himalayan salt
1 tablespoon Chinese rice vinegar
1 tablespoon mustard

1 teaspoon Chinese Five-spice powder
6 tablespoons honey
1/4 teaspoon Sichuan pepper
1 tablespoon sweet chili sauce
2 tablespoons soy sauce

Directions

Preheat your Air Fryer to 360 degrees F.

Brush the sesame oil all over the turkey thighs. Season them with spices.

Cook for 23 minutes, turning over once or twice. Make sure to work in batches to ensure even cooking

In the meantime, combine the remaining Ingredients in a wok (or similar type pan) that is preheated over medium-high heat. Cook and stir until the sauce reduces by about a third.

Add the fried turkey thighs to the wok; gently stir to coat with the sauce. Let the turkey rest for 10 minutes before slicing and serving. Enjoy!

Per serving: 279 Calories; 10.1g Fat; 19g Carbs; 27.7g Protein;

Easy Hot Chicken Drumsticks

(**Ready in about** 40 minutes | **Servings** 6)

Ingredients

6 chicken drumsticks Sauce:
3 tablespoons olive oil
1 teaspoon dried thyme

6 ounces hot sauce
3 tablespoons tamari sauce
1/2 teaspoon dried oregano

Directions

Spritz the sides and bottom of the cooking basket with a nonstick cooking spray.

Cook the chicken drumsticks at 380 degrees F for 35 minutes, flipping them over halfway through.

Meanwhile, heat the hot sauce, olive oil, tamari sauce, thyme, and oregano in a pan over medium-low heat; reserve.

Drizzle the sauce over the prepared chicken drumsticks; toss to coat well and serve. Bon appétit!

Per serving: 280 Calories; 18.7g Fat; 2.6g Carbs; 24.1g Protein

Crunchy Munchy Chicken Tenders with Peanuts

(**Ready in about** 25 minutes | **Servings** 4)

Ingredients

1 ½ pounds chicken tenderloins
Sea salt and ground black pepper, to taste
2 tablespoons peanuts, roasted and roughly chopped
1/2 cup tortilla chips, crushed
2 tablespoons peanut oil
1 teaspoon red pepper flakes
1/2 teaspoon garlic powder

Directions

Begin by preheating your Air Fryer to 360°F. Brush the chicken tenderloins on all sides with peanut oil.

Combine the crushed chips, salt, black pepper, garlic powder, and red pepper flakes in a mixing bowl. Dredge the chicken in the breading, shaking off any excess.

Place the tenderloins in the cooking basket. Cook for 12 to 13 minutes, or until the centre is no longer pink. Working in batches, an instant-read thermometer should read at least 165 degrees Fahrenheit.

Serve garnished with roasted peanuts. Bon appétit!

Per serving: 343 Calories; 16.4g Fat; 10.6g Carbs; 36.8g Protein

Tarragon Turkey Tenderloins with Baby Potatoes

(**Ready in about** 50 minutes | **Servings** 6)

Ingredients

2 pounds turkey tenderloins
2 teaspoons olive oil
1 teaspoon smoked paprika
1 pound baby potatoes, rubbed
Salt and ground black pepper, to taste
2 tablespoons dry white wine
1 tablespoon fresh tarragon leaves, chopped

Directions

Brush the turkey tenderloins with olive oil. Season with salt, black pepper, and paprika.

Afterwards, add the white wine and tarragon.

Cook the turkey tenderloins at 350 degrees F for 30 minutes, flipping them over halfway through. Let them rest for 5 to 9 minutes before slicing and serving.

After that, spritz the sides and bottom of the cooking basket with the remaining 1 teaspoon of olive oil.

Then, preheat your Air Fryer to 400 degrees F; cook the baby potatoes for 15 minutes. Serve with the turkey and enjoy!

Per serving: 317 Calories; 7.4g Fat; 14.2g Carbs; 45.7g Protein

Asian Chicken Filets with Cheese

(**Ready in about** 50 minutes | **Servings** 2)

Ingredients

4 rashers smoked bacon
1/4 teaspoon black pepper, preferably freshly ground
1 teaspoon garlic, minced
1 teaspoon black mustard seeds
1/2 cup Pecorino Romano cheese, freshly grated
1/2 teaspoon coarse sea salt
1 (2-inch) piece ginger, peeled and minced
2 chicken filets
1/3 cup tortilla chips, crushed
1 teaspoon mild curry powder
1/2 cup coconut milk

Directions

Start by preheating your Air Fryer to 400 degrees F. Add the smoked bacon and cook in the preheated Air Fryer for 5 to 7 minutes. Reserve.

In a mixing bowl, place the chicken fillets, salt, black pepper, garlic, ginger, mustard seeds, curry powder, and milk. Let it marinate in your refrigerator about 30 minutes.

In another bowl, mix the crushed chips and grated Pecorino Romano cheese.

Dredge the chicken fillets through the chips mixture and transfer them to the cooking basket. Reduce the temperature to 380 degrees F and cook the chicken for 6 minutes.

Turn them over and cook for a further 6 minutes. Repeat the process until you have run out of Ingredients.

Serve with reserved bacon. Enjoy!

Per serving: 376 Calories; 19.6g Fat; 12.1g Carbs; 36.2g Protein

Paprika Chicken Legs with Brussels Sprouts

(**Ready in about** 30 minutes | **Servings** 2)

Ingredients

2 chicken legs
1/2 teaspoon black pepper
1 pound Brussels sprouts
1/2 teaspoon paprika
1 teaspoon dill, fresh or dried
1/2 teaspoon kosher salt

Directions

Start by preheating your Air Fryer to 370 degrees F.

Now, season your chicken with paprika, salt, and pepper. Transfer the chicken legs to the cooking basket. Cook for 10 minutes.

Flip the chicken legs and cook an additional 10 minutes. Reserve.

Add the Brussels sprouts to the cooking basket; sprinkle with dill. Cook at 380 degrees F for 15 minutes, shaking the basket halfway through.

Serve with the reserved chicken legs. Bon appétit!

Per serving: 355 Calories; 20.1g Fat; 5.3g Carbs; 36.6g Protein

Chinese Duck (Xiang Su Ya)

(**Ready in about** 30 minutes + marinating time | **Servings** 6)

Ingredients

2 pounds duck breast, boneless	1 tablespoon light soy sauce
1 teaspoon Chinese 5-spice powder	2 green onions, chopped
1 teaspoon Szechuan peppercorns	1/2 teaspoon ground black pepper Glaze:
1 teaspoon coarse salt	3 tablespoons Shaoxing rice wine
1/4 cup molasses	1 tablespoon soy sauce
	3 tablespoons orange juice

Directions

In a ceramic bowl, place the duck breasts, green onions, light soy sauce, Chinese 5-spice powder, Szechuan peppercorns, and Shaoxing rice wine. Let it marinate for 1 hour in your refrigerator.

Preheat your Air Fryer to 400 degrees F for 5 minutes.

Now, discard the marinade and season the duck breasts with salt and pepper. Cook the duck breasts for 12 to 15 minutes or until they are golden brown.

Repeat with the other Ingredients.In the meantime, add the reserved marinade to the saucepan that is preheated over medium-high heat. Add the molasses, orange juice, and 1 tablespoon of soy sauce. Bring to a simmer and then, whisk constantly until it gets syrupy. Brush the surface of duck breasts with glaze so they are completely covered.

Place duck breasts back in the Air Fryer basket; cook an additional 5 minutes. Enjoy!

Per serving: 403 Calories; 25.3g Fat; 16.4g Carbs; 27.5g Protein

Turkey Bacon with Scrambled Eggs

(**Ready in about** 25 minutes | **Servings** 4)

Ingredients

1/2 pound turkey bacon	1/3 cup milk
2 tablespoons yogurt	1 bell pepper, finely chopped
1/2 teaspoon sea salt	4 eggs
2 green onions, finely chopped	1/2 cup Colby cheese, shredded

Directions

Place the turkey bacon in the cooking basket.

Cook at 360 degrees F for 9 to 11 minutes. Work in batches. Reserve the fried bacon.

In a mixing bowl, thoroughly whisk the eggs with milk and yogurt. Add salt, bell pepper, and green onions.

Brush the sides and bottom of the baking pan with the reserved 1 teaspoon of bacon grease.

Pour the egg mixture into the baking pan. Cook at 355 degrees F about 5 minutes. Top with shredded Colby cheese and cook for 5 to 6 minutes more.

Serve the scrambled eggs with the reserved bacon and enjoy!

Per serving: 456 Calories; 38.3g Fat; 6.3g Carbs; 21.4g Protein

Italian Chicken and Cheese Frittata

(**Ready in about** 25 minutes | **Servings** 4)

Ingredients

1 (1-pound) fillet chicken breast	Sea salt and ground black pepper, to taste
4 eggs	1/2 teaspoon cayenne pepper
1 tablespoon olive oil	1/2 cup Mascarpone cream
1/4 cup Asiago cheese, freshly grated	

Directions

Flatten the chicken breast with a meat mallet. Season with salt and pepper.

Heat the olive oil in a frying pan over medium flame. Cook the chicken for 10 to 12 minutes; slice into small strips, and reserve.

Then, in a mixing bowl, thoroughly combine the eggs, and cayenne pepper; season with salt to taste. Add the cheese and stir to combine.

Add the reserved chicken. Then, pour the mixture into a lightly greased pan; put the pan into the cooking basket.

Cook in the preheated Air Fryer at 355 degrees F for 10 minutes, flipping over halfway through.

Per serving: 329 Calories; 25.3g Fat; 3.4g Carbs; 21.1g Protein

Thanksgiving Turkey Tenderloin with Gravy

(**Ready in about** 40 minutes | **Servings** 4)

Ingredients

2 ½ pounds turkey tenderloin, sliced into pieces	1 dried marjoram
1 teaspoon cayenne pepper	1/2 head of garlic, peeled and halved
Sea salt and ground black pepper, to taste	Gravy:
3 cups vegetable broth	1/3 cup all-purpose flour
	Sea salt and ground black pepper, to taste

Directions

Start by preheating your Air Fryer to 350 degrees F.

Rub the turkey tenderloins with garlic halves; add marjoram, salt, black pepper, and cayenne pepper.

Cook the turkey tenderloins at 350 degrees F for 30 minutes or until an instant-read thermometer inserted into the center of the breast reaches 165 degrees F; flip them over halfway through.

In a saucepan, place the drippings from the roasted turkey. Add 1 cup of broth and 1/6 cup of flour to the pan; whisk until it makes a smooth paste.

Once it gets a golden brown color, add the rest of the chicken broth and flour. Sprinkle with salt and pepper to taste.

Let it simmer over medium heat, stirring constantly for 6 to 7 minutes. Serve with warm turkey tenderloin and enjoy!

Per serving: 374 Calories; 8.1g Fat; 20.5g Carbs; 52g Protein;

Roasted Citrus Turkey Drumsticks

(**Ready in about** 55 minutes | **Servings** 3)

Ingredients

3 medium turkey drumsticks, bone-in skin-on
1 teaspoon cayenne pepper
1 teaspoon dried parsley flakes
Zest of one orange
1/4 cup orange juice
Sea salt and ground black pepper, to taste
1 teaspoon fresh garlic, minced
1 teaspoon onion powder
1/2 butter stick, melted

Directions

Rub all Ingredients onto the turkey drumsticks.

Preheat your Air Fryer to 400 degrees F. Cook the turkey drumsticks for 16 minutes in the preheated Air Fryer.

Loosely cover with foil and cook an additional 24 minutes.

Once cooked, let it rest for 10 minutes before slicing and serving. Bon appétit!

Per serving: 352 Calories; 23.4g Fat; 5.2g Carbs; 29.3g Protein

Garden Vegetable and Chicken Casserole

(**Ready in about** 30 minutes | **Servings** 4)

Ingredients

2 teaspoons peanut oil
1/2 medium-sized leek, sliced
2 carrots, sliced
1 tablespoon all-purpose flour
1 thyme sprig
2 cups vegetable broth
2 pounds chicken drumettes
1 cup cauliflower florets
1 garlic clove, minced
1/4 cup dry white wine
1 rosemary sprig

Directions

Preheat your Air Fryer to 370 degrees F. Then, drizzle the chicken drumettes with peanut oil and cook them for 10 minutes. Transfer the chicken drumettes to a lightly greased pan.

Add the garlic, leeks, carrots, and cauliflower.

Mix the remaining Ingredients in a bowl. Pour the flour mixture into the pan. Cook at 380 degrees F for 15 minutes.

Serve warm.

Per serving: 333 Calories; 10.7g Fat; 5.4g Carbs; 50g Protein;

Creole Turkey with Peppers

(**Ready in about** 35 minutes | **Servings** 4)

Ingredients

2 pounds turkey thighs, skinless and boneless
1 habanero pepper, deveined and minced
1 carrot, sliced
1 tablespoon fish sauce
2 cups chicken broth
2 bell peppers, deveined and sliced
1 tablespoon Creole seasoning mix
1 red onion, sliced

Directions

Preheat your Air Fryer to 360° F. Using a nonstick cooking spray, spritz the bottom and sides of the casserole dish.

In the casserole dish, arrange the turkey thighs. Combine the onion, pepper, and carrot in a mixing bowl. Season with Creole seasoning.

After that, stir in the fish sauce and chicken broth. Cook for 30 minutes in a preheated Air Fryer. Serve immediately and enjoy!

Per serving: 426 Calories; 15.4g Fat; 12.4g Carbs; 51g Protein;

Peanut Chicken and Pepper Wraps

(**Ready in about** 25 minutes | **Servings** 4)

Ingredients

1 ½ pounds chicken breast, boneless and skinless
1 tablespoon soy sauce
2 teaspoons rice vinegar
1 teaspoon fresh garlic, minced
4 tortillas
1 teaspoon brown sugar
1 tablespoon sesame oil
1/4 cup peanut butter
1 teaspoon fresh ginger, peeled and grated
2 tablespoons lemon juice, freshly squeezed
1 bell pepper, julienned

Directions

Start by preheating your Air Fryer to 380 degrees F.

Cook the chicken breasts in the preheated Air Fryer approximately 6 minutes. Turn them over and cook an additional 6 minutes.

Meanwhile, make the sauce by mixing the peanut butter, sesame oil, soy sauce, vinegar, ginger, garlic, sugar, and lemon juice.

Slice the chicken crosswise across the grain into 1/4-inch strips. Toss the chicken into the sauce.

Decrease temperature to 390 degrees F. Spoon the chicken and sauce onto each tortilla; add bell peppers and wrap them tightly.

Drizzle with a nonstick cooking spray and bake about 7 minutes. Serve warm.

Per serving: 529 Calories; 25.5g Fat; 31.5g Carbs; 40.1g Protein

Turkey Wings with Butter Roasted Potatoes

(**Ready in about** 55 minutes | **Servings** 4)

Ingredients

4 large-sized potatoes, peeled and cut into 1-inch chunks
1 teaspoon garlic salt
1 ½ pounds turkey wings
2 tablespoons olive oil
1/2 teaspoon cayenne pepper

1 teaspoon rosemary
1 tablespoon butter, melted
1/2 teaspoon ground black pepper
1 tablespoon Dijon mustard
2 garlic cloves, minced

Directions

Add the potatoes, butter, rosemary, salt, and pepper to the cooking basket.

Cook at 400 degrees F for 12 minutes. Reserve the potatoes, keeping them warm.

Now, place the turkey wings in the cooking basket that is previously cleaned

and greased with olive oil. Add the garlic, mustard, and cayenne pepper.

Cook in the preheated Air Fryer at 350 degrees f for 25 minutes. Turn them over and cook an additional 15 minutes.

Test for doneness with a meat thermometer. Serve with warm potatoes.

Per serving: 567 Calories; 14.3g Fat; 65.7g Carbs; 46.1g Protein

Smoked Duck with Rosemary-Infused Gravy

(**Ready in about** 30 minutes | **Servings** 4)

Ingredients

1 ½ pounds smoked duck breasts, boneless
1 teaspoon agave syrup
12 pearl onions peeled
1 teaspoon rosemary, finely chopped

2 tablespoons ketchup
1 tablespoon yellow mustard
5 ounces chicken broth
1 tablespoon flour

Directions

Cook the smoked duck breasts in the preheated Air Fryer at 365 degrees F for 15 minutes.

Smear the mustard, ketchup, and agave syrup on the duck breast. Top with pearl onions. Cook for a further 7 minutes or until the skin of the duck breast looks crispy and golden brown.

Slice the duck breasts and reserve. Drain off the duck fat from the pan.

Then, add the reserved 1 tablespoon of duck fat to the pan and warm it over medium heat; add flour and cook until your roux is dark brown.

Add the chicken broth and rosemary to the pan. Reduce the heat to low and cook until the gravy has thickened slightly. Spoon the warm gravy over the reserved duck breasts. Enjoy!

Per serving: 485 Calories; 19.7g Fat; 24.1g Carbs; 51.3g Protein

Farmhouse Roast Turkey

(**Ready in about** 50 minutes | **Servings** 6)

Ingredients

2 pounds turkey
1 teaspoon sea salt
1/2 teaspoon ground black pepper

1 tablespoon fresh rosemary, chopped
1 celery stalk, chopped
1 onion, chopped

Directions

Start by preheating your Air Fryer to 360 degrees F. Spritz the sides and bottom of the cooking basket with a nonstick cooking spray.

Place the turkey in the cooking basket. Add the rosemary, salt, and black pepper. Cook for 30 minutes in the preheated Air Fryer.

Add the onion and celery and cook an additional 15 minutes. Bon appétit!

Per serving: 316 Calories; 24.2g Fat; 2.5g Carbs; 20.4g Protein

Chicken with Golden Roasted Cauliflower

(**Ready in about** 30 minutes | **Servings** 4)

Ingredients

2 pounds chicken legs
2 tablespoons olive oil
1 teaspoon sea salt
1 teaspoon dried marjoram
2 garlic cloves, minced
1/3 cup Pecorino Romano cheese, freshly grated

1/2 teaspoon ground black pepper
1 teaspoon smoked paprika
1 (1-pound) head cauliflower, broken into small florets
1/2 teaspoon dried thyme
Salt, to taste

Directions

Toss the chicken legs with the olive oil, salt, black pepper, paprika, and marjoram.

Cook in the preheated Air Fryer at 380 degrees F for 11 minutes. Flip the chicken legs and cook for a further 5 minutes.

Toss the cauliflower florets with garlic, cheese, thyme, and salt.

Increase the temperature to 400 degrees F; add the cauliflower florets and cook for 12 more minutes. Serve warm.

Per serving: 388 Calories; 18.9g Fat; 5.6g Carbs; 47.3g Protein

Adobo Seasoned Chicken with Veggies

(**Ready in about** 1 hour 30 minutes | **Servings** 4)

Ingredients

2 pounds chicken wings, rinsed and patted dry
1/2 teaspoon red pepper flakes, crushed
1 teaspoon granulated onion
1 teaspoon ground turmeric
2 tablespoons tomato powder
2 cloves garlic, peeled but not chopped
2 bell peppers, seeded and sliced
4 carrots, trimmed and halved
1/4 teaspoon ground black pepper
1 teaspoon paprika
1 teaspoon coarse sea salt
1 tablespoon dry Madeira wine
2 stalks celery, diced
1 large Spanish onion, diced
1 teaspoon ground cumin
2 tablespoons olive oil

Directions

In a large mixing bowl, combine all of the ingredients. Cover and place in the refrigerator for 1 hour.

Place the chicken wings in a baking dish.

Cook the chicken wings for 7 minutes in a preheated Air Fryer at 380 degrees F.

Cook for 15 minutes more after adding the vegetables, shaking the basket once or twice. Serve hot.

Per serving: 427 Calories; 15.3g Fat; 18.5g Carbs; 52.3g Protein

Chicken and Brown Rice Bake

(**Ready in about** 50 minutes | **Servings** 3)

Ingredients

1 cup brown rice
1 tablespoon butter, melted
1 onion, chopped
Kosher salt and ground black pepper, to taste
1 cup tomato puree
2 cups vegetable broth
2 garlic cloves, minced
1/2 cup water
3 chicken fillets
1 teaspoon cayenne pepper
1 tablespoon fresh chives, chopped

Directions

Heat the brown rice, vegetable broth and water in a pot over high heat. Bring it to a boil; turn the stove down to simmer and cook for 35 minutes.

Grease a baking pan with butter.

Spoon the prepared rice mixture into the baking pan. Add the onion, garlic, salt, black pepper, cayenne pepper, and chicken. Spoon the tomato puree over the chicken.

Cook in the preheated Air Fryer at 380 degrees F for 12 minutes. Serve garnished with fresh chives. Enjoy!

Per serving: 508 Calories; 18.3g Fat; 61g Carbs; 24.5g Protein;

Sticky Exotic Chicken Drumettes

(**Ready in about** 25 minutes | **Servings** 4)

Ingredients

2 tablespoons peanut oil
1 tablespoon yellow mustard
2 tablespoons honey
1/2 teaspoon sambal oelek
1/4 cup chicken broth
1 ½ pounds chicken drumettes, bone-in
Salt and ground white pepper, to taste
1 tablespoon tamari sauce
1 clove garlic, peeled and minced
2 tablespoons fresh orange juice
1/2 cup raw onion rings, for garnish

Directions

Start by preheating your Air Fryer to 380 degrees F.

Line the cooking basket with parchment paper. Lightly grease the parchment paper with 1 tablespoon of peanut oil. In a mixing bowl, thoroughly combine the remaining 1 tablespoon of oil honey, tamari sauce, mustard, garlic, orange juice, and sambal oelek. Whisk to combine well.

Arrange the chicken drumettes in the prepared cooking basket. Season with salt and white pepper.

Spread 1/2 of the honey mixture evenly all over each breast. Pour in the chicken broth. Cook for 12 minutes.

Turn them over, add the remaining 1/2 of the honey mixture, and cook an additional 10 minutes. Garnish with onion rings and serve immediately.

Per serving: 317 Calories; 12.5g Fat; 11.5g Carbs; 38.4g Protein

Spanish Chicken with Golden Potatoes

(**Ready in about** 25 minutes | **Servings** 4)

Ingredients

2 tablespoons butter, melted
1 pound Yukon Gold potatoes, peeled and diced
1 teaspoon dried rosemary, crushed
1 teaspoon dried thyme, crushed
1/3 teaspoon freshly ground black pepper
4 chicken drumsticks, bone-in
1 teaspoon fresh garlic, minced
1 teaspoon cayenne pepper
1 lemon, 1/2 juiced, 1/2 cut into wedges
Kosher salt, to taste
2 tablespoons sherry

Directions

Start by preheating your Air Fryer to 370 degrees F. Then, grease a baking pan with the melted butter. Arrange the chicken drumsticks in the baking pan. Bake in the preheated Air Fryer for 8 minutes. Add the diced potatoes.

Drizzle chicken and potatoes with lemon juice. Sprinkle with garlic, rosemary, thyme, cayenne pepper, black pepper, and salt. Turn the temperature to 400 degrees F and cook for a further 12 minutes. Make sure to shake the basket once or twice. Remove from the Air Fryer basket and sprinkle sherry on top. Serve with the lemon wedges. Enjoy!

Per serving: 382 Calories; 17.9g Fat; 26.1g Carbs; 26.7g Protein

Turkey Breakfast Frittata

(**Ready in about** 50 minutes | **Servings** 4)

Ingredients

1 tablespoon olive oil
3 tablespoons Greek yogurt
6 large-sized eggs
1/4 teaspoon red pepper flakes, crushed Himalayan salt, to taste
1 green bell pepper, seeded and sliced

1 pound turkey breasts, slices
3 tablespoons Cottage cheese, crumbled
1 red bell pepper, seeded and sliced
1/4 teaspoon ground black pepper

Directions

Grease the cooking basket with olive oil. Add the turkey and cook in the preheated Air Fryer at 350 degrees F for 30 minutes, flipping them over halfway through. Cut into bite-sized strips and reserve.

Now, beat the eggs with Greek yogurt, cheese, black pepper, red pepper, and salt. Add the bell peppers to a baking pan that is previously lightly greased with a cooking spray.

Add the turkey strips; pour the egg mixture over all Ingredients.

Bake in the preheated Air Fryer at 360 degrees F for 15 minutes. Serve right away!

Per serving: 327 Calories; 13.4g Fat; 3.5g Carbs; 45.4g Protein

Nana's Turkey Chili

(**Ready in about** 1 hour | **Servings** 4)

Ingredients

1/2 medium-sized leek, chopped
1 jalapeno pepper, seeded and minced
2 cups tomato puree
1 pound ground turkey, 85% lean 15% fat
1/2 teaspoon black peppercorns
1 teaspoon mustard seeds

2 garlic cloves, minced
1/2 red onion, chopped
2 tablespoons olive oil
1 bell pepper, seeded and chopped
2 cups chicken stock
Salt, to taste
1 teaspoon chili powder
1 teaspoon ground cumin
1 (12-ounce) can kidney beans, rinsed and drained

Directions

Start by preheating your Air Fryer to 365 degrees F.

Place the leeks, onion, garlic and peppers in a baking pan; drizzle olive oil evenly over the top. Cook for 4 to 6 minutes.

Add the ground turkey. Cook for 6 minutes more or until the meat is no longer pink.

Now, add the tomato puree, 1 cup of chicken stock, black peppercorns, salt, chili powder, mustard seeds, and cumin to the baking pan. Cook for 24 minutes, stirring every 7 to 10 minutes. Stir in the canned beans and the remaining 1 cup of stock; let it cook for a further 9 minutes; make sure to stir halfway through. Bon appétit!

Per serving: 327 Calories; 13.4g Fat; 3.5g Carbs; 45.4g Protein

Authentic Chicken-Fajitas with Salsa

(**Ready in about** 30 minutes | **Servings** 4)

Ingredients

1 pound chicken tenderloins, chopped
1 teaspoon fajita seasoning
1 teaspoon shallot powder
Salsa
4 flour tortillas
1 bunch fresh coriander, roughly chopped
1 lime

Sea salt and ground black pepper, to your liking
2 bell peppers, seeded and diced
1 ancho chili pepper, seeded and finely chopped
2 tablespoons extra-virgin olive oil
2 ripe tomatoes, crushed

Directions

Toss the chicken in a bowl with the salt, pepper, shallot powder, and fajita seasoning mix.

9 minutes in a preheated Air Fryer at 390 degrees F. Roast for an additional 8 minutes after adding the bell peppers

Combine the chilli, tomatoes, and coriander for the salsa. Squeeze 1 lime juice over the top; add olive oil and stir well to combine.

Warm the tortillas in your Air Fryer for 10 minutes at 200 degrees F. Serve the chicken fajitas with tortillas and salsa on the side. Enjoy!

Per serving: 433 Calories; 14.5g Fat; 44.9g Carbs; 30.2g Protein

Pizza Spaghetti Casserole

(**Ready in about** 30 minutes | **Servings** 4)

Ingredients

8 ounces spaghetti
2 tomatoes, pureed
1/2 cup Asiago cheese, shredded
3 tablespoons Romano cheese, grated

1 pound smoked chicken sausage, sliced
1 tablespoon Italian seasoning mix
1 tablespoon fresh basil leaves, chiffonade

Directions

Bring a large pot of lightly salted water to a boil. Cook your spaghetti for 10 minutes or until al dente; drain and reserve, keeping warm.

Stir in the chicken sausage, tomato puree, Asiago cheese, and Italian seasoning mix.

Then, spritz a baking pan with cooking spray; add the spaghetti mixture to the pan. Bake in the preheated Air Fryer at 325 degrees F for 11 minutes.

Top with the grated Romano cheese. Turn the temperature to 390 degrees F and cook an additional 5 minutes or until everything is thoroughly heated and the cheese is melted.

Garnish with fresh basil leaves. Bon appétit!

Per serving: 472 Calories; 23.1g Fat; 28.6g Carbs; 38.2g Protein

Vermouth Bacon and Turkey Burgers

(**Ready in about** 30 minutes | **Servings** 4)

Ingredients

2 tablespoons vermouth
2 strips Canadian bacon, sliced
2 garlic cloves, minced 2 tablespoons fish sauce
4 soft hamburger rolls
1 teaspoon red pepper flakes
4 (1-ounce) slices Cheddar cheese
4 lettuce leaves

1 tablespoon honey
1/2 shallot, minced
1 pound ground turkey
Sea salt and ground black pepper, to taste
4 tablespoons tomato ketchup
4 tablespoons mayonnaise

Directions

Start by preheating your Air Fryer to 400 degrees F.

Whisk the vermouth and honey in a mixing bowl; brush the Canadian bacon with the vermouth mixture.

Cook for 3 minutes. Flip the bacon over and cook an additional 3 minutes.

Then, thoroughly combine the ground turkey, shallots, garlic, fish sauce, salt, black pepper, and red pepper. Form the meat mixture into 4 burger patties.

Bake in the preheated Air Fryer at 370 degrees F for 10 minutes. Flip them over and cook another 10 minutes.

Spread the ketchup and mayonnaise on the inside of the hamburger rolls and place the burgers on the rolls; top with bacon, cheese and lettuce; serve immediately.

Per serving: 564 Calories; 30.6g Fat; 32.9g Carbs; 37.7g Protein

Chicken Taquitos with Homemade Guacamole

(**Ready in about** 35 minutes | **Servings** 4)

Ingredients

1 tablespoon peanut oil
1 pound chicken breast
1 teaspoon chili powder
1 teaspoon garlic powder
1/2 cup sour cream
1 ripe avocado, pitted and peeled
1 tablespoon fresh cilantro, chopped
1 lime, juiced
1 teaspoon fresh garlic, minced

Seasoned salt and ground black pepper, to taste
1 cup Colby cheese, shredded
8 corn tortillas
Guacamole:
1/2 onion, finely chopped
1 teaspoon ground cumin
1 tomato, crushed
1 chili pepper, seeded and minced
Sea salt and black pepper, to taste

Directions

Toss the chicken with the salt, pepper, shallot powder, and fajita seasoning mix in a mixing bowl.

9 minutes in a 390° F preheated Air Fryer. After adding the bell peppers, roast for an additional 8 minutes.

For the salsa, combine the chilli, tomatoes, and coriander. Squeeze 1 lime juice over the top, then drizzle with olive oil and mix well.

Warm the tortillas in an Air Fryer at 200°F for 10 minutes. With tortillas and salsa on the side, serve the chicken fajitas. Enjoy!

Per serving: 512 Calories; 35.2g Fat; 15.9g Carbs; 34.9g Protein

VEGETABLES & SIDE DISHES

Roasted Broccoli and Cauliflower with Tahini Sauce

(**Ready in about** 15 minutes | **Servings** 3)

Ingredients

1/2 pound broccoli, broken into florets
1/2 pound cauliflower, broken into florets
1 teaspoon onion powder
1 tablespoons tahini
Salt and chili flakes, to taste
1/2 teaspoon porcini powder
1/4 teaspoon cumin powder
1/2 teaspoon granulated garlic
1 teaspoon olive oil
2 tablespoons soy sauce
1 teaspoon white vinegar

Directions

Start by preheating your Air Fryer to 400 degrees F.

Now, toss the vegetables with the onion powder, porcini powder cumin powder, garlic and olive oil. Transfer your vegetables to the lightly greased cooking basket.

Air Fry your veggies in the preheated Air Fryer at 400 degrees F for 6 minutes. Remove the broccoli florets from the cooking basket. Continue to cook the cauliflower for 5 to 6 minutes more.

Meanwhile, make the tahini sauce by simply whisking the remaining Ingredients in a small bowl. Spoon the sauce over the warm vegetables and serve immediately. Bon appétit!

Per serving: 178 Calories; 11.9g Fat; 14.6g Carbs; 6.8g Protein

Sweet & Sticky Baby Carrots

(**Ready in about** 45 minutes | **Servings** 3)

Ingredients

1 tablespoon coconut oil
1 pound baby carrots
2 lemongrasses, finely chopped
3 tablespoons honey
1 teaspoon fresh ginger, peeled and grated
1 teaspoon lemon thyme

Directions

Toss all Ingredients in a mixing bowl and let it stand for 30 minutes. Transfer the baby carrots to the cooking basket.

Cook the baby carrots at 380 degrees F for 15 minutes, shaking the basket halfway through the cooking time to ensure even cooking.

Serve warm and enjoy!

Per serving: 157 Calories; 4.8g Fat; 29.3g Carbs; 1.2g Protein

Green Bean Salad with Goat Cheese and Almonds

(**Ready in about** 15 minutes | **Servings** 3)

Ingredients

1 ½ pounds green beans, trimmed and cut into small chunks
2 bell peppers, deseeded and sliced
1 tablespoon Shoyu sauce
Dressing:
1 teaspoon deli mustard
2 tablespoons extra-virgin olive oil
1 small-sized red onion, sliced
Sea salt and ground black pepper, to taste
1/4 cup almonds
1/2 cup goat cheese, crumbled
1 tablespoon champagne vinegar
1 clove garlic, pressed

Directions

Season the green beans with salt and black pepper to your liking. Brush them with a nonstick cooking oil.

Place the green beans in the Air Fryer cooking basket. Cook the green beans at 400 degrees F for 5 minutes and transfer to a salad bowl. Stir in the onion and bell peppers.

Then, add the raw almonds to the cooking basket. Roast the almonds at 350 degrees F for 5 minutes, shaking the basket periodically to ensure even cooking.

In the meantime, make the dressing by blending all Ingredients until well incorporated.

Dress your salad and top with goat cheese and roasted almonds. Enjoy!

Per serving: 290 Calories; 17.3g Fat; 25.6g Carbs; 13.8g Protein

Roasted Asparagus with Pecorino Romano Cheese

(**Ready in about** 10 minutes | **Servings** 3)

Ingredients

1 pound asparagus spears, trimmed
1/2 teaspoon shallot powder
1/4 teaspoon cumin powder
1/2 teaspoon dried rosemary
1 tablespoon sesame seeds, toasted
1/2 teaspoon garlic powder
1 teaspoon sesame oil
Coarse sea salt and ground black pepper, to taste 4 tablespoons Pecorino Romano cheese, grated

Directions

Begin by preheating your Air Fryer to 400°F.

Toss the asparagus with the sesame oil, spices, and cheese before placing it in the Air Fryer cooking basket.

Cook the asparagus for 5 to 6 minutes in a preheated Air Fryer, shaking the basket halfway through to ensure even browning. Serve warm, garnished with toasted sesame seeds. Good appetite!

Per serving: 109 Calories; 5.9g Fat; 8.5g Carbs; 7.8g Protein

Mediterranean-Style Roasted Broccoli

(**Ready in about** 10 minutes | **Servings** 3)

Ingredients

1 pound broccoli florets
1 teaspoon butter, melted
Sea salt, to taste
1 tablespoon fresh lemon juice

1 teaspoon mixed peppercorns, crushed
1/4 cup mayonnaise
1 teaspoon deli mustard
2 cloves garlic, minced

Directions

Toss the broccoli florets with butter, salt and crushed peppercorns until well coated on all sides.

Cook in the preheated Air Fryer at 400 degrees F for 6 minutes until they've softened.

In the meantime, make your aioli by mixing the mayo, lemon juice, mustard and garlic in a bowl.

Serve the roasted broccoli with the sauce on the side. Enjoy!

Per serving: 199 Calories; 15.6g Fat; 11.3g Carbs; 4.6g Protein

Hot Cheesy Roasted Eggplants

(**Ready in about** 15 minutes | **Servings** 2)

Ingredients

1 pound eggplants, sliced
1 teaspoon sesame oil
1/4 teaspoon chili flakes
1/2 teaspoon parsley flakes
1 teaspoon garlic, pressed

Sea salt and freshly ground black pepper, to taste
1/2 cup cream cheese, at room temperature

Directions

Brush the eggplants with sesame oil and season with salt and black pepper before placing them in the Air Fryer cooking basket.

Cook your eggplants for 10 minutes at 400 degrees F.

In the meantime, combine the remaining ingredients to make the rub. Cook for 5 minutes more after topping the eggplants with the chilli cheese mixture.

Arrange the eggplants on a serving platter. Good appetite!

Per serving: 257 Calories; 19.8g Fat; 16g Carbs; 6.6g Protein

Stuffed and Baked Sweet Potatoes

(**Ready in about** 35 minutes | **Servings** 2)

Ingredients

2 medium sweet potatoes
1 tablespoon butter, cold
2 tablespoons cilantro, chopped
Coarse sea salt and ground black pepper, to taste

6 ounces canned kidney beans
1/4 cup Cotija cheese, crumbled

Directions

Poke the sweet potatoes all over using a small knife; transfer them to the Air Fryer cooking basket.

Cook in the preheated Air Fryer at 380 degrees F for 20 to 25 minutes. Then, scrape the sweet potato flesh using a spoon; mix sweet potato flesh with kidney beans, cheese, butter, salt and pepper.

Bake for a further 10 minutes until cooked through.

Place the sweet potatoes on serving plates. Garnish with cilantro and serve.

Per serving: 277 Calories; 13.7g Fat; 31.4g Carbs; 8.1g Protein

Spring Beet and Feta Cheese Salad

(**Ready in about** 45 minutes | **Servings** 2)

Ingredients

2 medium beets, scrubbed and trimmed
2 scallions stalks, chopped
1 tablespoon maple syrup
1 tablespoon orange juice concentrate
1/2 teaspoon Dijon mustard
Salt and black pepper, to taste
2 ounces feta cheese, crumbled

6 ounces mixed greens
1 teaspoon olive oil
2 stalks green garlic, finely chopped
2 tablespoons extra-virgin olive oil
1/4 teaspoon ground cumin seeds
2 tablespoons white vinegar

Directions

Toss your beets with 1 teaspoon of olive oil. Cook your beets in the preheated Air Fryer at 400 degrees F for 40 minutes, turning them over once or twice to ensure even cooking.

Let your beets cool completely and then, slice them with a sharp knife. Place the beets in a salad bowl and add in the mixed greens, scallions and garlic.

In a small mixing dish, whisk the maple syrup, orange juice concentrate, vinegar, 2 tablespoons of extra-virgin olive oil, Dijon mustard, salt, black pepper and ground cumin.

Dress your salad, toss to combine and garnish with feta cheese. Bon appétit!

Per serving: 349 Calories; 23.1g Fat; 28.8g Carbs; 11.1g Protein

Roasted Chermoula Parsnip

(**Ready in about** 20 minutes | **Servings** 3)

Ingredients

1 pound parsnip, trimmed, peeled and cut into 1/2 inch pieces
1/2 teaspoon saffron strands
2 garlic cloves
1 teaspoon ground cumin
1/2 teaspoon ground coriander
1 tablespoon freshly squeezed lemon juice
1 tablespoon fresh cilantro leaves
1 tablespoon fresh parsley leaves
Salt and black pepper, to taste
1/2 teaspoon cayenne pepper
4 tablespoons extra-virgin olive oil

Directions

Place your parsnips in the Air Fryer cooking basket; spritz the parsnip with a nonstick cooking oil.

Cook the parsnip in the preheated Air Fryer at 380 degrees F for 15 minutes, shaking the basket halfway through the cooking time to ensure even browning.

Add the remaining Ingredients to a bowl of your food processor or blender. Blend until smooth and well combined.

Spoon the Chermoula dressing over roasted parsnip and serve. Bon appétit!

Per serving: 201 Calories; 8.7g Fat; 30g Carbs; 2.4g Protein;

Roasted Cherry Tomato Pasta

(**Ready in about** 15 minutes | **Servings** 3)

Ingredients

1 pound cherry tomatoes
1 teaspoon olive oil
1/2 teaspoon oregano
1/2 teaspoon dried basil
1 pound fettuccine pasta
Sea salt and ground black pepper, to taste

Directions

Toss the cherry tomatoes with the olive oil, salt, black pepper, oregano, and basil until well combined.

Cook for 4 minutes in a preheated Air Fryer at 400 degrees F, tossing the basket halfway through to ensure even cooking.

Cook the pasta as directed on the package. Enjoy the roasted tomatoes over the hot pasta!

Per serving: 573 Calories; 3.9g Fat; 90g Carbs; 24g Protein;

Mexican-Style Roasted Zucchini

(**Ready in about** 15 minutes | **Servings** 3)

Ingredients

1 pound zucchini, sliced into thick rounds
1/2 teaspoon garlic powder
1/8 teaspoon cayenne pepper
1 teaspoon Mexican oregano
1 teaspoon chili oil
1 tablespoon fresh cilantro, roughly chopped
1/2 teaspoon red pepper flakes, crushed
Kosher salt and black pepper, to taste
1/2 cup Cotija cheese, crumbled

Directions

Toss your zucchini with the chili oil, red pepper flakes, garlic powder, cayenne pepper, Mexican oregano, salt and black pepper.

Transfer your zucchini to the Air Fryer cooking basket.

Cook your zucchini at 400 degrees F for 7 minutes. Turn over the slices of zucchini and top them with crumbled cheese.

Continue to cook for 5 minutes more. Garnish with cilantro and serve.

Per serving: 137 Calories; 8.8g Fat; 6.9g Carbs; 9.9g Protein

Mediterranean Herb-Crusted Cauliflower

(**Ready in about** 15 minutes | **Servings** 3)

Ingredients

1 ½ pounds cauliflower, cut into florets
1 teaspoon garlic, minced
1 teaspoon lemon zest
1 teaspoon dried rosemary
1/2 teaspoon dried thyme
1/4 cup breadcrumbs
1 teaspoon olive oil
Sea salt and ground black pepper, to taste
1 tablespoon fresh Italian parsley, chopped
1/4 cup Parmesan cheese, grated
1/4 cup Kalamata olives

Directions

Toss the cauliflower florets with all Ingredients, except for the Kalamata olives.

Cook the cauliflower at 400 degrees F for 12 minutes, shaking the basket once or twice to ensure even browning.

Garnish the roasted cauliflower with Kalamata olives and serve immediately. Enjoy!

Per serving: 137 Calories; 5.8g Fat; 16.5g Carbs; 7.4g Protein;

Creamed Sweet Potato Casserole

(**Ready in about** 30 minutes | **Servings** 3)

Ingredients

1 cup heavy cream
1/2 teaspoon dried parsley flakes
1 ½ ponds sweet potatoes, peeled and thinly sliced
1/2 cup Colby cheese, grated
1/2 teaspoon garlic, minced
A pinch of freshly grated nutmeg
1 teaspoon rosemary
1 teaspoon basil

Direction

Begin by preheating your Air Fryer to 330°F. Brush nonstick cooking oil on the sides and bottom of a casserole dish.

Except for the cheese, thoroughly combine all ingredients in a mixing bowl. Fill the casserole dish halfway with the mixture.

Bake for 25 minutes in a preheated Air Fryer. Bake for an additional 5 minutes after adding the cheese. Good appetite!

Per serving: 421 Calories; 22g Fat; 46.5g Carbs; 9.6g Protein

Classic Brussels Sprouts with Bacon

(**Ready in about** 20 minutes | **Servings** 2)

Ingredients

3/4 pound Brussels sprouts, trimmed and halved
1/2 teaspoon smoked paprika
1 teaspoon garlic, minced
1 tablespoon white wine
3 ounces bacon, sliced
Sea salt and ground black pepper, to taste
1 teaspoon lemon juice, freshly squeezed
1 teaspoon butter, melted

Directions

Toss the Brussels sprouts with butter, salt, black pepper, paprika, garlic, lemon juice and wine. Transfer your Brussels sprouts to the Air Fryer cooking basket.

Top your Brussels sprouts with bacon and cook them at 380 degrees F for 15 minutes, shaking the basket once or twice to ensure even cooking.

Serve warm and enjoy!

Per serving: 277 Calories; 19.2g Fat; 18.7g Carbs; 11.6g Protein

Cauliflower Tater Tots

(**Ready in about** 20 minutes | **Servings** 3)

Ingredients

1 ½ pounds cauliflower
1 tablespoon corn flour
1 tablespoon butter
1 teaspoon dried parsley flakes
1/2 teaspoon dried basil
2 tablespoons plain flour
1 teaspoon shallot powder
1/2 teaspoon garlic powder
Sea salt and freshly ground black pepper, to taste

Directions

Blanch the cauliflower in salted boiling water for 4 minutes, or until al dente. Drain the cauliflower and pulse it in a food processor.

Place the cauliflower in a mixing bowl and set aside. Mix in the remaining ingredients until well combined. To make bite-sized tots, roll the mixture into balls.

Cook for 16 minutes in a preheated Air Fryer at 375 degrees F, shaking the basket halfway through to ensure even browning.

Good appetite!

Per serving: 127 Calories; 4.6g Fat; 17.6g Carbs; 5.2g Protein

Fried Peppers with Roasted Garlic Sauce

(**Ready in about** 50 minutes | **Servings** 2)

Ingredients

4 bell peppers
Sea salt and black pepper to taste
1/4 cup mayonnaise
6 cloves garlic
1 teaspoon fresh lime juice
1 teaspoon olive oil
1 tablespoon fresh parsley, roughly chopped Dipping Sauce:
1/4 cup sour cream
1/4 teaspoon paprika

Directions

Brush the peppers with olive oil and transfer them to the cooking basket.

Roast the peppers at 400 degrees F for 15 minutes, turning your peppers over halfway through the cooking time; roast the peppers until the skin blisters and turns black.

Transfer the peppers to a plastic bag until cool; the skins should peel away off of the peppers easily; season the peppers with salt and pepper and reserve.

To make the sauce, place the garlic on a sheet of aluminum foil and spritz with cooking spray. Wrap the garlic in the foil.

Cook in the preheated Air Fryer at 400 degrees for 12 minutes. Then, open the top of the foil and continue to cook for a further 10 minutes.

Let it cool for about 10 minutes; remove the cloves by squeezing them out of the skins; mash the garlic and combine it with the sour cream, mayonnaise, fresh lime juice and paprika.

Garnish the roasted peppers with parsley and serve with the sauce on the side and enjoy!

Per serving: 307 Calories; 26.2g Fat; 16.3g Carbs; 4.2g Protein

Greek-Style Air Grilled Tomatoes with Feta

(**Ready in about** 15 minutes | **Servings** 3)

Ingredients

3 medium tomatoes, quartered, pat dry
3 ounces feta cheese, sliced
1 teaspoon oregano
1 teaspoon parsley
Sea salt and ground black pepper, to season
1 teaspoon basil
1 tablespoon extra-virgin olive oil
1 teaspoon cilantro
1/2 teaspoon rosemary
2 tablespoons Greek black olives, pitted and sliced

Directions

Brush your tomatoes with olive oil. Sprinkle them with spices until well coated on all sides. Now, transfer your tomatoes to the Air Fryer cooking basket

Cook your tomatoes at 350 degrees F for approximately 12 minutes, turning them over halfway through the cooking time.

Garnish with black olives and feta cheese and serve. Enjoy!

Per serving: 147 Calories; 11.2g Fat; 7.6g Carbs; 5.2g Protein

Rainbow Vegetable Croquettes

(**Ready in about** 15 minutes | **Servings** 3)

Ingredients

1/3 canned green peas
1/3 sweet corn kernels
1/4 cup plain flour
1/2 cup cheddar cheese, grated
1 egg
1/2 teaspoon fresh garlic, pressed
Kosher salt and freshly ground black pepper, to taste
1/3 pound zucchini, grated and squeezed
1/4 cup chickpea flour
1 teaspoon fresh coriander, chopped
1 teaspoon fresh parsley, chopped
1/2 teaspoon cayenne pepper
1 tablespoon olive oil

Directions

In a mixing bowl, thoroughly combine the vegetables, flour, cheese, egg, coriander, parsley; sprinkle with all spices and stir until everything is well incorporated.

Shape the mixture into small patties and transfer them to the lightly oiled Air Fryer cooking basket.

Cook the vegetable croquettes in the preheated Air Fryer at 365 degrees F for 6 minutes. Turn them over and cook for a further 6 minutes

Serve immediately and enjoy!

Per serving: 234 Calories; 10.8g Fat; 23.4g Carbs; 11.8g Protein

Sweet Potato Hash Browns

(**Ready in about** 50 minutes | **Servings** 3)

Ingredients

1 pound sweet potatoes, grated
1/2 teaspoon garlic, finely chopped
1/4 teaspoon ground allspice
1 tablespoon peanut oil
1 bell pepper, chopped
1/2 cup scallion, chopped
Sea salt and ground black pepper, to your liking
1 teaspoon peanut oil

Directions

Allow your sweet potatoes to soak in cold water for 25 minutes. Remove from the water and pat dry with a paper towel.

Stir in the remaining ingredients until everything is thoroughly combined.

Cook for 25 minutes at 395°F in a preheated Air Fryer, turning halfway through the cooking time. Good appetite!

Per serving: 188 Calories; 6.2g Fat; 30.4g Carbs; 4g Protein

Authentic Japanese Vegetable Tempura

(**Ready in about** 15 minutes | **Servings** 3)

Ingredients

1 cup plain flour 1 egg
1 pound green beans
2 tablespoons soy sauce
1 tablespoon mirin Himalayan salt, to taste
1 cup ice-cold water
1 white onion, slice into rings
1 teaspoon dashi granules

Directions

Sift the flour in a bowl. In another bowl, whisk the egg until pale and frothy; pour in the water.

Fold the sifted flour into the egg/water mixture and stir to combine. Dip the green beans and onion in the prepared tempura.

Cook your veggies in the preheated Air Fryer at 400 degrees F for 10

minutes, shaking the basket halfway through the cooking time; work with batches.

Meanwhile, whisk the dashi granules, soy sauce and mirin; salt to taste and set the sauce aside.

Serve the vegetable tempura with the sauce on the side. Serve immediately!

Per serving: 268 Calories; 6.2g Fat; 42.4g Carbs; 9.7g Protein;

Spanish Patatas Bravas

(**Ready in about** 15 minutes | **Servings** 3)

Ingredients

1 pound russet potatoes, cut into 1-inch cubes
1 cup tomatoes, crushed
1/2 teaspoon paprika
2 garlic cloves, crushed
A pinch of brown sugar
Salt and ground black pepper, to taste
1/2 teaspoon chili powder
2 teaspoons canola oil

Directions

Toss the potatoes with 1 teaspoon of oil, salt and black pepper. Transfer the potato chunks to the lightly oiled Air Fryer cooking basket.

Cook the potatoes in your Air Fryer at 400 degrees F for 12 minutes total, shaking the basket halfway through the cooking time.

In the meantime, heat the remaining teaspoon of oil in a saucepan over medium-high heat. Once hot, stir in the other Ingredients cook for 8 to 10 minutes until cooked through.

Spoon the sauce over roasted potatoes and serve immediately. Enjoy!

Per serving: 166 Calories; 3.9g Fat; 32g Carbs; 4.5g Protein;

Vegetable Oatmeal Fritters

(**Ready in about** 20 minutes | **Servings** 3)

Ingredients

1 cup rolled oats
1/2 teaspoon shallot powder
1/2 teaspoon porcini powder
1/2 teaspoon garlic powder
1/2 cup celery, grated
1/2 teaspoon mustard seeds
1 ½ cups water
2 tablespoons soy sauce
1 cup white mushrooms, chopped
1 carrot, grated
1/2 teaspoon cumin
2 tablespoons tomato ketchup

Directions

Start by preheating your Air Fryer to 380 degrees F.

Thoroughly combine all Ingredients. Shape the batter into equal patties and place them in the cooking basket. Spritz your patties with a nonstick cooking spray.

Cook the fritters in the preheated Air Fryer for 15 minutes, turning them over halfway through the cooking time.

Serve with your favorite dipping sauce. Bon appétit!

Per serving: 263 Calories; 5.9g Fat; 42.8g Carbs; 11.4g Protein

Favorite Winter Bliss Bowl

(**Ready in about** 25 minutes | **Servings** 3)

Ingredients

1 pound cauliflower florets
9 ounces frozen crab cakes
1 teaspoon olive oil
1 cup iceberg lettuce
1 red bell pepper, deseeded and sliced
2 tablespoons fresh lemon juice
2 tablespoons cilantro leaves, chopped
Sea salt and freshly ground black pepper, to taste
1 cup quinoa
1 cup baby spinach
1 tablespoon extra-virgin olive oil
1 teaspoon yellow mustard

Directions

Brush the cauliflower and crab cakes with olive oil; season them with salt and black pepper and transfer them to the cooking basket.
Cook the cauliflower at 400 degrees F for about 12 minutes total, shaking the basket halfway through the cooking time. Then, cook the crab cakes at 400 degrees F for about 12 minutes total, flipping them halfway through the cooking time.
In the meantime, rinse your quinoa, drain it and transfer to a soup pot with 2 cups of lightly salted water; bring to a boil. Turn heat to a simmer and continue to cook, covered, for about 20 minutes; fluff with a fork and transfer to a serving bowl.
Add the cauliflower and crab cakes to the bowl. Add your greens and bell pepper to the bowl. In a small mixing dish, whisk the lemon juice, extra- virgin olive oil and yellow mustard.
Drizzle the dressing over all Ingredients, garnish with fresh cilantro and serve immediately. Bon appétit!
Per serving: 166 Calories; 3.9g Fat; 32g Carbs; 4.5g Protein

Mexican-Style Roasted Corn Salad

(**Ready in about** 15 minutes | **Servings** 2)

Ingredients

2 ears of corn, husked
4 ounces Cotija cheese crumbled
1/2 red onion, finely chopped
1/2 teaspoon Mexican oregano
1 cup Mexican Escabeche
2 tablespoons extra-virgin olive oil
Fresh juice of 1 lime
Kosher salt and freshly ground black pepper, to taste

Directions

Start by preheating your Air Fryer to 390 degrees F.

Place the corn on the cob in the lightly greased cooking basket; cook the corn on the cob for 10 minutes, turning over halfway through the cooking time.

Once the corn has cooled, use a sharp knife to cut off the kernels into a salad bowl. Toss the corn kernels with the remaining Ingredients and serve immediately. Enjoy!

Per serving: 373 Calories; 28.5g Fat; 19.7g Carbs; 13g Protein

Traditional Indian Bhajiya

(**Ready in about** 20 minutes | **Servings** 3)

Ingredients

1 cup carrot, grated
1 small garlic clove, finely chopped
1/2 cup chickpea flour
1 teaspoon Chaat masala
1 cup cabbage, shredded
Himalayan salt and ground black pepper, to taste
1 small onion, chopped
1 teaspoon coriander, minced
1 teaspoon olive oil

Directions

Combine all ingredients in a mixing bowl until well combined.

After that, spoon 2 tablespoons of the mixture into the cooking basket and flatten with a wide spatula.

Cook for 7 to 8 minutes at 350 degrees F, then flip and cook for another 8 minutes, or until golden brown on top. Warm up and enjoy!

Per serving: 114 Calories; 2.7g Fat; 18.5g Carbs; 4.8g Protein

Easy Sweet Potato Bake

(**Ready in about** 35 minutes | **Servings** 3)

Ingredients

1 stick butter, melted
2 tablespoons honey
2 eggs, beaten
1/2 cup fresh breadcrumbs
1 pound sweet potatoes, mashed
1/3 cup coconut milk
1/4 cup flour

Directions

Start by preheating your Air Fryer to 325 degrees F. Spritz a casserole dish with cooking oil.

In a mixing bowl, combine all Ingredients, except for the breadcrumbs and 1

tablespoon of butter. Spoon the mixture into the prepared casserole dish.

Top with the breadcrumbs and brush the top with the remaining 1 tablespoon of butter. Bake in the preheated Air Fryer for 30 minutes. Bon appétit!

Per serving: 409 Calories; 26.1g Fat; 38.3g Carbs; 7.2g Protein

Avocado Fries with Roasted Garlic Mayonnaise

(**Ready in about** 50 minutes | **Servings** 4)

Ingredients

1/2 head garlic (6-7 cloves)
3/4 cup all-purpose flour
2 eggs
3 avocados, cut into wedges
1/2 cup mayonnaise
Sea salt and ground black pepper, to taste
1 cup tortilla chips, crushed
Sauce:
1 teaspoon lemon juice
1 teaspoon mustard

Directions

Place the garlic on a piece of aluminum foil and spritz with cooking spray. Wrap the garlic in the foil.

Cook in the preheated Air Fryer at 400 degrees for 12 minutes. Check the garlic, open the top of the foil and continue to cook for 10 minutes more.

Let it cool for 10 to 15 minutes; remove the cloves by squeezing them out of the skins; mash the garlic and reserve. In a shallow bowl, combine the flour, salt, and black pepper. In another shallow dish, whisk the eggs until frothy.

Place the crushed tortilla chips in a third shallow dish. Dredge the avocado wedges in the flour mixture, shaking off the excess. Then, dip in the egg mixture; lastly, dredge in crushed tortilla chips. Spritz the avocado wedges with cooking oil on all sides.

Cook in the preheated Air Fryer at 395 degrees F approximately 8 minutes, turning them over halfway through the cooking time.

Meanwhile, combine the sauce Ingredients with the smashed roasted garlic. To serve, divide the avocado fries between plates and top with the sauce.

Enjoy!

Per serving: 351 Calories; 27.7g Fat; 21.5g Carbs; 6.4g Protein

Roasted Broccoli with Sesame Seeds

(**Ready in about** 15 minutes | **Servings** 2)

Ingredients

1 pound broccoli florets
1/2 teaspoon porcini powder
1 teaspoon garlic powder
1/2 teaspoon cumin powder
1/4 teaspoon paprika
1/2 teaspoon shallot powder
Sea salt and ground black pepper, to taste
2 tablespoons sesame seeds
2 tablespoons sesame oil

Directions

Start by preheating the Air Fryer to 400 degrees F.
Blanch the broccoli in salted boiling water until al dente, about 3 to 4 minutes. Drain well and transfer to the lightly greased Air Fryer basket.
Add the sesame oil, shallot powder, porcini powder, garlic powder, salt, black pepper, cumin powder, paprika, and sesame seeds.
Cook for 6 minutes, tossing halfway through the cooking time. Bon appétit!
Per serving: 267 Calories; 19.5g Fat; 20.2g Carbs; 8.9g Protein

Corn on the Cob with Herb Butter

(**Ready in about** 15 minutes | **Servings** 2)

Ingredients

2 ears fresh corn, shucked and cut into halves
1 tbsp fresh rosmary chopped
1/2 teaspoon fresh ginger, grated
1 tablespoon fresh basil, chopped

1 teaspoon granulated garlic
2 tablespoons butter, room temperature
Sea salt and ground black pepper, to taste
2 tablespoons fresh chives, roughly chopped

Directions

Spritz the corn with cooking spray. Cook at 395 degrees F for 6 minutes, turning them over halfway through the cooking time.

In the meantime, mix the butter with the granulated garlic, ginger, salt, black pepper, rosemary, and basil.

Spread the butter mixture all over the corn on the cob. Cook in the preheated Air Fryer an additional 2 minutes. Bon appétit!

Per serving: 239 Calories; 13.3g Fat; 30.2g Carbs; 5.4g Protein

Rainbow Vegetable Fritters

(**Ready in about** 20 minutes | **Servings** 2)

Ingredients

1 zucchini, grated and squeezed
4 tablespoons all-purpose flour
1 tablespoon peanut oil
1 teaspoon fresh garlic, minced

1/2 cup canned green peas
1 cup corn kernels
2 tablespoons fresh shallots, minced
Sea salt and ground black pepper, to taste
1 teaspoon cayenne pepper

Directions

In a mixing bowl, thoroughly combine all Ingredients until everything is well incorporated.

Shape the mixture into patties. Spritz the Air Fryer basket with cooking spray.

Cook in the preheated Air Fryer at 365 degrees F for 6 minutes. Turn them over and cook for a further 6 minutes

Serve immediately and enjoy!

Per serving: 215 Calories; 8.4g Fat; 31.6g Carbs; 6g Protein

Easy Sweet Potato Hash Browns

(**Ready in about** 50 minutes | **Servings** 2)

Ingredients

1 pound sweet potatoes, peeled and grated
1 teaspoon fresh garlic, minced
1/2 teaspoon cinnamon
1 tablespoon peanut oil

1/4 cup scallions, chopped
1/4 teaspoon ground allspice
Sea salt and ground black pepper, to taste
2 eggs, whisked

Directions

Allow the sweet potatoes to soak in cold water for 25 minutes. Drain the sweet potatoes and pat them dry with a kitchen towel.

Stir in the remaining ingredients until well combined.

Cook for 20 minutes in a preheated Air Fryer at 395°F. Shake the basket a couple of times. With ketchup, of course.

Per serving: 381 Calories; 16.7g Fat; 44.8g Carbs; 14.3g Protein

American-Style Brussel Sprout Salad

(**Ready in about** 35 minutes | **Servings** 4)

Ingredients

1 pound Brussels sprouts
1 apple, cored and diced
1/2 cup pomegranate seeds
1/4 cup olive oil
4 eggs, hardboiled and sliced
Dressing
1 teaspoon honey

1/2 cup mozzarella cheese, crumbled
1 small red onion, chopped
2 tablespoons champagne vinegar
1 teaspoon Dijon mustard
Sea salt and ground black pepper, to taste

Directions

Start by preheating your Air Fryer to 380 degrees F.

Add the Brussels sprouts to the cooking basket. Spritz with cooking spray and cook for 15 minutes. Let it cool to room temperature about 15 minutes.

Toss the Brussels sprouts with the apple, cheese, pomegranate seeds, and red onion.

Mix all Ingredients for the dressing and toss to combine well. Serve topped with the hard-boiled eggs. Bon appétit!

Per serving: 319 Calories; 18.5g Fat; 27g Carbs; 14.7g Protein;

The Best Cauliflower Tater Tots

(**Ready in about** 25 minutes | **Servings** 4)

Ingredients

1 pound cauliflower florets
2 tablespoons scallions, chopped
1 garlic clove, minced
1/2 cup breadcrumbs
1 teaspoon paprika
1 tablespoon olive oil
1 cup Colby cheese, shredded
2 eggs
1/4 teaspoon dried dill weed
Sea salt and ground black pepper, to taste

Directions

Blanch the cauliflower for 3 to 4 minutes in salted boiling water, or until al dente. Drain thoroughly before pulsing in a food processor.

Mix in the remaining ingredients until well combined. Make bite-sized tots out of the cauliflower mixture.

Spritz the cooking spray into the Air Fryer basket.

Cook for 16 minutes, shaking, in a preheated Air Fryer at 375 degrees F.

halfway through the cooking time. Serve with your favorite sauce for dipping. Bon appétit!

Per serving: 267 Calories; 19.2g Fat; 9.6g Carbs; 14.9g Protein

Skinny Pumpkin Chips

(**Ready in about** 20 minutes | **Servings** 2)

Ingredients

1 pound pumpkin, cut into sticks
1/2 teaspoon basil
1/2 teaspoon rosemary
1 tablespoon coconut oil
Salt and ground black pepper, to taste

Directions

Start by preheating the Air Fryer to 395 degrees F. Brush the pumpkin sticks with coconut oil; add the spices and toss to combine.

Cook for 13 minutes, shaking the basket halfway through the cooking time. Serve with mayonnaise. Bon appétit!

Per serving: 118 Calories; 7g Fat; 14.7g Carbs; 2.2g Protein

Cheese Stuffed Roasted Peppers

(**Ready in about** 20 minutes | **Servings** 2)

Ingredients

2 red bell peppers, tops and seeds removed
1 cup cream cheese
2 pickles, chopped
2 yellow bell peppers, tops and seeds removed
4 tablespoons mayonnaise
Salt and pepper, to taste

Directions

Arrange the peppers in the lightly greased cooking basket. Cook in the preheated Air Fryer at 400 degrees F for 15 minutes, turning them over halfway through the cooking time.

Season with salt and pepper.

Then, in a mixing bowl, combine the cream cheese with the mayonnaise and chopped pickles. Stuff the pepper with the cream cheese mixture and serve. Enjoy!

Per serving: 367 Calories; 21.8g Fat; 21.9g Carbs; 21.5g Protein

Classic Onion Rings

(**Ready in about** 30 minutes | **Servings** 2)

Ingredients

1 medium-sized onion, slice into rings
Coarse sea salt and ground black pepper, to your liking
3/4 cup bread crumbs
1 teaspoon baking powder
1 cup all-purpose flour
2 eggs, beaten
1/2 cup yogurt
1 teaspoon onion powder
1 teaspoon garlic powder
1/2 teaspoon celery seeds

Directions

Place the onion rings in the bowl with cold water; let them soak approximately 20 minutes; drain the onion rings and pat dry using a pepper towel.

In a shallow bowl, mix the flour, baking powder, salt, and black pepper. Add the yogurt and eggs and mix well to combine.

In another shallow bowl, mix the bread crumbs, onion powder, garlic powder, and celery seeds. Dip the onion rings in the flour/egg mixture; then, dredge in the breadcrumb mixture.

Spritz the Air Fryer basket with cooking spray; arrange the breaded onion rings in the basket.

Cook in the preheated Air Fryer at 400 degrees F for 4 to 5 minutes, turning them over halfway through the cooking time. Bon appétit!

Per serving: 440 Calories; 12.7g Fat; 60g Carbs; 19.2g Protein

Greek-Style Roasted Tomatoes with Feta

(**Ready in about** 20 minutes | **Servings** 2)

Ingredients

3 medium-sized tomatoes, cut into four slices, pat dry
1/4 teaspoon red pepper flakes, crushed
1 teaspoon dried oregano
1 teaspoon dried basil
3 slices Feta cheese
1/2 teaspoon sea salt

Directions

Spritz the tomatoes with cooking oil and transfer them to the Air Fryer basket. Sprinkle with seasonings.

Cook at 350 degrees F approximately 8 minutes turning them over halfway through the cooking time.

Top with the cheese and cook an additional 4 minutes. Bon appétit!

Per serving: 148 Calories; 9.4g Fat; 9.4g Carbs; 7.8g Protein

Sweet Corn Fritters with Avocado

(**Ready in about** 20 minutes | **Servings** 3)

Ingredients

2 cups sweet corn kernels
2 eggs, whisked
2 tablespoons fresh cilantro, chopped
Sea salt and ground black pepper, to taste
1 avocado, peeled, pitted and diced
1 small-sized onion, chopped
1 teaspoon baking powder
2 tablespoons sweet chili sauce
1 garlic clove, minced

Directions

In a mixing bowl, thoroughly combine the corn, onion, garlic, eggs, baking powder, cilantro, salt, and black pepper.

Shape the corn mixture into 6 patties and transfer them to the lightly greased Air Fryer basket.

Cook in the preheated Air Fry at 370 degrees for 8 minutes; turn them over and cook for 7 minutes longer.

Serve the fritters with the avocado and chili sauce.

Per serving: 383 Calories; 21.3g Fat; 42.8g Carbs; 12.7g Protein

Cauliflower and Goat Cheese Croquettes

(**Ready in about** 30 minutes | **Servings** 2)

Ingredients

1/2 pound cauliflower florets
Sea salt and ground black pepper, to taste
1 cup sour cream
1/2 teaspoon shallot powder
1 cup goat cheese, shredded
1/4 teaspoon cumin powder
2 garlic cloves, minced
1 teaspoon Dijon mustard

Directions

Place the cauliflower florets in a saucepan of water; bring to the boil; reduce the heat and cook for 10 minutes or until tender.

Mash the cauliflower using your blender; add the garlic, cheese, and spices; mix to combine well.

Form the cauliflower mixture into croquettes shapes.

Cook in the preheated Air Fryer at 375 degrees F for 16 minutes, shaking halfway through the cooking time. Serve with the sour cream and mustard. Bon appétit!

Per serving: 297 Calories; 21.7g Fat; 11.7g Carbs; 15.3g Protein

Greek-Style Vegetable Bake

(**Ready in about** 35 minutes | **Servings** 4)

Ingredients

1 eggplant, peeled and sliced
1 red onion, sliced
1 teaspoon fresh garlic, minced
1 teaspoon dried oregano
Salt and ground black pepper, to taste
1 tomato, sliced
2 bell peppers, seeded and sliced
1 teaspoon mustard
4 tablespoons olive oil
1 teaspoon smoked paprika
6 ounces halloumi cheese, sliced lengthways

Directions

Start by preheating your Air Fryer to 370 degrees F. Spritz a baking pan with nonstick cooking spray.

Place the eggplant, peppers, onion, and garlic on the bottom of the baking pan. Add the olive oil, mustard, and spices. Transfer to the cooking basket and cook for 14 minutes.

Top with the tomatoes and cheese; increase the temperature to 390 degrees F and cook for 5 minutes more until bubbling. Let it sit on a cooling rack for 10 minutes before serving.

Bon appétit!

Per serving: 296 Calories; 22.9g Fat; 16.1g Carbs; 9.3g Protein

Baked Cholula Cauliflower

(**Ready in about** 20 minutes | **Servings** 4)

Ingredients

1/2 cup all-purpose flour	Salt, to taste
1/2 teaspoon ground black pepper	1/2 teaspoon garlic powder
1/2 teaspoon cayenne pepper	1/2 cup water
2 tablespoons olive oil	1 pound cauliflower, broken into small florets
1/4 cup Cholula sauce	1/2 teaspoon shallot powder

Directions

Start by preheating your Air Fryer to 400 degrees F. Lightly grease a baking pan with cooking spray.

In a mixing bowl, combine the flour, water, spices, and olive oil. Coat the cauliflower with the prepared batter; arrange the cauliflower on the baking pan.

Then, bake in the preheated Air Fryer for 8 minutes or until golden brown.

Brush the Cholula sauce all over the cauliflower florets and bake an additional 4 to 5 minutes. Bon appétit!

Per serving: 153 Calories; 7.3g Fat; 19.3g Carbs; 4.1g Protein

Fall Vegetables with Spiced Yogurt

(**Ready in about** 25 minutes | **Servings** 2)

Ingredients

1 pound celeriac, cut into 1 1/2-inch pieces	2 red onions, cut into 1 1/2-inch pieces
2 carrots, cut into 1 1/2-inch pieces	1/2 teaspoon sea salt
1 tablespoon sesame oil	1/2 teaspoon mustard seeds
1/2 teaspoon chili powder	1/2 teaspoon ground black pepper, to taste
Spiced Yogurt:	1/4 cup Greek yogurt
1 tablespoon mayonnaise	1 tablespoon honey

Directions

Place the vegetables in a single layer in the lightly greased cooking basket. Drizzle the sesame oil over vegetables.

Sprinkle with black pepper and sea salt.

Cook at 390 degrees F for 20 minutes, shaking the basket halfway through the cooking time.

Meanwhile, make the sauce by whisking all Ingredients. Spoon the sauce over the roasted vegetables. Bon appétit!

Per serving: 319 Calories; 14.1g Fat; 46g Carbs; 6.4g Protein

Sweet-and-Sour Mixed Veggies

(**Ready in about** 25 minutes | **Servings** 4)

Ingredients

1/2 pound asparagus, cut into 1 1/2-inch pieces	2 tablespoons peanut oil
1/2 pound broccoli, cut into 1 1/2-inch pieces	1/2 pound carrots, cut into 1 1/2-inch pieces
Some salt and white pepper, to taste	1/2 cup water
2 tablespoon honey	4 tablespoons raisins
	2 tablespoons apple cider vinegar

Directions

Place the vegetables in a single layer in the lightly greased cooking basket. Drizzle the peanut oil over the vegetables.

Sprinkle with salt and white pepper.

Cook at 380 degrees F for 15 minutes, shaking the basket halfway through the cooking time.

Add 1/2 cup of water to a saucepan; bring to a rapid boil and add the raisins, honey, and vinegar. Cook for 5 to 7 minutes or until the sauce has reduced by half.

Spoon the sauce over the warm vegetables and serve immediately. Bon appétit!

Per serving: 153 Calories; 7.1g Fat; 21.6g Carbs; 3.6g Protein

Roasted Corn Salad

(**Ready in about** 15 minutes + chilling time | **Servings** 3)

Ingredients

2 ears of corn, husked	3 tablespoons sour cream
1 garlic clove, minced	1 jalapeño pepper, seeded and minced
1/4 cup plain yogurt	2 bell peppers, seeded and thinly sliced
Pink salt and white pepper, to your liking	1 tbsp fresh lemon juice
1 shallot, chopped	1/4 cup Queso Fresco, crumbled
2 tablespoons fresh parsley, chopped	

Directions

Start by preheating the Air Fryer to 390 degrees F. Spritz the Air Fryer grill pan with cooking spray.

Place the corn on the grill pan and cook for 10 minutes, turning over halfway through the cooking time. Set aside.

Once the corn has cooled to the touch, use a sharp knife to cut off the kernels into a salad bowl.

While the corn is resting, whisk the sour cream, yogurt, garlic, jalapeño pepper, fresh lemon juice, salt, and white pepper.

Add the shallot, pepper, and parsley to the salad bowl and toss to combine well. Toss with the sauce and serve topped with cheese. Enjoy!

Per serving: 205 Calories; 9.5g Fat; 27g Carbs; 7.5g Protein

Rainbow Vegetable and Parmesan Croquettes

(**Ready in about** 40 minutes | **Servings** 4)

Ingredients

1 pound potatoes, peeled	2 tablespoons butter
Salt and black pepper, to taste	1 carrot, grated
1/2 cup mushrooms, chopped	4 tablespoons milk
1/4 cup broccoli, chopped	1/2 teaspoon cayenne pepper
1 clove garlic, minced	2 tablespoons olive oil
1/2 cup panko bread crumbs	3 tablespoons scallions, minced
1/2 cup all-purpose flour	2 eggs
	1/2 cup parmesan cheese, grated

Directions

In a large saucepan, boil the potatoes for 17 to 20 minutes. Drain the potatoes and mash with the milk, butter, salt, black pepper, and cayenne pepper.

Add the mushrooms, broccoli, carrots, garlic, scallions, and olive oil; stir to combine well. Shape the mixture into patties.

In a shallow bowl, place the flour; beat the eggs in another bowl; in a third bowl, combine the breadcrumbs with the parmesan cheese.

Dip each patty into the flour, followed by the eggs, and then the breadcrumb mixture; press to adhere.

Cook in the preheated Air Fryer at 375 degrees F for 16 minutes, shaking halfway through the cooking time. Bon appétit!

Per serving: 377 Calories; 19.1g Fat; 40.2g Carbs; 12.1g Protein

Quick Shrimp and Vegetable Bake

(**Ready in about** 25 minutes | **Servings** 4)

Ingredients

1 pound shrimp cleaned and deveined	1 cup cauliflower, cut into florets
1 carrot, sliced	2 bell pepper, sliced
1 shallot, sliced	1 cup broccoli, cut into florets
1 cup tomato paste	
2 tablespoons sesame oil	

Directions

Begin by preheating your Air Fryer to 360°F. Coat the baking dish with cooking spray.

Arrange the shrimp and vegetables in the baking dish now. Then pour the sesame oil over the vegetables. Over the vegetables, pour the tomato paste.

In a preheated Air Fryer, cook for 10 minutes. Cook for another 12 minutes, stirring occasionally. Serve hot.

Per serving: 269 Calories; 8.8g Fat; 21.7g Carbs; 28.2g Protein

Roasted Brussels Sprout Salad

(**Ready in about** 35 minutes + chilling time | **Servings** 2)

Ingredients

1/2 pound Brussels sprouts	Coarse sea salt and ground black pepper, to taste
1 tablespoon olive oil	
2 ounces baby arugula	2 ounces pancetta, chopped
Lemon Vinaigrette:	2 tablespoons extra virgin olive oil
1 shallot, thinly sliced	
1 teaspoon Dijon mustard	2 tbsp fresh lemon juice
1 tablespoon honey	

Directions

Start by preheating your Air Fryer to 380 degrees F.

Add the Brussels sprouts to the cooking basket. Brush with olive oil and cook for 15 minutes. Let it cool to room temperature about 15 minutes.

Toss the Brussels sprouts with the salt, black pepper, baby arugula, and shallot.

Mix all Ingredients for the dressing. Then, dress your salad, garnish with pancetta, and serve well chilled. Bon appétit!

Per serving: 316 Calories; 16.6g Fat; 33.2g Carbs; 13.8g Protein

Winter Bliss Bowl

(**Ready in about** 45 minutes | **Servings** 3)

Ingredients

1 cup pearled barley	1 (1-pound) head cauliflower, broken into small florets
sea salt and ground black pepper, to taste	Coarse
2 tablespoons champagne vinegar	1 teaspoon yellow mustard
4 tablespoons olive oil, divided	4 tablespoons mayonnaise
2 tablespoons cilantro leaves, chopped	10 ounces ounce canned sweet corn, drained

Directions

Cook the barley in a saucepan with salted water. Bring to a boil and cook approximately 28 minutes. Drain and reserve.

Start by preheating the Air Fryer to 400 degrees F.

Place the cauliflower florets in the lightly greased Air Fryer basket. Season with salt and black pepper; cook for 12 minutes, tossing halfway through the cooking time.

Toss with the reserved barley. Add the champagne vinegar, mayonnaise, mustard, olive oil, and corn. Garnish with fresh cilantro. Bon appétit!

Per serving: 387 Calories; 25.3g Fat; 38.5g Carbs; 6g Protein

Tater Tot Vegetable Casserole

(**Ready in about** 40 minutes | **Servings** 6)

Ingredients

1 tablespoon olive oil
1 red bell pepper, seeded and sliced
1 shallot, sliced
1 (28-ounce) bag frozen tater tots
Sea salt and ground black pepper, to your liking
1 cup Swiss cheese, shredded

2 cloves garlic, minced
1 yellow bell pepper, seeded and sliced
1 ½ cups kale
1 cup milk
6 eggs
4 tablespoons seasoned breadcrumbs

Directions

Heat the olive oil in a saucepan over medium-high heat. Sauté the shallot, garlic, and peppers for 2 to 3 minutes. Add the kale and cook until wilted.

Arrange the tater tots evenly over the bottom of a lightly greased casserole

dish. Spread the sautéed mixture over the top.

In a mixing bowl, thoroughly combine the eggs, milk, salt, pepper, and shredded cheese. Pour the mixture into the casserole dish.

Lastly, top with the seasoned breadcrumbs. Bake at 330 degrees F for 30 minutes or until top is golden brown. Bon appétit!

Per serving: 493 Calories; 26.1g Fat; 49.6g Carbs; 17.1g Protein

Fried Asparagus with Goat Cheese

(**Ready in about** 15 minutes | **Servings** 3)

Ingredients

1 bunch of asparagus, trimmed
1/4 teaspoon cracked black pepper, to taste
1/2 teaspoon dried dill weed

1/2 teaspoon kosher salt
1 tablespoon olive oil
1/2 cup goat cheese, crumbled

Directions

Place the asparagus spears in the lightly greased cooking basket. Toss the asparagus with the olive oil, salt, black pepper, and dill.

Cook in the preheated Air Fryer at 400 degrees F for 9 minutes. Serve garnished with goat cheese. Bon appétit!

Per serving: 132 Calories; 11.2g Fat; 2.2g Carbs; 6.5g Protein

FISH & SEAFOOD

Colorful Salmon and Fennel Salad

(**Ready in about** 20 minutes | **Servings** 3)

Ingredients
1 pound salmon
Sea salt and ground black pepper, to taste
1/2 teaspoon paprika
1 tablespoon lime juice
1 tablespoon sesame seeds, lightly toasted
1 cucumber, sliced
1 fennel, quartered
1 tablespoon balsamic vinegar
1 teaspoon olive oil
1 tomato, sliced
1 tablespoon extra-virgin olive oil

Directions
Toss the salmon and fennel with 1 teaspoon olive oil, salt, black pepper, and paprika in a mixing bowl.

Cook for 12 minutes in a preheated Air Fryer at 380 degrees F, shaking the basket once or twice.

Transfer the salmon to a salad bowl and cut it into bite-sized strips.

Combine the fennel, balsamic vinegar, lime juice, 1 tablespoon extra-virgin olive oil, tomato, and cucumber in a mixing bowl.

Toss well to combine and serve topped with lightly toasted sesame seeds. Enjoy!

Per serving: 306 Calories; 16.3g Fat; 5.6g Carbs; 32.2g Protein

Parmesan Chip-Crusted Tilapia

(**Ready in about** 15 minutes | **Servings** 3)

Ingredients
1 ½ pounds tilapia, slice into 4 portions Sea
salt and ground black pepper, to taste
1/4 cup parmesan cheese, preferably freshly grated
2 tablespoons buttermilk
1 teaspoon granulated garlic
1/4 cup almond flour
1/2 teaspoon cayenne pepper
1 cup tortilla chips, crushed
1 egg, beaten

Directions
Generously season your tilapia with salt, black pepper and cayenne pepper.
Prepare a bread station. Add the granulated garlic, almond flour and parmesan cheese to a rimmed plate.
Whisk the egg and buttermilk in another bowl and place crushed tortilla chips in the third bowl.
Dip the tilapia pieces in the flour mixture, then in the egg/buttermilk mixture and finally roll them in the crushed chips, pressing to adhere well.
Cook in your Air Fryer at 400 degrees F for 10 minutes, flipping halfway through the cooking time. Serve with chips if desired. Bon appétit!
Per serving: 356 Calories; 10.5g Fat; 11.9g Carbs; 52g Protein

Keto Cod Fillets

(**Ready in about** 15 minutes | **Servings** 2)

Ingredients
2 cod fish fillets
1 teaspoon Old Bay seasoning
1 egg, beaten
1 teaspoon butter, melted
2 tablespoons coconut milk, unsweetened
1/3 cup coconut flour, unsweetened

Directions
Place the cod fish fillets, butter and Old Bay seasoning in a Ziplock bag; shake until the fish is well coated on all sides.

In a shallow bowl, whisk the egg and coconut milk until frothy.

In another bowl, place the coconut flour. Dip the fish fillets in the egg mixture, then, coat them with coconut flour, pressing to adhere.

Cook the fish at 390 degrees F for 6 minutes; flip them over and cook an additional 6 minutes until your fish flakes easily when tested with a fork. Bon appétit!

Per serving: 218 Calories; 12.5g Fat; 3.5g Carbs; 22g Protein

Easiest Lobster Tails Ever

(**Ready in about** 10 minutes | **Servings** 2)

Ingredients
2 (6-ounce) lobster tails
1/2 teaspoon dried rosemary
1/2 teaspoon garlic, pressed
1 teaspoon deli mustard
1 teaspoon olive oil
1 teaspoon fresh cilantro, minced
Sea salt and ground black pepper, to taste

Directions
Toss the lobster tails with the other Ingredients until they are well coated on all sides.

Cook the lobster tails at 370 degrees F for 3 minutes. Then, turn them and cook on the other side for 3 to 4 minutes more until they are opaque.

Serve warm and enjoy!

Per serving: 147 Calories; 3.5g Fat; 2.5g Carbs; 25.5g Protein

Salmon Bowl with Lime Drizzle

(**Ready in about** 15 minutes | **Servings** 3)

Ingredients

1 pound salmon steak
2 teaspoons sesame oil
1/2 teaspoon coriander seeds
1 lime, juiced
1 teaspoon honey

Sea salt and Sichuan pepper, to taste
2 tablespoons reduced-sodium soy sauce

Directions

Pat the salmon dry and drizzle it with 1 teaspoon of sesame oil.

Season the salmon with salt, pepper and coriander seeds. Transfer the salmon to the Air Fryer cooking basket.

Cook the salmon at 400 degrees F for 5 minutes; turn the salmon over and continue to cook for 5 minutes more or until opaque.

Meanwhile, warm the remaining Ingredients in a small saucepan to make the lime drizzle.

Slice the fish into bite-sized strips, drizzle with the sauce and serve immediately. Enjoy!

Per serving: 307 Calories; 15g Fat; 4.5g Carbs; 32.3g Protein

Classic Crab Cakes

(**Ready in about** 15 minutes | **Servings** 3)

Ingredients

1 egg, beaten
2 crustless bread slices
1 pound lump crabmeat
1 teaspoon deli mustard
Sea salt and ground black pepper, to taste
4 lemon wedges, for serving

2 tablespoons milk
2 tablespoons scallions, chopped
1 teaspoon Sriracha sauce
1 garlic clove, minced

Directions

Whisk the egg and milk until pale and frothy; add in the bread and let it soak for a few minutes.

Stir in the other Ingredients, except for the lemon wedges; shape the mixture into 4 equal patties. Place your patties in the Air Fryer cooking basket. Spritz your patties with a nonstick cooking spray.

Cook the crab cakes at 400 degrees F for 5 minutes. Turn them over and cook on the other side for 5 minutes.

Serve warm, garnished with lemon wedges. Bon appétit!

Per serving: 180 Calories; 4.4g Fat; 10.5g Carbs; 24.4g Protein

Salmon Fillets with Herbs and Garlic

(**Ready in about** 15 minutes | **Servings** 3)

Ingredients

1 pound salmon fillets
1 tablespoon olive oil
1 sprig thyme
2 cloves garlic, minced
1 lemon, sliced

Sea salt and ground black pepper, to taste
2 sprigs rosemary

Directions

Pat the salmon fillets dry and season them with salt and pepper; drizzle salmon fillets with olive oil and place in the Air Fryer cooking basket.

Cook the salmon fillets at 380 degrees F for 7 minutes; turn them over, top with thyme, rosemary and garlic and continue to cook for 5 minutes more.

Serve topped with lemon slices and enjoy!

Per serving: 248 Calories; 11.2g Fat; 3.1g Carbs; 31.4g Protein

Grouper with Miso-Honey Sauce

(**Ready in about** 15 minutes | **Servings** 2)

Ingredients

3/4 pound grouper fillets
1 teaspoon water
1 tablespoon sesame oil
1 tablespoon mirin
1 tablespoon Shoyu sauce

Salt and white pepper, to taste
1 teaspoon deli mustard or Dijon mustard
1 tablespoon honey
1/4 cup white miso

Directions

Sprinkle the grouper fillets with salt and white pepper; drizzle them with a nonstick cooking oil.

Cook the fish at 400 degrees F for 5 minutes; turn the fish fillets over and cook an additional 5 minutes.

Meanwhile, make the sauce by whisking the remaining. Serve the warm fish with the miso-honey sauce on the side. Bon appétit!

Per serving: 307 Calories; 15g Fat; 4.5g Carbs; 32.3g Protein

Fish Sticks with Vidalia Onions

(**Ready in about** 12 minutes | **Servings** 2)

Ingredients

1/2 pound fish sticks, frozen
1 teaspoon sesame oil
Sea salt and ground black pepper, to taste
1/4 teaspoon mustard seeds
4 tablespoons Greek-style yogurt

1/2 pound Vidalia onions, halved
4 tablespoons mayonnaise
1/2 teaspoon red pepper flakes
1 teaspoon chipotle chili in adobo, minced

Directions

Drizzle the fish sticks and Vidalia onions with sesame oil. Toss them with salt, black pepper and red pepper flakes.

Transfer them to the Air Fryer cooking basket.

Cook the fish sticks and onions at 400 degreed F for 5 minutes. Shake the basket and cook an additional 5 minutes or until cooked through.

Meanwhile, mix the mayonnaise, Greek-style yogurt, mustard seeds and chipotle chili.

Serve the warm fish sticks garnished with Vidalia onions and the sauce on the side. Bon appétit!

Per serving: 571 Calories; 41.7g Fat; 36.2g Carbs; 14.2g Protein

Moroccan Harissa Shrimp

(**Ready in about** 10 minutes | **Servings** 3)

Ingredients

1 pound breaded shrimp, frozen
1 teaspoon coriander seeds
1 teaspoon caraway seeds
1 teaspoon fresh garlic, minced

Sea salt and ground black pepper, to taste
1 teaspoon crushed red pepper
1 teaspoon extra-virgin olive oil

Directions

Toss the breaded shrimp with olive oil and transfer to the Air Fryer cooking basket.

Cook in the preheated Air Fryer at 400 degrees F for 5 minutes; shake the basket and cook an additional 4 minutes.

Meanwhile, mix the remaining Ingredients until well combined. Taste and adjust seasonings. Toss the warm shrimp with the harissa sauce and serve immediately. Enjoy!

Per serving: 240 Calories; 5.1g Fat; 20.2g Carbs; 25.2g Protein

Classic Pancetta-Wrapped Scallops

(**Ready in about** 10 minutes | **Servings** 3)

Ingredients

1 pound sea scallops
1/4 teaspoon shallot powder
1/4 teaspoon garlic powder
1/2 teaspoon dried dill
2 tablespoons soy sauce

1 tablespoon deli mustard
Sea salt and ground black pepper, to taste
4 ounces pancetta slices

Directions

Pat dry the sea scallops and transfer them to a mixing bowl. Toss the sea scallops with the deli mustard, soy sauce, shallot powder, garlic powder, dill, salt and black pepper.

Wrap a slice of bacon around each scallop and transfer them to the Air Fryer cooking basket.

Cook in your Air Fryer at 400 degrees F for 4 minutes; turn them over and cook an additional 3 minutes.

Serve with hot sauce for dipping if desired. Bon appétit!

Per serving: 403 Calories; 24.5g Fat; 5.1g Carbs; 40.1g Protein

Fish Cakes with Bell Pepper

(**Ready in about** 15 minutes | **Servings** 3)

Ingredients

1 pound haddock
2 tablespoons milk
2 stalks fresh scallions, minced
1/2 teaspoon fresh garlic, minced
1/4 teaspoon celery seeds

1 egg
1 bell pepper, deveined and finely chopped
1/2 teaspoon cumin seeds
Sea salt and ground black pepper, to taste
1/2 cup breadcrumbs
1 teaspoon olive oil

Directions

Except for the breadcrumbs and olive oil, thoroughly combine all ingredients until well combined.

Roll the mixture into three patties and coat with breadcrumbs, pressing to adhere. Drizzle olive oil over the patties and place them in the cooking basket of an Air Fryer.

Cook the fish cakes for 5 minutes at 400 degrees F, then flip them over and cook for another 5 minutes, or until cooked through.

Good appetite!

Per serving: 226 Calories; 6.5g Fat; 10.9g Carbs; 31.4g Protein

Greek Sardeles Psites

(**Ready in about** 40 minutes | **Servings** 2)

Ingredients

4 sardines, cleaned
Sea salt and ground black pepper, to taste
1/4 cup sweet white wine
1/2 teaspoon fresh garlic, minced
1 tomato, crushed
1/4 cup baby capers, drained
1/4 cup all-purpose flour
1/2 red onion, chopped
4 tablespoons extra-virgin olive oil
1 tablespoon fresh coriander, minced
1/4 teaspoon chili paper flakes

Directions

Coat the sardines in all-purpose flour until they are evenly coated on all sides.

Arrange your sardines in the cooking basket and season with salt and black pepper. Cook for 35 to 40 minutes at 325 degrees F in your Air Fryer, or until the skin is crispy.

Meanwhile, in a frying pan over medium heat, heat the olive oil. Now, begin to sauté

4 to 5 minutes, or until the onion and garlic are tender and aromatic

Stir in the remaining ingredients, cover, and cook for 15 minutes, or until the sauce has thickened and reduced. Serve the sauce immediately over the warm sardines. Enjoy!

Per serving: 349 Calories; 17.5g Fat; 19g Carbs; 26.3g Protein

Thai-Style Jumbo Scallops

(**Ready in about** 40 minutes | **Servings** 2)

Ingredients

8 jumbo scallops
Sea salt and red pepper flakes, to season
1 tablespoon coconut oil
1 tablespoon oyster sauce
1 tablespoon soy sauce
1/4 cup coconut milk
1 teaspoon sesame oil
1 Thai chili, deveined and minced
1 teaspoon garlic, minced
2 tablespoons fresh lime juice

Directions

Pat the jumbo scallops dry and toss them with 1 teaspoon of sesame oil, salt and red pepper.

Cook the jumbo scallops in your Air Fryer at 400 degrees F for 4 minutes; turn them over and cook an additional 3 minutes. While your scallops are cooking, make the sauce in a frying pan. Heat the coconut oil in a pan over medium-high heat.

Once hot, cook the Thai chili and garlic for 1 minute or so until just tender and fragrant. Add in the oyster sauce, soy sauce and coconut milk and continue to simmer, partially covered, for 5 minutes longer.

Lastly, stir in fresh lime juice and stir to combine well. Add the warm scallops to the sauce and serve immediately.

Per serving: 200 Calories; 10.5g Fat; 10.2g Carbs; 16.3g Protein

Southwestern Prawns with Asparagus

(**Ready in about** 10 minutes | **Servings** 3)

Ingredients

1 pound prawns, deveined
1 teaspoon butter, melted
1/4 teaspoon oregano
1/2 cup chunky-style salsa
1 ripe avocado
Salt, to taste
1/2 pound asparagus spears, cut into1-inch chinks
1/2 teaspoon mixed peppercorns, crushed
1 lemon, sliced

Directions

Toss your prawns and asparagus with melted butter, oregano, salt and mixed peppercorns.

Cook the prawns and asparagus at 400 degrees F for 5 minutes, shaking the basket halfway through the cooking time. Divide the prawns and asparagus between serving plates and garnish with avocado and lemon slices. Serve with the salsa on the side. Bon appétit!

Per serving: 280 Calories; 12.1g Fat; 12.8g Carbs; 34.1g Protein

Classic Old Bay Fish with Cherry Tomatoes

(**Ready in about** 15 minutes | **Servings** 3)

Ingredients

1 pound swordfish steak
Salt and black pepper, to season
2 teaspoon olive oil
1 teaspoon Old Bay seasoning
1 pound cherry tomatoes
1/2 cup cornflakes, crushed

Directions

Toss the swordfish steak with cornflakes, Old Bay seasoning, salt, black pepper and 1 teaspoon of olive oil.

Cook the swordfish steak in your Air Fryer at 400 degrees F for 6 minutes.

Now, turn the fish over, top with tomatoes and drizzle with the remaining teaspoon of olive oil. Continue to cook for 4 minutes.

Serve with lemon slices if desired. Bon appétit!

Per serving: 291 Calories; 13.5g Fat; 10.4g Carbs; 31.9g Protein

Haddock Steaks with Decadent Mango Salsa

(**Ready in about** 15 minutes | **Servings** 2)

Ingredients

2 haddock steaks
Sea salt and ground black
pepper, to taste Mango salsa:
1/4 cup red onion, chopped
1 teaspoon cilantro, chopped
2 tablespoons fresh lemon
juice

1 teaspoon butter, melted
1/2 mango, diced
1 tablespoon white wine
1 chili pepper, deveined and
minced

Directions

Toss the haddock with butter, wine, salt and black pepper.

Cook the haddock in your Air Fryer at 400 degrees F for 5 minutes. Flip the haddock and cook on the other side for 5 minutes more.

Meanwhile, make the mango salsa by mixing all Ingredients. Serve the warm haddock with the chilled mango salsa and enjoy!

Per serving: 411 Calories; 25.5g Fat; 18.4g Carbs; 26.3g Protein

Homemade Fish Fingers

(**Ready in about** 15 minutes | **Servings** 2)

Ingredients

3/4 pound tilapia
4 tablespoons chickpea flour
1/2 teaspoon red chili flakes
1/4 cup pork rinds
1 egg

2 tablespoons milk
1/2 cup breadcrumbs
Coarse sea salt and black
pepper, to season

Directions

Rinse the tilapia and pat it dry using kitchen towels. Then, cut the tilapia into strips.

Then, whisk the egg, milk and chickpea flour in a rimmed plate.

Add the pork rinds and breadcrumbs to another plate; stir in red chili flakes, salt and black pepper and stir to combine well.

Dip the fish strips in the egg mixture, then, roll them over the breadcrumb mixture. Transfer the fish fingers to the Air Fryer cooking basket and spritz them with a nonstick cooking spray.

Cook in the preheated Air Fryer at 400 degrees F for 10 minutes, shaking the basket halfway through to ensure even browning. Serve warm and enjoy!

Per serving: 332 Calories; 10.5g Fat; 12.2g Carbs; 46.3g Protein

Ahi Tuna with Peppers and Tartare Sauce

(**Ready in about** 15 minutes | **Servings** 2)

Ingredients

2 ahi tuna steaks
1/2 teaspoon garlic powder
1 teaspoon olive oil
4 tablespoons mayonnaise
2 tablespoons sour cream
2 tablespoons white onion,
minced

2 Spanish peppers, quartered
Salt and freshly ground black
pepper, to taste Tartare sauce:
1 tablespoon baby capers,
drained
1 tablespoon gherkins,
drained and chopped

Directions

Pat the ahi tuna dry using kitchen towels.

Toss the ahi tuna and Spanish peppers with olive oil, garlic powder, salt and black pepper.

Cook the ahi tuna and peppers in the preheated Air Fryer at 400 degrees F for 10 minutes, flipping them halfway through the cooking time.

Meanwhile, whisk all the sauce Ingredients until well combined. Plate the ahi tuna steaks and arrange Spanish peppers around them. Serve with tartare sauce on the side and enjoy!

Per serving: 485 Calories; 24.3g Fat; 7.7g Carbs; 56.3g Protein

Fried Oysters with Kaffir Lime Sauce

(**Ready in about** 10 minutes | **Servings** 2)

Ingredients

8 fresh oysters, shucked
3/4 cup breadcrumbs
1/3 cup plain flour
1 habanero pepper, minced
1 teaspoon coconut sugar
1 teaspoon olive oil

1 egg
1/2 teaspoon Italian
seasoning mix
1 lime, freshly squeezed
1 kaffir lime leaf, shredded

Directions

Clean the oysters and set them aside. Add the flour to a rimmed plate. Whisk the egg in another rimmed plate. Mix the breadcrumbs and Italian seasoning mix in a third plate.

Dip your oysters in the flour, shaking off the excess. Then, dip them in the egg mixture and finally, coat your oysters with the breadcrumb mixture.

Spritz the breaded oysters with a nonstick cooking spray.

Cook your oysters in the preheated Air Fryer at 400 degrees F for 2 to 3 minutes, shaking the basket halfway through the cooking time.

Meanwhile, blend the remaining Ingredients to make the sauce. Serve the warm oysters with the kaffir lime sauce on the side. Bon appétit!

Per serving: 295 Calories; 8.7g Fat; 23.4g Carbs; 30g Protein

Tuna Steak with Roasted Cherry Tomatoes

(**Ready in about** 15 minutes | **Servings** 2)

Ingredients

1 pound tuna steak
1 teaspoon extra-virgin olive oil
1 teaspoon garlic, finely chopped

1 cup cherry tomatoes
2 sprigs rosemary, leaves picked and crushed
1 tablespoon lime juice
Sea salt and red pepper flakes, to taste

Directions

Toss the tuna steaks and cherry tomatoes with olive oil, rosemary leaves, salt, black pepper and garlic.
Place the tuna steaks in a lightly oiled cooking basket; cook tuna steaks at 440 degrees F for about 6 minutes.
Turn the tuna steaks over, add in the cherry tomatoes and continue to cook for 4 minutes more. Drizzle the fish with lime juice and serve warm garnished with roasted cherry tomatoes!
Per serving: 231 Calories; 3.3g Fat; 6.2g Carbs; 45.2g Protein;

Salmon Filets with Fennel Slaw

(**Ready in about** 15 minutes | **Servings** 3)

Ingredients

1 pound salmon filets
Sea salt and ground black pepper, to taste Fennel Slaw:
1 Lebanese cucumber, thinly sliced
1/2 ounce tarragon

1 teaspoon Cajun spice mix
1 pound fennel bulb, thinly sliced
1/2 red onion, thinly sliced
2 tablespoons tahini
2 tablespoons lemon juice
1 tablespoon soy sauce

Directions

Rinse the salmon filets and pat them dry with a paper towel. Then, toss the salmon filets with the Cajun spice mix, salt and black pepper.

Cook the salmon filets in the preheated Air Fryer at 380 degrees F for 6 minutes; flip the salmon filets and cook for a further 6 minutes.

Meanwhile, make the fennel slaw by stirring fennel, cucumber, red onion and tarragon in a salad bowl. Mix the remaining Ingredients to make the dressing.

Dress the salad and transfer to your refrigerator until ready to serve. Serve the warm fish with chilled fennel slaw. Bon appétit!

Per serving: 337 Calories; 13.6g Fat; 19.3g Carbs; 36.3g Protein

Seed-Crusted Codfish Fillets

(**Ready in about** 15 minutes | **Servings** 2)

Ingredients

codfish fillets
Sea salt and black pepper, to taste
1 teaspoon sesame seeds

1 teaspoon sesame oil
1 tablespoon chia seeds

Directions

Start by preheating your Air Fryer to 380 degrees F.

Add the sesame oil, salt, black pepper, sesame seeds and chia seeds to a rimmed plate. Coat the top of the codfish with the seed mixture, pressing it down to adhere.

Lower the codfish fillets, seed side down, into the cooking basket and cook for 6 minutes. Turn the fish fillets over and cook for a further 6 minutes.

Serve warm and enjoy!

Per serving: 263 Calories; 8.3g Fat; 8.2g Carbs; 37.7g Protein;

Scallops with Pineapple Salsa and Pickled Onions

(**Ready in about** 15 minutes | **Servings** 3)

Ingredients

12 scallops
1/4 teaspoon dried rosemary
1/2 teaspoon dried tarragon
1/2 teaspoon dried basil
1/2 cup pickled onions, drained
1 cup pineapple, diced
1 jalapeño, deveined and minced
1 small-sized red onion, minced
Sea salt and ground black pepper, to taste

1 teaspoon sesame oil
1/4 teaspoon red pepper flakes, crushed Coarse sea salt and black pepper, to taste Pineapple Salsa:
2 tablespoons fresh cilantro, roughly chopped
1/2 teaspoon coconut sugar
1 teaspoon ginger root, peeled and grated

Directions

Toss the scallops sesame oil, rosemary, tarragon, basil, red pepper, salt and black pepper.

Cook in the preheated Air Fryer at 400 degrees F for 6 to 7 minutes, shaking the basket once or twice to ensure even cooking.

Meanwhile, process all the salsa Ingredients in your blender; cover and place the salsa in your refrigerator until ready to serve.

Serve the warm scallops with pickled onions and pineapple salsa on the side. Bon appétit!

Per serving: 177 Calories; 2.6g Fat; 22.3g Carbs; 15.6g Protein

Tuna Steaks with Pearl Onions

(**Ready in about** 20 minutes | **Servings** 4)

Ingredients

4 tuna steaks
1 teaspoon dried rosemary
1 teaspoon dried marjoram
1/2 teaspoon sea salt
1 lemon, sliced

1 pound pearl onions
1 tablespoon cayenne pepper
4 teaspoons olive oil
1/2 teaspoon black pepper,
preferably freshly cracked

Directions

Place the tuna steaks in the lightly greased cooking basket. Top with the pearl onions; add the olive oil, rosemary, marjoram, cayenne pepper, salt, and black pepper.

Bake in the preheated Air Fryer at 400 degrees F for 9 to 10 minutes. Work in two batches.

Serve warm with lemon slices and enjoy!

Per serving: 332 Calories; 5.9g Fat; 10.5g Carbs; 56.1g Protein

English-Style Flounder Fillets

(**Ready in about** 20 minutes | **Servings** 2)

Ingredients

1 flounder fillets
1/2 teaspoon Worcestershire sauce
1/2 teaspoon coarse sea salt
1/4 teaspoon chili powder

1/4 cup all-purpose flour
1/2 teaspoon lemon pepper
1 egg
1/2 cup bread crumbs

Directions

The flounder fillets should be rinsed and patted dry. In a large saucepan, combine the flour and salt.

In a shallow bowl, whisk together the egg and Worcestershire sauce. Separately, combine the bread crumbs, lemon pepper, salt, and chilli powder in a separate bowl.

Dredge the fillets in the flour and shake off any excess. After that, dip them in the egg mixture. Finally, coat the fish fillets in the breadcrumb mixture, coating all sides.

Spritz with cooking spray before placing in the Air Fryer basket. Cook for 7 minutes at 390°F.

Turn them over, spritz the other side with cooking spray, and cook for another 5 minutes. Good appetite!

Per serving: 432 Calories; 16.7g Fat; 29g Carbs; 38.4g Protein

Cod and Shallot Frittata

(**Ready in about** 20 minutes | **Servings** 3)

Ingredients

2 cod fillets
1/2 cup milk
2 garlic cloves, minced
1/2 teaspoon red pepper flakes, crushed

6 eggs
1 shallot, chopped
Sea salt and ground black pepper, to taste

Directions

Bring a pot of salted water to a boil. Boil the cod fillets for 5 minutes or until it is opaque. Flake the fish into bite-sized pieces.

In a mixing bowl, whisk the eggs and milk. Stir in the shallots, garlic, salt, black pepper, and red pepper flakes. Stir in the reserved fish.

Pour the mixture into the lightly greased baking pan.

Cook in the preheated Air Fryer at 360 degrees F for 9 minutes, flipping over halfway through. Bon appétit!

Per serving: 454 Calories; 30.8g Fat; 10.3g Carbs; 32.4g Protein

Crispy Tilapia Fillets

(**Ready in about** 20 minutes | **Servings** 5)

Ingredients

5 tablespoons all-purpose flour
Sea salt and white pepper, to taste
5 tilapia fillets, slice into halves

2 tablespoons extra virgin olive oil 1/2 cup cornmeal
1 teaspoon garlic paste

Directions

Combine the flour, salt, white pepper, garlic paste, olive oil, and cornmeal in a Ziploc bag. Add the fish fillets and shake to coat well.

Spritz the Air Fryer basket with cooking spray. Cook in the preheated Air Fryer at 400 degrees F for 10 minutes; turn them over and cook for 6 minutes more. Work in batches.

Serve with lemon wedges if desired. Enjoy!

Per serving: 315 Calories; 9.1g Fat; 19.4g Carbs; 38.5g Protein

Saucy Garam Masala Fish

(**Ready in about** 25 minutes | **Servings** 2)

Ingredients

2 teaspoons olive oil
1 teaspoon Garam masala
1/4 cup coconut milk
1/4 cup coriander, roughly chopped
1 garlic clove, minced

1/2 teaspoon cayenne pepper
1/4 teaspoon Kala namak (Indian black salt)
1/2 teaspoon fresh ginger, grated
2 catfish fillets

Directions

Preheat your Air Fryer to 390 degrees F. Then, spritz the baking dish with a nonstick cooking spray.

In a mixing bowl, whisk the olive oil, milk, cayenne pepper, Garam masala, Kala namak, ginger, and garlic.

Coat the catfish fillets with the Garam masala mixture. Cook the catfish fillets in the preheated Air Fryer approximately 18 minutes, turning over halfway through the cooking time.

Garnish with fresh coriander and serve over hot noodles if desired.

Per serving: 301 Calories; 12.1g Fat; 2.3g Carbs; 43g Protein

Grilled Salmon Steaks

(**Ready in about** 45 minutes | **Servings** 4)

Ingredients

2 cloves garlic, minced
Sea salt and ground black pepper, to taste
1 teaspoon smoked paprika
4 salmon steaks

4 tablespoons butter, melted
1/2 teaspoon onion powder
1 tablespoon lime juice
1/4 cup dry white wine

Directions

Place all Ingredients in a large ceramic dish. Cover and let it marinate for 30 minutes in the refrigerator.

Arrange the salmon steaks on the grill pan. Bake at 390 degrees for 5 minutes, or until the salmon steaks are easily flaked with a fork.

Flip the fish steaks, baste with the reserved marinade, and cook another 5 minutes. Bon appétit!

Per serving: 420 Calories; 23g Fat; 2.5g Carbs; 48.5g Protein

Delicious Snapper en Papillote

(**Ready in about** 20 minutes | **Servings** 2)

Ingredients

1 snapper fillets
1 bell pepper, sliced
2 garlic cloves, halved
1 tablespoon olive oil
1 tomato, sliced
Sea salt, to taste 2 bay leaves

1 shallot, peeled and sliced
1 small-sized serrano pepper, sliced
1/4 teaspoon freshly ground black pepper
1/2 teaspoon paprika

Directions

Place two parchment sheets on a working surface. Place the fish in the center of one side of the parchment paper.

Top with the shallot, garlic, peppers, and tomato. Drizzle olive oil over the fish and vegetables. Season with black pepper, paprika, and salt. Add the bay leaves

Fold over the other half of the parchment. Now, fold the paper around the edges tightly and create a half moon shape, sealing the fish inside.

Cook in the preheated Air Fryer at 390 degrees F for 15 minutes. Serve warm.

Per serving: 329 Calories; 9.8g Fat; 12.7g Carbs; 46.7g Protein

Halibut Cakes with Horseradish Mayo

(**Ready in about** 20 minutes | **Servings** 4)

Ingredients

Halibut Cakes:
2 tablespoons olive oil
2 tablespoons cilantro, chopped
1 shallot, chopped
1/2 cup Romano cheese, grated
1 tablespoon Worcestershire sauce Mayo Sauce:
1/2 cup mayonnaise

1 pound halibut
1/2 teaspoon cayenne pepper
2 garlic cloves, minced
1/4 teaspoon black pepper
Salt, to taste
1 egg, whisked
1/2 cup breadcrumbs
1 teaspoon horseradish, grated

Directions

Begin by preheating your Air Fryer to 380°F. Cooking oil should be sprayed into the Air Fryer basket.

In a mixing bowl, combine all of the ingredients for the halibut cakes; knead with your hands until everything is well combined.

Make equal-sized patties out of the mixture. Place the patties in the Air Fryer basket. Cook the fish patties for 10 minutes, flipping halfway through.

Combine the horseradish and mayonnaise in a mixing bowl. With the horseradish mayo, serve the halibut cakes. Good appetite!

Per serving: 470 Calories; 38.2g Fat; 6.3g Carbs; 24.4g Protein

Dilled and Glazed Salmon Steaks

(**Ready in about** 20 minutes | **Servings** 2)

Ingredients

2 salmon steaks Coarse sea salt, to taste
2 tablespoons honey
1 tablespoon fresh lemon juice
1 teaspoon garlic, minced
1/2 teaspoon dried dill
1/4 teaspoon freshly ground black pepper, or more to taste
1 tablespoon sesame oil
1/2 teaspoon smoked cayenne pepper
Zest of 1 lemon

Directions

Preheat your Air Fryer to 380 degrees F. Pat dry the salmon steaks with a kitchen towel.

In a ceramic dish, combine the remaining Ingredients until everything is well whisked.

Add the salmon steaks to the ceramic dish and let them sit in the refrigerator for 1 hour. Now, place the salmon steaks in the cooking basket. Reserve the marinade.

Cook for 12 minutes, flipping halfway through the cooking time.

Meanwhile, cook the marinade in a small sauté pan over a moderate flame. Cook until the sauce has thickened.

Pour the sauce over the steaks and serve with mashed potatoes if desired. Bon appétit!

Per serving: 421 Calories; 16.8g Fat; 19.9g Carbs; 46.7g Protein

Easy Prawns alla Parmigiana

(**Ready in about** 20 minutes | **Servings** 4)

Ingredients

2 egg whites
1 cup Parmigiano-Reggiano, grated
1/2 cup fine breadcrumbs
1 teaspoon garlic powder
1/2 teaspoon ground black pepper
1 ½ pounds prawns, deveined
1 cup all-purpose flour
1/2 teaspoon celery seeds
1/2 teaspoon porcini powder
1/2 teaspoon onion powder
1/2 teaspoon dried rosemary
1/2 teaspoon sea salt

Directions

To make a breading station, whisk the egg whites in a shallow dish. In a separate dish, place the all-purpose flour.

In a third dish, thoroughly combine the Parmigiano-Reggiano, breadcrumbs,

and seasonings; mix to combine well.

Dip the prawns in the flour, then, into the egg whites; lastly, dip them in the parm/breadcrumb mixture. Roll until they are covered on all sides.

Cook in the preheated Air Fryer at 390 degrees F for 5 to 7 minutes or until golden brown. Work in batches. Serve with lemon wedges if desired.

Per serving: 442 Calories; 10.3g Fat; 40.4g Carbs; 43.7g Protein

Indian Famous Fish Curry

(**Ready in about** 25 minutes | **Servings** 4)

Ingredients

2 tablespoons sunflower oil
1 tablespoon coriander powder
Salt and white pepper, to taste
1/2 teaspoon fenugreek seeds
1 shallot, minced
2 red chilies, chopped
1 cup coconut milk
1/2 pound fish, chopped
1 garlic clove, minced
1 ripe tomato, pureed
1 teaspoon curry paste

Directions

Preheat your Air Fryer to 380 degrees F; brush the cooking basket with 1 tablespoon of sunflower oil.

Cook your fish for 10 minutes on both sides. Transfer to the baking pan that is previously greased with the remaining tablespoon of sunflower oil.

Add the remaining Ingredients and reduce the heat to 350 degrees F. Continue to cook an additional 10 to 12 minutes or until everything is heated through. Enjoy!

Per serving: 449 Calories; 29.1g Fat; 20.4g Carbs; 27.3g Protein

Snapper Casserole with Gruyere Cheese

(**Ready in about** 25 minutes | **Servings** 4)

Ingredients

2 tablespoons olive oil
2 garlic cloves, minced
Sea salt and ground black pepper, to taste
1 teaspoon cayenne pepper
1 cup Gruyere cheese, shredded
1 ½ pounds snapper fillets
1 shallot, thinly sliced
1/2 teaspoon dried basil
1/2 cup tomato puree
1/2 cup white wine

Directions

Heat 1 tablespoon of olive oil in a saucepan over medium-high heat. Now, cook the shallot and garlic until tender and aromatic.

Preheat your Air Fryer to 370 degrees F.

Grease a casserole dish with 1 tablespoon of olive oil. Place the snapper fillet in the casserole dish. Season with salt, black pepper, and cayenne pepper.

Add the sautéed shallot mixture.

Add the basil, tomato puree and wine to the casserole dish. Cook for 10 minutes in the preheated Air Fryer.

Top with the shredded cheese and cook an additional 7 minutes. Serve immediately.

Per serving: 406 Calories; 19.9g Fat; 9.3g Carbs; 46.4g Protein

Monkfish Fillets with Romano Cheese

(**Ready in about** 15 minutes | **Servings** 2)

Ingredients

2 monkfish fillets
2 tablespoons butter, melted
1/2 teaspoon dried rosemary
1/4 teaspoon cracked black pepper
4 tablespoons Romano cheese, grated
1 teaspoon garlic paste
1/2 teaspoon Aleppo chili powder
1/2 teaspoon sea salt

Directions

Start by preheating the Air Fryer to 320 degrees F. Spritz the Air Fryer basket with cooking oil.

Spread the garlic paste all over the fish fillets.

Brush the monkfish fillets with the melted butter on both sides. Sprinkle with the chili powder, rosemary, black pepper, and salt. Cook for 7 minutes in the preheated Air Fryer.

Top with the Romano cheese and continue to cook for 2 minutes more or until heated through. Bon appétit!

Per serving: 415 Calories; 22.5g Fat; 3.7g Carbs; 47.4g Protein

Grilled Hake with Garlic Sauce

(**Ready in about** 20 minutes | **Servings** 3)

Ingredients

3 hake fillets
1 tablespoon fresh lime juice
1 cup panko crumbs
1/4 teaspoon ground black pepper, or more to taste
2 tablespoons olive oil
2 cloves garlic, minced
6 tablespoons mayonnaise
Salt, to taste
1 teaspoon Dijon mustard
1/4 cup Greek-style yogurt
Garlic Sauce
1/2 teaspoon tarragon leaves, minced

Directions

Pat dry the hake fillets with a kitchen towel.

In a shallow bowl, whisk together the mayo, mustard, and lime juice. In another shallow bowl, thoroughly combine the panko crumbs with salt, and black pepper.

Spritz the Air Fryer grill pan with non-stick cooking spray. Grill in the preheated Air Fry at 395 degrees F for 10 minutes, flipping halfway through the cooking time.

Serve immediately.

Per serving: 479 Calories; 22g Fat; 29.1g Carbs; 39.1g Protein

Grilled Tilapia with Portobello Mushrooms

(**Ready in about** 20 minutes | **Servings** 2)

Ingredients

2 tilapia fillets
1/2 teaspoon red pepper flakes, crushed
1/2 teaspoon dried sage, crushed
1 teaspoon dried parsley flakes
1 tablespoon avocado oil
1/4 teaspoon lemon pepper
1/2 teaspoon sea salt
A few drizzles of liquid smoke
4 medium-sized Portobello mushrooms

Directions

Toss all Ingredients in a mixing bowl; except for the mushrooms.

Transfer the tilapia fillets to a lightly greased grill pan. Preheat your Air Fryer to 400 degrees F and cook the tilapia fillets for 5 minutes.

Now, turn the fillets over and add the Portobello mushrooms. Continue to cook for 5 minutes longer or until mushrooms are tender and the fish is opaque. Serve immediately.

Per serving: 320 Calories; 11.4g Fat; 29.1g Carbs; 49.3g Protein

Authentic Mediterranean Calamari Salad

(**Ready in about** 15 minutes | **Servings** 3)

Ingredients

1 pound squid, cleaned, sliced into rings
2 tablespoons sherry wine
1/2 teaspoon ground black pepper
1 cup grape tomatoes
1 teaspoon yellow mustard
1/3 cup Kalamata olives, pitted and sliced
1/2 teaspoon granulated garlic Salt, to taste
1/2 teaspoon basil
1/2 teaspoon dried rosemary
1/2 cup mayonnaise
1 small red onion, thinly sliced
1/2 cup fresh flat-leaf parsley leaves, coarsely chopped

Directions

Start by preheating the Air Fryer to 400 degrees F. Spritz the Air Fryer basket with cooking oil.

Toss the squid rings with the sherry wine, garlic, salt, pepper, basil, and rosemary. Cook in the preheated Air Fryer for 5 minutes, shaking the basket halfway through the cooking time.

Work in batches and let it cool to room temperature. When the squid is cool enough, add the remaining Ingredients.

Gently stir to combine and serve well chilled. Bon appétit!

Per serving: 457 Calories; 31.3g Fat; 18.4g Carbs; 25.1g Protein

Filet of Flounder Cutlets

(**Ready in about** 15 minutes | **Servings** 2)

Ingredients

1 egg
1/2 cup Pecorino Romano cheese, grated
2 flounder fillets
1 teaspoon dried parsley flakes
1/2 cup cracker crumbs
1/2 teaspoon cayenne pepper
Sea salt and white pepper, to taste

Directions

To make a breading station, whisk the egg until frothy.

In another bowl, mix the cracker crumbs, Pecorino Romano cheese, and spices.

Dip the fish in the egg mixture and turn to coat evenly; then, dredge in the cracker crumb mixture, turning a couple of times to coat evenly.

Cook in the preheated Air Fryer at 390 degrees F for 5 minutes; turn them over and cook another 5 minutes. Enjoy!

Per serving: 330 Calories; 20.3g Fat; 12.1g Carbs; 24.8g Protein

King Prawns with Lemon Butter Sauce

(**Ready in about** 15 minutes | **Servings** 4)

Ingredients

King Prawns:
2 cloves garlic, minced
1/2 cup Pecorino Romano cheese, grated
1 teaspoon garlic powder
1 teaspoon mustard seeds
2 tablespoons olive oil Sauce:
2 tablespoons fresh lemon juice
1/2 teaspoon Worcestershire sauce
1 ½ pounds king prawns, peeled and deveined
Sea salt and ground white pepper, to your
2 tablespoons butter
liking 1/2 teaspoon onion powder
1/4 teaspoon ground black pepper

Directions

All ingredients for the king prawns should be thoroughly combined in a plastic closeable bag; shake to combine well.

Place the coated king prawns in the Air Fryer basket that has been lightly greased.

Cook for 6 minutes at 390°F in a preheated Air Fryer, shaking the basket halfway through. Working in batches is recommended.

Meanwhile, melt the butter in a small saucepan over medium heat and add the remaining ingredients.

Reduce the heat to low and whisk for 2 to 3 minutes, or until thoroughly heated. Pour the sauce over the hot king prawns. Good appetite!

Per serving: 302 Calories; 17.2g Fat; 3.2g Carbs; 32.2g Protein

Crusty Catfish with Sweet Potato Fries

(**Ready in about** 50 minutes | **Servings** 2)

Ingredients

1/2 pound catfish
1/2 cup bran cereal
Sea salt and ground black pepper, to taste
1/4 teaspoon ground bay leaf
4 sweet potatoes, cut French fries
1/4 cup parmesan cheese, grated
1 teaspoon garlic powder
1 teaspoon smoked paprika
2 tablespoons butter, melted
1 egg

Directions

Pat the catfish dry with a kitchen towel.

Combine the bran cereal with the parmesan cheese and all spices in a shallow bowl. Whisk the egg in another shallow bowl.

Dip the fish in the egg mixture and turn to coat evenly; then, dredge in the bran cereal mixture, turning a couple of times to coat evenly. Spritz the Air Fryer basket with cooking spray. Cook the catfish in the preheated Air Fryer at 390 degrees F for 10 minutes; turn them over and cook for 4 minutes more.

Then, drizzle the melted butter all over the sweet potatoes; cook them in the preheated Air Fryer at 380 degrees F for 30 minutes, shaking occasionally. Serve over the warm fish fillets. Bon appétit!

Per serving: 481 Calories; 25.4g Fat; 37.5g Carbs; 31.3g Protein

Crunchy Topped Fish Bake

(**Ready in about** 20 minutes | **Servings** 4)

Ingredients

1 tablespoon butter, melted
1 tablespoon chicken stock
1 tablespoon dry white wine
1 pound tuna
Sea salt and ground black pepper, to taste
1/2 teaspoon dried thyme
2 ripe tomatoes, pureed
1/4 cup breadcrumbs
1 medium-sized leek, thinly sliced
1/2 teaspoon red pepper flakes, crushed
1/2 teaspoon dried basil
1/2 teaspoon dried rosemary
1/4 cup Parmesan cheese, grated

Directions

Melt 1/2 tablespoon of butter in a sauté pan over medium-high heat. Now, cook the leek and garlic until tender and aromatic. Add the stock and wine to deglaze the pan.

Preheat your Air Fryer to 370 degrees F.

Grease a casserole dish with the remaining 1/2 tablespoon of melted butter. Place the fish in the casserole dish. Add the seasonings. Top with the sautéed leek mixture.

Add the tomato puree. Cook for 10 minutes in the preheated Air Fryer. Top with the breadcrumbs and cheese; cook an additional 7 minutes until the crumbs are golden. Bon appétit!

Per serving: 455 Calories; 12.4g Fat; 9.9g Carbs; 73.6g Protein

Creamed Trout Salad

(**Ready in about** 20 minutes | **Servings** 2)

Ingredients

1/2 pound trout fillets, skinless
1 tablespoon fresh lemon juice
6 ounces chickpeas, canned and drained
1 red onion, thinly sliced
1 teaspoon mustard
2 tablespoons horseradish, prepared, drained
Salt and ground white pepper, to taste
1 cup Iceberg lettuce, torn into pieces
1/4 cup mayonnaise

Directions

Spritz the Air Fryer basket with cooking spray.

Cook the trout fillets in the preheated Air Fryer at 395 degrees F for 10 minutes or until opaque. Make sure to turn them halfway through the cooking time.

Break the fish into bite-sized chunks and place in the refrigerator to cool. Toss your fish with the remaining Ingredients. Bon appétit!

Per serving: 490 Calories; 26.4g Fat; 30.3g Carbs; 33.9g Protein

Quick Thai Coconut Fish

(**Ready in about** 20 minutes + marinating time | **Servings** 2)

Ingredients

1 cup coconut milk
2 tablespoons Shoyu sauce
Salt and white pepper, to taste
1 teaspoon turmeric powder
2 tablespoons olive oil
2 tablespoons lime juice
1/2 Thai Bird's Eye chili, seeded and finely chopped
1 pound tilapia
1/2 teaspoon ginger powder

Directions

In a mixing bowl, thoroughly combine the coconut milk with the lime juice, Shoyu sauce, salt, pepper, turmeric, ginger, and chili pepper. Add tilapia and let it marinate for 1 hour.

Brush the Air Fryer basket with olive oil. Discard the marinade and place the tilapia fillets in the Air Fryer basket.

Cook the tilapia in the preheated Air Fryer at 400 degrees F for 6 minutes; turn them over and cook for 6 minutes more. Work in batches.

Serve with some extra lime wedges if desired. Enjoy!

Per serving: 435 Calories; 21.5g Fat; 11.6g Carbs; 50.2g Protein

Double Cheese Fish Casserole

(**Ready in about** 30 minutes | **Servings** 4)

Ingredients

1 tablespoon avocado oil
Sea salt and ground white pepper, to taste
2 tablespoons shallots, chopped
1/2 cup Cottage cheese
1 teaspoon yellow mustard
1 tablespoon lime juice
1 teaspoon garlic powder
1 bell pepper, seeded and chopped
1 pound hake fillets
1/2 cup sour cream
1 egg, well whisked
1/2 cup Swiss cheese, shredded

Directions

Brush the bottom and sides of a casserole dish with avocado oil. Add the hake fillets to the casserole dish and sprinkle with garlic powder, salt, and pepper.

Add the chopped shallots and bell peppers.

In a mixing bowl, thoroughly combine the Cottage cheese, sour cream, egg, mustard, and lime juice. Pour the mixture over fish and spread evenly.

Cook in the preheated Air Fryer at 370 degrees F for 10 minutes.

Top with the Swiss cheese and cook an additional 7 minutes. Let it rest for 10 minutes before slicing and serving. Bon appétit!

Per serving: 456 Calories; 30.1g Fat; 8.8g Carbs; 36.7g Protein

Rosemary-Infused Butter Scallops

(**Ready in about** 1 hour 10 minutes | **Servings** 4)

Ingredients

2 pounds sea scallops
2 sprigs rosemary, only leaves
1/2 cup beer
4 tablespoons butter
Sea salt and freshly cracked black pepper, to taste

Directions

In a ceramic dish, mix the sea scallops with beer; let it marinate for 1 hour.

Meanwhile, preheat your Air Fryer to 400 degrees F. Melt the butter and add the rosemary leaves. Stir for a few minutes.

Discard the marinade and transfer the sea scallops to the Air Fryer basket. Season with salt and black pepper.

Cook the scallops in the preheated Air Fryer for 7 minutes, shaking the basket halfway through the cooking time. Work in batches.

Bon appétit!

Per serving: 317 Calories; 17.3g Fat; 9.2g Carbs; 29.4g Protein

Shrimp Kabobs with Cherry Tomatoes

(**Ready in about** 30 minutes | **Servings** 4)

Ingredients

1 ½ pounds jumbo shrimp, cleaned, shelled and deveined
1 tablespoons Sriracha sauce
1/2 teaspoon dried oregano
1/2 teaspoon dried basil
1/2 teaspoon marjoram
1/2 teaspoon mustard seeds
2 tablespoons butter, melted
1 pound cherry tomatoes
Sea salt and ground black pepper, to taste
1 teaspoon dried parsley flakes

Directions

Toss all Ingredients in a mixing bowl until the shrimp and tomatoes are covered on all sides.

Soak the wooden skewers in water for 15 minutes.

Thread the jumbo shrimp and cherry tomatoes onto skewers. Cook in the preheated Air Fryer at 400 degrees F for 5 minutes, working with batches. Bon appétit!

Per serving: 267 Calories; 6.8g Fat; 18.1g Carbs; 35.4g Protein

Snapper with Coconut Milk Sauce

(**Ready in about** 20 minutes + marinating time | **Servings** 2)

Ingredients

1/2 cup full-fat coconut milk
2 tablespoons lemon juice
2 snapper fillets
1 tablespoon cornstarch
1 teaspoon fresh ginger, grated
1 tablespoon olive oil
Salt and white pepper, to taste

Directions

In a glass bowl, combine the milk, lemon juice, and ginger; add the fish and marinate for 1 hour.

Placed the fish in the Air Fryer basket after removing it from the milk mixture. Drizzle olive oil over the fillets of fish.

Cook for 15 minutes in a preheated Air Fryer at 390 degrees F.

Meanwhile, bring the milk mixture to a rapid boil over medium-high heat, stirring constantly. Reduce to a simmer and add the cornstarch, salt, and pepper; cook for another 12 minutes.

Serve the sauce over the warm snapper fillets right away. Good appetite

Per serving: 431 Calories; 17.3g Fat; 18.5g Carbs; 48.4g Protein

SNACKS & APPETIZERS

Root Vegetable Chips with Dill Mayonnaise

(**Ready in about** 40 minutes | **Servings** 4)

Ingredients

1/2 pound red beetroot, julienned
1/2 pound golden beetroot, julienned
1/2 cup mayonnaise

Sea salt and ground black pepper, to taste
1 teaspoon olive oil
1/4 pound carrot, julienned
1 teaspoon garlic, minced
1/4 teaspoon dried dill weed

Directions

Toss your veggies with salt, black pepper and olive oil.

Arrange the veggie chips in a single layer in the Air Fryer cooking basket.

Cook the veggie chips in the preheated Air Fryer at 340 degrees F for 20 minutes; tossing the basket occasionally to ensure even cooking. Work with two batches.

Meanwhile, mix the mayonnaise, garlic and dill until well combined.

Serve the vegetable chips with the mayo sauce on the side. Bon appétit!

Per serving: 187 Calories; 11.2g Fat; 20.1g Carbs; 2.6g Protein

Parmesan Squash Chips

(**Ready in about** 20 minutes | **Servings** 3)

Ingredients

3/4 pound butternut squash, cut into thin rounds
1 teaspoon butter
1/2 cup ketchup

Sea salt and ground black pepper, to taste
1 teaspoon Sriracha sauce
1/2 cup Parmesan cheese, grated

Directions

Toss the butternut squash with Parmesan cheese, salt, black pepper and butter.

Transfer the butternut squash rounds to the Air Fryer cooking basket.

Air Fryer at 400 degrees F for 12 minutes. Shake the Air Fryer basket periodically to ensure even cooking. Work with batches.

While the parmesan squash chips are baking, whisk the ketchup and sriracha and set it aside.

Serve the parmesan squash chips with Sriracha ketchup and enjoy!

Per serving: 174 Calories; 6.1g Fat; 26.1g Carbs; 6.4g Protein

Paprika and Cheese French Fries

(**Ready in about** 15 minutes | **Servings** 2)

Ingredients

8 ounces French fries, frozen
Sea salt, to taste

1/2 cup Monterey-Jack cheese, grated
1 teaspoon paprika

Directions

Cook the French fries in your Air Fryer at 400 degrees F for about 7 minutes. Shake the basket and continue to cook for a further 6 minutes.

Top the French fries with cheese, paprika and salt cheese. Continue to cook for 1 minute more or until the cheese has melted. Serve warm and enjoy!

Per serving: 368 Calories; 17.1g Fat; 37.2g Carbs; 16.4g Protein

Mexican Crunchy Cheese Straws

(**Ready in about** 15 minutes | **Servings** 3)

Ingredients

1/2 cup almond flour
1/4 teaspoon shallot powder
1/4 teaspoon garlic powder
1 ounce Manchego cheese, grated

1/4 teaspoon xanthan gum
1/4 teaspoon ground cumin
1 egg yolk, whisked
2 ounces Cotija cheese, grated

Directions

Mix all Ingredients until everything is well incorporated.

Twist the batter into straw strips and place them inside your Air Fryer on a baking mat.

Cook the cheese straws in your Air Fryer at 360°F for 5 minutes, then flip them over and cook for another 5 minutes.

Before serving, allow the cheese straws to cool. Enjoy!

Per serving: 138 Calories; 11g Fat; 0.8g Carbs; 7.8g Protein

Greek-Style Zucchini Rounds

(**Ready in about** 15 minutes | **Servings** 3)

Ingredients

1/2 pound zucchini, cut into thin rounds

1/2 teaspoon oregano

Coarse sea salt and ground black pepper, to taste Greek dipping sauce:

1/2 teaspoon fresh lemon juice

2 tablespoons mayonnaise

1/2 teaspoon dried sage, crushed

1/4 teaspoon ground bay leaf

1/2 cup Greek yogurt

1 teaspoon extra-virgin olive oil

1/2 teaspoon garlic, pressed

Directions

Toss the zucchini rounds with olive oil and spices and place them in the Air Fryer cooking basket.

Cook in the preheated Air Fryer at 400 degrees F for 10 minutes; shaking the basket halfway through the cooking time.

Let it cool slightly and cook an additional minute or so until crispy and golden brown.

Meanwhile, make the sauce by whisking all the sauce Ingredients; place the sauce in the refrigerator until ready to serve.

Serve the crispy zucchini rounds with Greek dipping sauce on the side. Enjoy!

Per serving: 128 Calories; 1.2g Fat; 6.2g Carbs; 3.9g Protein

Beer-Battered Vidalia Onion Rings

(**Ready in about** 15 minutes | **Servings** 2)

Ingredients

1/2 cup all-purpose flour 1

1/4 teaspoon dried oregano

/2 teaspoon baking powder

1/4 cup beer

1/2 pound Vidalia onions, cut into rings

1/4 teaspoon cayenne pepper

Kosher salt and ground black pepper, to taste

1 cup crushed tortilla chips

1 large egg, beaten

Directions

In a mixing bowl, thoroughly combine the flour, baking powder, cayenne pepper, oregano, salt, black pepper, egg and beer; mix to combine well.

In another shallow bowl, place the crushed tortilla chips.

Dip the Vidalia rings in the beer mixture; then, coat the rings with the crushed tortilla chips, pressing to adhere.

Transfer the onion rings to the Air Fryer cooking basket and spritz them with a nonstick spray.

Cook the onion rings at 380 degrees F for about 8 minutes, shaking the basket halfway through the cooking time to ensure even browning. Bon appétit!

Per serving: 269 Calories; 4.1g Fat; 48.1g Carbs; 7.9g Protein

Italian-Style Tomato Chips

(**Ready in about** 20 minutes | **Servings** 2)

Ingredients

2 tomatoes, cut into thick rounds

1 teaspoon Italian seasoning mix

1/4 cup Romano cheese, grated

Sea salt and fresh ground pepper, to taste

1 teaspoon extra-virgin olive oil

Directions

Start by preheating your Air Fryer to 350 degrees F.

Toss the tomato sounds with remaining Ingredients. Transfer the tomato rounds to the cooking basket without overlapping.

Cook your tomato rounds in the preheated Air Fryer for 5 minutes. Flip them over and cook an additional 5 minutes. Work with batches.

Bon appétit!

Per serving: 119 Calories; 6.5g Fat; 9.1g Carbs; 6.6g Protein

Bacon Chips with Chipotle Dipping Sauce

(**Ready in about** 15 minutes | **Servings** 3)

Ingredients

6 ounces bacon, cut into strips

Chipotle Dipping Sauce:

6 tablespoons sour cream

1/2 teaspoon chipotle chili powder

Directions

Place the bacon strips in the Air Fryer cooking basket.

Cook the bacon strips at 360 degrees F for 5 minutes; turn them over and cook for another 5 minutes.

Meanwhile, make the chipotle dipping sauce by whisking the sour cream and chipotle chili powder; reserve.

Serve the bacon chips with the chipotle dipping sauce and enjoy!

Per serving: 265 Calories; 24.5g Fat; 2.4g Carbs; 8.1g Protein;

Sea Scallops and Bacon Kabobs

(**Ready in about** 10 minutes | **Servings** 2)

Ingredients

10 sea scallops, frozen
1 teaspoon paprika
4 ounces bacon, diced

1 teaspoon garlic powder
Sea salt and ground black pepper, to taste

Directions

Assemble the skewers alternating sea scallops and bacon. Sprinkle the garlic powder, paprika, salt and black pepper all over your kabobs. Bake your kabobs in the preheated Air Fryer at 400 degrees F for 6 minutes. Serve warm with your favorite sauce for dipping. Enjoy!

Per serving: 403 Calories; 22g Fat; 4.3g Carbs; 43.6g Protein;

Hot Cheesy Mushrooms Bites

(**Ready in about** 10 minutes | **Servings** 3)

Ingredients

1 teaspoon butter, melted
4 ounces cheddar cheese, grated
4 tablespoons tortilla chips, crushed
12 button mushrooms, stalks removed and chopped

1 teaspoon fresh garlic, finely minced
1/2 teaspoon hot sauce
1 tablespoon fresh coriander, chopped
Sea salt and ground black pepper, to taste

Directions

In a mixing bowl, thoroughly combine the butter, garlic, cheddar cheese, tortilla chips, coriander, hot sauce and chopped mushrooms.

Divide the filling among mushroom caps and transfer them to the air Fryer cooking basket; season them with salt and black pepper.

Cook your mushrooms in the preheated Air Fryer at 400 degrees F for 5 minutes. Transfer the warm mushrooms to a serving platter and serve at room temperature. Bon appétit!

Per serving: 203 Calories; 14.3g Fat; 7.4g Carbs; 13.3g Protein

Cinnamon Pear Chips

(**Ready in about** 10 minutes | **Servings** 2)

Ingredients

1 large pear, cored and sliced
1 teaspoon coconut oil
1 teaspoon honey

1 teaspoon apple pie spice blend

Directions

Toss the pear slices with the spice blend, coconut oil and honey.

Then, place the pear slices in the Air Fryer cooking basket and cook at 360 degrees F for about 8 minutes.

Shake the basket once or twice to ensure even cooking. Pear chips will crisp up as it cools

Per serving: 94 Calories; 2.6g Fat; 18.1g Carbs; 0.7g Protein

Pecorino Romano Meatballs

(**Ready in about** 15 minutes | **Servings** 2)

Ingredients

1/2 pound ground turkey
1 egg, beaten
1 teaspoon stone-ground mustard
2 tablespoons scallions, chopped
1/2 teaspoon red pepper flakes, crushed

2 tablespoons tomato ketchup
1/4 Pecorino-Romano cheese, grated
1 garlic clove, minced
Sea salt and ground black pepper, to taste

Directions

In a mixing bowl, thoroughly combine all Ingredients.

Shape the mixture into 6 equal meatballs. Transfer the meatballs to the Air Fryer cooking basket that is previously greased with a nonstick cooking spray.

Cook the meatballs at 360 degrees F for 10 to 11 minutes, shaking the basket occasionally to ensure even cooking. An instant thermometer should read 165 degrees F.

Bon appétit!

Per serving: 264 Calories; 14.6g Fat; 3.7g Carbs; 29.7g Protein

Crunchy Roasted Chickpeas

(**Ready in about** 20 minutes | **Servings** 2)

Ingredients

1 tablespoon extra-virgin olive oil
8 ounces can chickpeas, drained
1/2 teaspoon smoked paprika

1/2 teaspoon ground cumin
1/2 teaspoon garlic powder
Sea salt, to taste

Directions

Drizzle olive oil over the drained chickpeas and transfer them to the Air Fryer cooking basket.

Cook your chickpeas in the preheated Air Fryer at 395 degrees F for 13 minutes. Turn your Air Fryer to 350 degrees F and cook an additional 6 minutes.

Toss the warm chickpeas with smoked paprika, cumin, garlic and salt. Bon appétit!

Per serving: 184 Calories; 6g Fat; 25.5g Carbs; 8.1g Protein

Pork Crackling with Sriracha Dip

(**Ready in about** 40 minutes | **Servings** 3)

Ingredients

1/2 pound pork rind
1/2 cup tomato sauce
1 teaspoon Sriracha sauce

Sea salt and ground black
pepper, to taste
1/2 teaspoon stone-ground
mustard

Directions

Rub sea salt and pepper on the skin side of the pork rind.
Allow it to sit for 30 minutes.

Then, cut the pork rind into chunks using kitchen scissors.

Roast the pork rind at 380 degrees F for 8 minutes; turn
them over and cook for a further 8 minutes or until
blistered.

Meanwhile, mix the tomato sauce with the Sriracha sauce
and mustard. Serve the pork crackling with the Sriracha dip
and enjoy!

Per serving: 525 Calories; 49.8g Fat; 10.6g Carbs; 6.8g Protein

Fish Sticks with Honey Mustard Sauce

(**Ready in about** 10 minutes | **Servings** 3)

Ingredients

10 ounces fish sticks
2 teaspoons honey

2 teaspoons yellow mustard
1/2 cup mayonnaise

Directions

Add the fish sticks to the Air Fryer cooking basket; drizzle
the fish sticks with a nonstick cooking spray.

Cook the fish sticks at 400 degrees F for 5 minutes; turn
them over and cook for another 5 minutes. Meanwhile,
mix the mayonnaise, yellow mustard and honey until well
combined. Serve the fish sticks with the honey mustard
sauce for dipping. Enjoy!

Per serving: 315 Calories; 19.8g Fat; 28.5g Carbs; 6.4g
Protein;

Prosciutto Stuffed Jalapeños

(**Ready in about** 15 minutes | **Servings** 2)

Ingredients

8 fresh jalapeño peppers,
deseeded and cut in half
lengthwise
1/2 teaspoon granulated
garlic

1/4 teaspoon cayenne pepper
4 ounces Ricotta cheese, at
room temperature
8 slices prosciutto, chopped

Directions

Place the fresh jalapeño peppers on a clean surface.

Mix the remaining Ingredients in a bowl; divide the filling
between the jalapeño peppers. Transfer the peppers to the
Air Fryer cooking basket. Cook the stuffed peppers at 400
degrees F for 15 minutes. Serve and enjoy!

Per serving: 178 Calories; 8.7g Fat; 11.7g Carbs; 14.3g
Protein

Salmon, Cheese and Cucumber Bites

(**Ready in about** 15 minutes | **Servings** 3)

Ingredients

1/2 pound salmon
1/2 teaspoon onion powder
1/4 teaspoon cumin powder
1 teaspoon granulated garlic
2 ounces cream cheese

1 teaspoon extra-virgin olive
oil
Sea salt and ground black
pepper, to taste
1 English cucumber, cut into
1-inch rounds

Directions

Pat the salmon dry and drizzle it with olive oil.

Season the salmon with onion powder, cumin, granulated
garlic, salt and black pepper. Transfer the salmon to the Air
Fryer cooking basket.

Cook the salmon at 400 degrees F for 5 minutes; turn the
salmon over and continue to cook for 5 minutes more or
until opaque. Cut the salmon into bite-sized pieces.

Spread 1 teaspoon of cream cheese on top of each
cucumber slice; top each slice with a piece of salmon.

Insert a tiny party fork down the center to keep in place.
Bon appétit!

Per serving: 184 Calories; 10.6g Fat; 4.3g Carbs; 17.3g Protein

Easy Mexican Elote

(**Ready in about** 10 minutes | **Servings** 2)

Ingredients

2 ears of corn, husked
4 tablespoons Mexican cheese
blend, crumbled
1 tablespoon fresh cilantro,
chopped

4 tablespoons Mexican crema
Sea salt and chili powder, to
taste
1 teaspoon fresh lime juice

Directions

Cook the corn for about 6 minutes in a 390°F preheated
Air Fryer.

In a mixing bowl, combine the Mexican crema, Mexican
cheese blend, lime juice, salt, and chilli powder.

After that, insert a wooden stick into the core to serve as a
handle. Rub the topping mixture over each ear of corn.

Garnish with fresh cilantro, if desired. Serve right away.

Per serving: 203 Calories; 7.6g Fat; 28.3g Carbs; 11.5g Protein

Classic Jiaozi (Chinese Dumplings)

(**Ready in about** 15 minutes | **Servings** 3)

Ingredients

1/2 pound ground pork
2 scallion stalks, chopped
1 ounce bamboo shoots, shredded
1/2 teaspoon garlic paste
1 teaspoon honey
Sauce:
1 tablespoon ketchup
1 teaspoon sesame seeds, lightly toasted

1 cup Napa cabbage, shredded
1 teaspoon fresh ginger, peeled and grated
8 ounces round wheat dumpling
2 tablespoons rice vinegar
1 teaspoon deli mustard
1/4 cup soy sauce

Directions

Cook the pork in a wok that is preheated over medium-high heat; cook until no longer pink and stir in the Napa cabbage, scallions, bamboo shoots, garlic paste and ginger; salt to taste and stir to combine well.

Divide the pork mixture between dumplings. Moisten the edge of each dumpling with water, fold the top half over the bottom half and press together firmly.

Place your dumplings in the Air Fryer cooking basket and spritz them with cooking spray. Cook your dumplings at 400 degrees F for 8 minutes. Work with batches.

While your dumplings are cooking, whisk the sauce Ingredients. Serve the warm dumplings with the sauce for dipping. Enjoy!

Per serving: 539 Calories; 23g Fat; 66.2g Carbs; 22.2g Protein;

Eggplant Parm Chips

(**Ready in about** 30 minutes | **Servings** 2)

Ingredients

1/2 pound eggplant, cut into rounds
1/2 teaspoon porcini powder
1/2 teaspoon garlic powder
1/4 teaspoon cayenne pepper

Kosher salt and ground black pepper, to taste
1/2 cup Parmesan cheese, grated
1/2 teaspoon shallot powder

Directions

Toss the eggplant rounds with the remaining Ingredients until well coated on both sides.

Bake the eggplant chips at 400 degrees F for 15 minutes; shake the basket and continue to cook for 15 minutes more.

Let cool slightly, eggplant chips will crisp up as it cools. Bon appétit!

Per serving: 148 Calories; 7.2g Fat; 13.5g Carbs; 8.2g Protein;

Apple Chips with Walnuts

(**Ready in about** 35 minutes | **Servings** 2)

Ingredients

1 apples, peeled, cored and sliced
1/4 cup walnuts

1 teaspoon cinnamon
1/2 teaspoon ground cloves

Directions

Toss the apple slices with ground cloves and cinnamon.

Place the apple slices in the Air Fryer cooking basket and cook at 360 degrees F for 10 minutes or until crisp. Reserve.

Then, toast the walnuts at 300 degrees F for 10 minutes; now, shake the basket and cook for another 10 minutes.

Chop the walnuts and scatter them over the apple slices. Bon appétit!

Per serving: 163 Calories; 6.8g Fat; 27.3g Carbs; 2.1g Protein;

Sticky Glazed Wings

(**Ready in about** 30 minutes | **Servings** 2)

Ingredients

1/2 pound chicken wings
1 tablespoon Worcestershire sauce
1 tablespoon hot sauce

2 tablespoons brown sugar
1 tablespoon balsamic vinegar
1 tablespoon sesame oil

Directions

Brush the chicken wings with sesame oil and transfer them to the Air Fryer cooking basket.

Cook the chicken wings at 370 degrees F for 12 minutes; turn them over and cook for a further 10 minutes.

Meanwhile, bring the other Ingredients to a boil in a saucepan; cook for 2 to 3 minutes or until thoroughly cooked.

Toss the warm chicken wings with the sauce and place them on a serving platter. Serve and enjoy!

Per serving: 318 Calories; 19.3g Fat; 11.6g Carbs; 22.1g Protein

Barbecue Little Smokies

(**Ready in about** 20 minutes | **Servings** 6)

Ingredients

1 pound beef cocktail wieners   10 ounces barbecue sauce

Directions

Start by preheating your Air Fryer to 380 degrees F.

Prick holes into your sausages using a fork and transfer them to the baking pan.

Cook for 13 minutes. Spoon the barbecue sauce into the pan and cook an additional 2 minutes.

Serve with toothpicks. Bon appétit!

Per serving: 182 Calories; 4.6g Fat; 19.2g Carbs; 15.9g Protein;

Greek-Style Deviled Eggs

(**Ready in about** 20 minutes | **Servings** 2)

Ingredients

4 eggs
2 tablespoons Kalamata olives, pitted and chopped
1 tablespoon Greek-style yogurt
Sea salt and crushed red pepper flakes, to taste

1 tablespoon chives, chopped
1 teaspoon habanero pepper, seeded and chopped
1 tablespoon parsley, chopped

Directions

Place the wire rack in the Air Fryer basket and lower the eggs onto the rack. Cook the eggs at 260 degrees F for 15 minutes.

Transfer the eggs to an ice-cold water bath to stop cooking. Peel the eggs

under cold running water; slice them into halves, separating the whites and yolks.

Mash the egg yolks with the remaining Ingredients and mix to combine. Spoon the yolk mixture into the egg whites and serve well chilled. Enjoy!

Per serving: 154 Calories; 9.3g Fat; 3.6g Carbs; 12.1g Protein;

Mini Plantain Cups

(**Ready in about** 10 minutes | **Servings** 3)

Ingredients

2 blackened plantains, chopped
1/2 cup milk
1 teaspoon fresh ginger, peeled and minced

1/2 cup cornmeal
1/4 cup all-purpose flour
1 tablespoon coconut oil
A pinch of ground cinnamon
A pinch of salt

Directions

In a mixing bowl, thoroughly combine all Ingredients until everything is well incorporated.

Spoon the batter into a greased mini muffin tin.

Bake the mini plantain cups in your Air Fryer at 330 degrees F for 6 to 7 minutes or until golden brown.

Bon appétit!

Per serving: 322 Calories; 7.1g Fat; 63g Carbs; 5.5g Protein;

Baby Carrots with Asian Flair

(**Ready in about** 20 minutes | **Servings** 3)

Ingredients

1 pound baby carrots
1/2 teaspoon Szechuan pepper
1 large garlic clove, crushed
1 tablespoon honey

2 tablespoons sesame oil
1 teaspoon Wuxiang powder (Five-spice powder)
1 (1-inch) piece fresh ginger root, peeled and grated
2 tablespoons tamari sauce

Directions

Start by preheating your Air Fryer to 380 degrees F.

Toss all Ingredients together and place them in the Air Fryer basket.

Cook for 15 minutes, shaking the basket halfway through the cooking time. Enjoy!

Per serving: 165 Calories; 9.3g Fat; 20.6g Carbs; 1.6g Protein;

Sweet Potato Fries with Spicy Dip

(**Ready in about** 50 minutes | **Servings** 3)

Ingredients

3 medium sweet potatoes, cut into 1/3-inch sticks
Spicy Dip:
1/4 teaspoon Dijon mustard
1 teaspoon hot sauce

1 teaspoon kosher salt
2 tablespoons olive oil
1/4 cup mayonnaise
1/4 cup Greek yogurt

Directions

Soak the sweet potato for 30 minutes in icy cold water. Drain and pat the sweet potatoes dry with paper towels.

Toss the sweet potatoes in a bowl with the olive oil and salt.

Place in a cooking basket that has been lightly oiled. Cook for 14 minutes in a preheated Air Fryer at 360°F. Cook in small batches.

While the sweet potatoes are cooking, whisk together the remaining ingredients for the spicy dip. Keep refrigerated until ready to serve. Enjoy!

Per serving: 332 Calories; 23.6g Fat; 27.9g Carbs; 3g Protein;

Crunchy Broccoli Fries

(**Ready in about** 15 minutes | **Servings** 4)

Ingredients

1 pound broccoli florets
1/2 teaspoon cayenne pepper
1/2 teaspoon onion powder
4 tablespoons parmesan cheese, preferably freshly grated

1 teaspoon granulated garlic
Sea salt and ground black pepper, to taste
2 tablespoons sesame oil

Directions

Start by preheating the Air Fryer to 400 degrees F.

Blanch the broccoli in salted boiling water until al dente, about 3 to 4 minutes. Drain well and transfer to the lightly greased Air Fryer basket.

Add the onion powder, garlic, cayenne pepper, salt, black pepper, and sesame oil.

Cook for 6 minutes, tossing halfway through the cooking time. Bon appétit!

Per serving: 127 Calories; 8.6g Fat; 9.9g Carbs; 4.9g Protein;

Kale Chips with Tahini Sauce

(**Ready in about** 15 minutes | **Servings** 4)

Ingredients

5 cups kale leaves, torn into 1-inch pieces
1 teaspoon garlic powder
1/4 teaspoon porcini powder
1/2 teaspoon mustard seeds
1 teaspoon salt

1/2 teaspoon shallot powder
1 ½ tablespoons sesame oil
1/3 cup tahini (sesame butter)
1 tablespoon fresh lemon juice
2 cloves garlic, minced

Directions

Toss the kale with the sesame oil and seasonings.

Bake in the preheated Air Fryer at 350 degrees F for 10 minutes, shaking the cooking basket occasionally.

Bake until the edges are brown. Work in batches.

Meanwhile, make the sauce by whisking all Ingredients in a small mixing bowl. Serve and enjoy!

Per serving: 170 Calories; 15g Fat; 7.1g Carbs; 4.2g Protein;

Famous Blooming Onion with Mayo Dip

(**Ready in about** 25 minutes | **Servings** 3)

Ingredients

1 large Vidalia onion 1/2 cup all-purpose flour
1 teaspoon salt
1/2 teaspoon dried thyme
2 eggs
1/4 cup milk Mayo Dip:
3 tablespoons sour cream
Kosher salt and freshly ground black pepper, to taste

1/2 teaspoon ground black pepper
1 teaspoon cayenne pepper
1/2 teaspoon dried oregano
1/2 teaspoon ground cumin
3 tablespoons mayonnaise
1 tablespoon horseradish

Directions

Cut off the top 1/2 inch of the Vidalia onion; peel your onion and place it cut-side down. Starting 1/2 inch from the root, cut the onion in half. Make a second cut that splits each half in two. You will have 4 quarters held together by the root.

Repeat these cuts, splitting the 4 quarters to yield eighths; then, you should split them again until you have 16 evenly spaced cuts. Turn the onion over and gently separate the outer pieces using your fingers.

In a mixing bowl, thoroughly combine the flour and spices. In a separate bowl, whisk the eggs and milk. Dip the onion into the egg mixture, followed by the flour mixture.

Spritz the onion with cooking spray and transfer to the lightly greased cooking basket. Cook for 370 degrees F for 12 to 15 minutes.

Meanwhile, make the mayo dip by whisking the remaining Ingredients. Serve and enjoy!

Per serving: 222 Calories; 9.9g Fat; 24.6g Carbs; 8.6g Protein;

Puerto Rican Tostones

(**Ready in about** 15 minutes | **Servings** 2)

Ingredients

1 ripe plantain, sliced
A pinch of kosher salt

1 tablespoon sunflower oil
A pinch of grated nutmeg

Directions

In a mixing bowl, combine the plantains, oil, nutmeg, and salt.

Cook for 10 minutes in a preheated Air Fryer at 400 degrees F, shaking the cooking basket halfway through.

Season with salt and pepper to taste, and serve immediately.

Per serving: 151 Calories; 7.1g Fat; 23.9g Carbs; 0.6g Protein;

Parsnip Chips with Spicy Citrus Aioli

(**Ready in about** 20 minutes | **Servings** 4)

Ingredients

1 pound parsnips, peel long strips
1 teaspoon red pepper flakes, crushed
Spicy Citrus Aioli:
1 tablespoon fresh lime juice
1 clove garlic, smashed

Sea salt and ground black pepper, to taste
1/2 teaspoon mustard seeds
2 tablespoons sesame oil
1/4 cup mayonnaise
Salt and black pepper, to taste
1/2 teaspoon curry powder

Directions

Start by preheating the Air Fryer to 380 degrees F.

Toss the parsnip chips with the sesame oil, salt, black pepper, red pepper, curry powder, and mustard seeds.

Cook for 15 minutes, shaking the Air Fryer basket periodically.

Meanwhile, make the sauce by whisking the mayonnaise, lime juice, garlic, salt, and pepper. Place in the refrigerator until ready to use. Bon appétit!

Per serving: 207 Calories; 12.1g Fat; 23.8g Carbs; 2.8g Protein

Classic Deviled Eggs

(**Ready in about** 20 minutes | **Servings** 3)

Ingredients

5 eggs
2 tablespoons sweet pickle relish Sea salt, to taste

2 tablespoons mayonnaise
1/2 teaspoon mixed peppercorns, crushed

Directions

Place the wire rack in the Air Fryer basket; lower the eggs onto the wire rack. Cook at 270 degrees F for 15 minutes.

Transfer them to an ice-cold water bath to stop the cooking. Peel the eggs under cold running water; slice them into halves.

Mash the egg yolks with the mayo, sweet pickle relish, and salt; spoon yolk mixture into egg whites. Arrange on a nice serving platter and garnish with the mixed peppercorns. Bon appétit!

Per serving: 261 Calories; 19.2g Fat; 5.5g Carbs; 15.5g Protein

Cajun Cheese Sticks

(**Ready in about** 15 minutes | **Servings** 4)

Ingredients

1/2 cup all-purpose flour
2 eggs
1 tablespoon Cajun seasonings
8 cheese sticks, kid-friendly

1/2 cup parmesan cheese, grated
1/4 cup ketchup

Directions

To begin, set up your breading station. Place the all-purpose flour in a shallow dish. In a separate dish, whisk the eggs.

Finally, mix the parmesan cheese and Cajun seasoning in a third dish.

Start by dredging the cheese sticks in the flour; then, dip them into the egg. Press the cheese sticks into the parmesan mixture, coating evenly.

Place the breaded cheese sticks in the lightly greased Air Fryer basket. Cook at 380 degrees F for 6 minutes.

Serve with ketchup and enjoy!

Per serving: 372 Calories; 22.7g Fat; 19.5g Carbs; 21.8g Protein

The Best Calamari Appetizer

(**Ready in about** 20 minutes | **Servings** 6)

Ingredients

1 ½ pounds calamari tubes, cleaned, cut into rings
1/4 cup buttermilk
1 cup cornmeal
1 egg, whisked

2 tablespoons lemon juice
Sea salt and ground black pepper, to taste
1 cup all-purpose flour
1 teaspoon paprika

Directions

Preheat your Air Fryer to 390 degrees F. Rinse the calamari and pat it dry. Season with salt and black pepper. Drizzle lemon juice all over the calamari.

Now, combine the cornmeal, flour, and paprika in a bowl; add the whisked egg and buttermilk.

Dredge the calamari in the egg/flour mixture.

Arrange them in the cooking basket. Spritz with cooking oil and cook for 9 to 12 minutes, shaking the basket occasionally. Work in batches.

Serve with toothpicks. Bon appétit!

Per serving: 274 Calories; 3.3g Fat; 36.8g Carbs; 22.9g Protein

Roasted Parsnip Sticks with Salted Caramel

(**Ready in about** 25 minutes | **Servings** 4)

Ingredients

1 pound parsnip, trimmed, scrubbed, cut into sticks
2 tablespoon avocado oil
2 tablespoons butter
2 tablespoons granulated sugar
1/2 teaspoon coarse salt
1/4 teaspoon ground allspice

Directions

Toss the parsnip with the avocado oil; bake in the preheated Air Fryer at 380 degrees F for 15 minutes, shaking the cooking basket occasionally to ensure even cooking.

Then, heat the sugar and 1 tablespoon of water in a small pan over medium heat. Cook until the sugar has dissolved; bring to a boil.

Keep swirling the pan around until the sugar reaches a rich caramel color. Pour in 2 tablespoons of cold water. Now, add the butter, allspice, and salt. The mixture should be runny.

Afterwards, drizzle the salted caramel over the roasted parsnip sticks and enjoy!

Per serving: 213 Calories; 13.1g Fat; 24.4g Carbs; 1.4g Protein

Greek-Style Squash Chips

(**Ready in about** 25 minutes | **Servings** 4)

Ingredients

1/2 cup seasoned breadcrumbs
1/4 teaspoon oregano
1/2 cup Parmesan cheese, grated
1 garlic clove, minced
1/2 cup Greek-style yogurt
Freshly ground black pepper, to your liking
Sea salt and ground black pepper, to taste
2 yellow squash, cut into slices
2 tablespoons grapeseed oil
Sauce:
1 tbsp fresh cilantro, chopped

Directions

In a shallow bowl, thoroughly combine the seasoned breadcrumbs, Parmesan, salt, black pepper, and oregano.

Dip the yellow squash slices in the prepared batter, pressing to adhere.

Brush with the grapeseed oil and cook in the preheated Air Fryer at 400 degrees F for 12 minutes. Shake the Air Fryer basket periodically to ensure

even cooking. Work in batches.

While the chips are baking, whisk the sauce Ingredients; place in your refrigerator until ready to serve. Enjoy!

Per serving: 180 Calories; 10.3g Fat; 13.3g Carbs; 5.8g Protein

Romano Cheese and Broccoli Balls

(**Ready in about** 25 minutes | **Servings** 4)

Ingredients

1/2 pound broccoli
2 garlic cloves, minced
1 shallot, chopped
2 tablespoons butter, at room temperature
Sea salt and ground black pepper, to taste
1/2 cup Romano cheese, grated
4 eggs, beaten
1/4 teaspoon dried basil
1/2 teaspoon paprika

Directions

Add the broccoli to your food processor and pulse until the consistency resembles rice.

Stir in the remaining Ingredients; mix until everything is well combined. Shape the mixture into bite-sized balls and transfer them to the lightly greased cooking basket.

Cook in the preheated Air Fryer at 375 degrees F for 16 minutes, shaking halfway through the cooking time. Serve with cocktail sticks and tomato ketchup on the side.

Per serving: 192 Calories; 15.2g Fat; 2.9g Carbs; 11.5g Protein

Summer Meatball Skewers

(**Ready in about** 20 minutes | **Servings** 6)

Ingredients

1/2 pound ground pork
1 teaspoon fresh garlic, minced
Salt and black pepper, to taste
1 red pepper, 1-inch pieces
1/2 cup barbecue sauce
1 teaspoon dried onion flakes
1 cup pearl onions
1/2 pound ground beef
1 teaspoon dried parsley flakes

Directions

Mix the ground meat with the onion flakes, garlic, parsley flakes, salt, and black pepper. Shape the mixture into 1-inch balls.

Thread the meatballs, pearl onions, and peppers alternately onto skewers. Microwave the barbecue sauce for 10 seconds.

Cook in the preheated Air Fryer at 380 degrees for 5 minutes. Turn the skewers over halfway through the cooking time. Brush with the sauce and cook for a further 5 minutes. Work in batches.

Serve with the remaining barbecue sauce and enjoy!

Per serving: 218 Calories; 13g Fat; 10.7g Carbs; 14.1g Protein;

Italian-Style Tomato-Parmesan Crisps

(**Ready in about** 20 minutes | **Servings** 4)

Ingredients

4 Roma tomatoes, sliced
2 tablespoons olive oil
1 teaspoon Italian seasoning mix

Sea salt and white pepper, to taste
4 tablespoons Parmesan cheese, grated

Directions

Begin by preheating your Air Fryer to 350°F. Grease the Air Fryer basket generously with nonstick cooking oil.

Toss the remaining ingredients with the sliced tomatoes. Place them in the cooking basket without overlapping them.

Cook for 5 minutes in a preheated Air Fryer. Cook for an additional 5 minutes after shaking the cooking basket. Working in batches is recommended.

If desired, serve with Mediterranean aioli for dipping. Good appetite!

Per serving: 90 Calories; 8.2g Fat; 2.7g Carbs; 1.8g Protein;

Loaded Tater Tot Bites

(**Ready in about** 20 minutes | **Servings** 6)

Ingredients

24 tater tots, frozen
6 tablespoons Canadian bacon, cooked and chopped

1 cup Swiss cheese, grated
1/4 cup Ranch dressing

Directions

Spritz the silicone muffin cups with non-stick cooking spray. Now, press the tater tots down into each cup.

Divide the cheese, bacon, and Ranch dressing between tater tot cups.

Cook in the preheated Air Fryer at 395 degrees for 10 minutes. Serve in paper cake cups. Bon appétit!

Per serving: 164 Calories; 9.7g Fat; 9.2g Carbs; 9.3g Protein;

Southern Cheese Straws

(**Ready in about** 30 minutes | **Servings** 6)

Ingredients

1 cup all-purpose flour
1/4 teaspoon smoked paprika
1/2 teaspoon celery seeds
1 sticks butter

Sea salt and ground black pepper, to taste
4 ounces mature Cheddar, cold, freshly grated

Directions

Start by preheating your air Fryer to 330 degrees F. Line the Air Fryer basket with parchment paper.

In a mixing bowl, thoroughly combine the flour, salt, black pepper, paprika, and celery seeds.

Then, combine the cheese and butter in the bowl of a stand mixer. Slowly stir in the flour mixture and mix to combine well.

Then, pack the dough into a cookie press fitted with a star disk. Pipe the long ribbons of dough across the parchment paper. Then cut into six-inch lengths.

Bake in the preheated Air Fryer for 15 minutes.

Repeat with the remaining dough. Let the cheese straws cool on a rack. You can store them between sheets of parchment in an airtight container. Bon appétit!

Per serving: 269 Calories; 19.3g Fat; 16.6g Carbs; 7.4g Protein

Sea Scallops and Bacon Skewers

(**Ready in about** 50 minutes | **Servings** 6)

Ingredients

1/2 pound sea scallops
1/2 cup coconut milk
6 ounces orange juice
1 shallot, diced
1 tablespoon vermouth

Sea salt and ground black pepper, to taste 1/2 pound bacon, diced
1 teaspoon garlic powder
1 teaspoon paprika

Directions

In a ceramic bowl, place the sea scallops, coconut milk, orange juice, vermouth, salt, and black pepper; let it marinate for 30 minutes.

Assemble the skewers alternating the scallops, bacon, and shallots. Sprinkle garlic powder and paprika all over the skewers.

Bake in the preheated air Fryer at 400 degrees F for 6 minutes. Serve warm and enjoy!

Per serving: 138 Calories; 3.6g Fat; 8.3g Carbs; 17.6g Protein;

Blue Cheesy Potato Wedges

(**Ready in about** 20 minutes | **Servings** 4)

Ingredients

2 Yukon Gold potatoes, peeled and cut into wedges
1/2 cup blue cheese, crumbled

Kosher salt, to taste
2 tablespoons ranch seasoning

Directions

Sprinkle the potato wedges with the ranch seasoning and salt. Grease generously the Air Fryer basket.

Place the potatoes in the cooking basket.

Roast in the preheated Air Fryer at 400 degrees for 12 minutes. Top with the cheese and roast an additional 3 minutes or until cheese begins to melt. Bon appétit!

Per serving: 157 Calories; 4.9g Fat; 22.1g Carbs; 6g Protein;

Cocktail Sausage and Veggies on a Stick

(**Ready in about** 25 minutes | **Servings** 4)

Ingredients

16 cocktail sausages, halved
16 pearl onions
1 green bell pepper, cut into 1 ½-inch pieces
Salt and cracked black pepper, to taste

1 red bell pepper, cut into 1 ½-inch pieces
1/2 cup tomato chili sauce

Directions

Thread the cocktail sausages, pearl onions, and peppers alternately onto skewers. Sprinkle with salt and black pepper.

Cook in the preheated Air Fryer at 380 degrees for 15 minutes, turning the skewers over once or twice to ensure even cooking.

Serve with the tomato chili sauce on the side. Enjoy!

Per serving: 190 Calories; 6.8g Fat; 18.5g Carbs; 13.3g Protein

Yakitori (Japanese Chicken Skewers)

(**Ready in about** 2 hours 15 minutes | **Servings** 4)

Ingredients

1/2 pound chicken tenders, cut bite-sized pieces
Sea salt and ground pepper, to taste
1 tablespoon fresh lemon juice
1 teaspoon sesame oil

1 teaspoon coriander seeds
1 clove garlic, minced
2 tablespoons sake
2 tablespoons Shoyu sauce

Directions

Place the chicken tenders, garlic, coriander, salt, black pepper, Shoyu sauce, sake, and lemon juice in a ceramic dish; cover and let it marinate for 2 hours.

Then, discard the marinade and tread the chicken tenders onto bamboo skewers.

Place the skewered chicken in the lightly greased Air Fryer basket. Drizzle sesame oil all over the skewered chicken.

Cook at 360 degrees for 6 minutes. Turn the skewered chicken over; brush

with the reserved marinade and cook for a further 6 minutes. Enjoy!

Per serving: 93 Calories; 2.7g Fat; 2.7g Carbs; 12.1g Protein

Paprika Zucchini Bombs with Goat Cheese

(**Ready in about** 20 minutes | **Servings** 4)

Ingredients

1 cup zucchini, grated, juice squeezed out
1/2 cup all-purpose flour
1/2 cup cornbread crumbs
1/2 cup goat cheese, grated
Salt and black pepper, to taste
1 teaspoon paprika

1 garlic clove, minced
1 egg
1/2 cup parmesan cheese, grated

Directions

Start by preheating your Air Fryer to 330 degrees F. Spritz the cooking basket with nonstick cooking oil.

Mix all Ingredients until everything is well incorporated. Shape the zucchini mixture into golf sized balls and place them in the cooking basket.

Cook in the preheated Air Fryer for 15 to 18 minutes, shaking the basket periodically to ensure even cooking.

Garnish with some extra paprika if desired and serve at room temperature. Bon appétit!

Per serving: 201 Calories; 9.5g Fat; 16.5g Carbs; 12.7g Protein

The Best Party Mix Ever

(**Ready in about** 15 minutes | **Servings** 10)

Ingredients

2 cups mini pretzels
1 cup mini crackers
1 cup peanuts
1 tablespoon Creole seasoning
2 tablespoons butter, melted

Directions

Toss all Ingredients in the Air Fryer basket.

Cook in the preheated Air Fryer at 360 degrees F approximately 9 minutes until lightly toasted. Shake the basket periodically. Enjoy!

Per serving: 228 Calories; 12.2g Fat; 24.7g Carbs; 5.9g Protein

Cauliflower Bombs with Sweet & Sour Sauce

(**Ready in about** 25 minutes | **Servings** 4)

Ingredients

Cauliflower Bombs:
2 ounces Ricotta cheese
1 egg
2 tablespoons olive oil
1 red bell pepper, jarred
1 clove garlic, minced
Salt and black pepper, to taste
1/2 pound cauliflower
1/3 cup Swiss cheese
1 tablespoon Italian seasoning mix Sweet & Sour Sauce:
1 teaspoon sherry vinegar
1 tablespoon tomato puree

Directions

Blanch the cauliflower in salted boiling water about 3 to 4 minutes until al dente. Drain well and pulse in a food processor.

Add the remaining Ingredients for the cauliflower bombs; mix to combine well.

Bake in the preheated Air Fryer at 375 degrees F for 16 minutes, shaking halfway through the cooking time.

In the meantime, pulse all Ingredients for the sauce in your food processor until combined. Season to taste. Serve the cauliflower bombs with the Sweet & Sour Sauce on the side. Bon appétit!

Per serving: 156 Calories; 11.9g Fat; 7.2g Carbs; 6.9g Protein

Crunchy Roasted Chickpeas

(**Ready in about** 25 minutes | **Servings** 4)

Ingredients

1 (15-ounce) can chickpeas, drained and patted dry
1/4 teaspoon mustard powder
1/2 teaspoon shallot powder
1/2 teaspoon red pepper flakes, crushed
1/8 cup Romano cheese, grated
1 teaspoon coriander, minced
1 tablespoon sesame oil
1/2 teaspoon garlic powder
Coarse sea salt and ground black pepper, to taste

Directions

Toss all Ingredients in a mixing bowl.

Roast in the preheated Air Fryer at 380 degrees F for 10 minutes, shaking the basket halfway through the cooking time.

Work in batches. Bon appétit!

Per serving: 226 Calories; 7.7g Fat; 28.4g Carbs; 11.1g Protein

DESSERTS

Homemade Chelsea Currant Buns

(**Ready in about** 50 minutes | **Servings** 4)

Ingredients

1/2 pound cake flour
1 teaspoon dry yeast
A pinch of sea salt
1/2 cup milk, warm
1 egg, whisked

1 tablespoons granulated sugar
4 tablespoons butter
1/2 cup dried currants
1 ounce icing sugar

Directions

Mix the flour, yeast, sugar and salt in a bowl; add in milk, egg and 2 tablespoons of butter and mix to combine well. Add lukewarm water as necessary to form a smooth dough.

Knead the dough until it is elastic; then, leave it in a warm place to rise for 30 minutes.

Roll out your dough and spread the remaining 2 tablespoons of butter onto the dough; scatter dried currants over the dough.

Cut into 8 equal slices and roll them up. Brush each bun with a nonstick

cooking oil and transfer them to the Air Fryer cooking basket.

Cook your buns at 330 degrees F for about 20 minutes, turning them over halfway through the cooking time.

Dust with icing sugar before serving. Bon appétit!

Per serving: 395 Calories; 14g Fat; 56.1g Carbs; 7.6g Protein;

Old-Fashioned Pinch-Me Cake with Walnuts

(**Ready in about** 20 minutes | **Servings** 4)

Ingredients

1 (10-ounces) can crescent rolls
1 teaspoon pumpkin pie spice blend
1 tablespoon dark rum

1/2 cup caster sugar
1/2 stick butter
1/2 cup walnuts, chopped

Directions

Start by preheating your Air Fryer to 350 degrees F.

Roll out the crescent rolls. Spread the butter onto the crescent rolls; scatter the sugar, spices and walnuts over the rolls. Drizzle with rum and roll them up.

Using your fingertips, gently press them to seal the edges.

Bake your cake for about 13 minutes or until the top is golden brown. Bon appétit!

Per serving: 455 Calories; 25.4g Fat; 52.1g Carbs; 6.1g Protein

Authentic Swedish Kärleksmums

(**Ready in about** 20 minutes | **Servings** 3)

Ingredients

2 tablespoons Swedish butter, at room temperature
1 tablespoon lingonberry jam
5 tablespoons all-purpose flour
A pinch of coarse sea salt

1 egg
4 tablespoons brown sugar
2 tablespoons cocoa powder
A pinch of grated nutmeg
1/2 teaspoon baking powder

Directions

Using an electric mixer, cream the butter and sugar together. Fold in the egg and lingonberry jam until well combined.

Mix in the flour, baking powder, cocoa powder, grated nutmeg, and salt until well combined. Pour the batter into a baking dish that has been lightly buttered.

Bake your cake for about 15 minutes, or until a tester inserted into the centre comes out dry and clean. Good appetite!

Per serving: 256 Calories; 11.5g Fat; 27.6g Carbs; 5.1g Protein

Air Grilled Peaches with Cinnamon-Sugar Butter

(**Ready in about** 25 minutes | **Servings** 2)

Ingredients

2 fresh peaches, pitted and halved
1/4 teaspoon ground cinnamon

2 tablespoons caster sugar
1 tablespoon butter

Directions

Mix the butter, sugar and cinnamon. Spread the butter mixture onto the peaches and transfer them to the Air Fryer cooking basket.

Cook your peaches at 320 degrees F for about 25 minutes or until the top is golden.

Serve with vanilla ice cream, if desired. Bon appétit!

Per serving: 146 Calories; 6.1g Fat; 22.6g Carbs; 1.4g Protein;

Chocolate Mug Cake

(**Ready in about** 10 minutes | **Servings** 2)

Ingredients

1/2 cup self-rising flour

5 tablespoons coconut milk

4 tablespoons unsweetened cocoa powder

2 eggs

6 tablespoons brown sugar

4 tablespoons coconut oil

A pinch of grated nutmeg

A pinch of salt

Directions

Mix all the Ingredients together; divide the batter between two mugs.

Place the mugs in the Air Fryer cooking basket and cook at 390 degrees F for about 10 minutes.

Bon appétit!

Per serving: 546 Calories; 34.1g Fat; 55.4g Carbs; 11.4g Protein

Easy Plantain Cupcakes

(**Ready in about** 10 minutes | **Servings** 4)

Ingredients

1 teaspoon baking powder

1/4 teaspoon ground cloves

1 cup all-purpose flour

2 ripe plantains, peeled and mashed with a fork

1 egg, whisked

1/4 cup brown sugar

1/4 teaspoon ground cinnamon

A pinch of salt

4 tablespoons coconut oil, room temperature

4 tablespoons pecans, roughly chopped

2 tablespoons raisins, soaked

Directions

In a mixing bowl, thoroughly combine all Ingredients until everything is well incorporated.

Spoon the batter into a greased muffin tin.

Bake the plantain cupcakes in your Air Fryer at 350 degrees F for about 10 minutes or until golden brown on the top. Bon appétit!

Per serving: 471 Calories; 22.5g Fat; 65.8g Carbs; 6.9g Protein

Strawberry Dessert Dumplings

(**Ready in about** 10 minutes | **Servings** 3)

Ingredients

9 wonton wrappers

1/3 strawberry jam

2 ounces icing sugar

Directions

Start by laying out the wonton wrappers.

Divide the strawberry jam between the wonton wrappers. Fold the wonton wrapper over the jam; now, seal the edges with wet fingers.

Cook your wontons at 400 degrees F for 8 minutes; working in batches. Bon appétit!

Per serving: 471 Calories; 22.5g Fat; 65.8g Carbs; 6.9g Protein;

Crunchy French Toast Sticks

(**Ready in about** 10 minutes | **Servings** 3)

Ingredients

1 egg

1 tablespoon brown sugar

1/4 teaspoon ground cloves

1/4 vanilla paste

1/4 cup milk

1/4 cup double cream

1/4 teaspoon ground cinnamon

3 thick slices of brioche bread, cut into thirds

1 cup crispy rice cereal

Directions

Thoroughly combine the egg, cream, milk, sugar, ground cloves, cinnamon and vanilla.

Dip each piece of bread into the cream mixture and then, press gently into the cereal, pressing to coat all sides.

Arrange the pieces of bread in the Air Fryer cooking basket and cook them at 380 degrees F for 2 minutes; flip and cook on the other side for 2 to 3 minutes longer.

Bon appétit!

Per serving: 188 Calories; 8.3g Fat; 21.9g Carbs; 6.2g Protein;

Old-Fashioned Apple Crumble

(**Ready in about** 35 minutes | **Servings** 4)

Ingredients

2 baking apples, peeled, cored and diced
1/4 teaspoon grated nutmeg
1/4 teaspoon ground cloves
1/2 teaspoon ground cinnamon
1/2 teaspoon vanilla essence
1/4 cup coconut oil
1 tablespoon cornstarch
2 tablespoons brown sugar
1/2 cup quick-cooking oats
1/4 cup self-rising flour
1/4 cup brown sugar
1/4 cup apple juice
1/2 teaspoon baking powder

Directions

Toss the apples with 2 tablespoons brown sugar and 2 tablespoons cornstarch. Place the apples in a baking pan that has been lightly greased with nonstick cooking spray.

Spray with cooking spray.

Combine the remaining topping ingredients in a mixing bowl. Over the apple layer, sprinkle the topping ingredients.

Bake your apple crumble for 35 minutes in a preheated Air Fryer at 330 degrees F. Good appetite!

Per serving: 261 Calories; 14.1g Fat; 35.7g Carbs; 1.9g Protein

Blueberry Fritters with Cinnamon Sugar

(**Ready in about** 20 minutes | **Servings** 4)

Ingredients

1/2 cup plain flour
A pinch of grated nutmeg
1 teaspoon brown sugar
1 cup fresh blueberries
1 egg
1 tablespoon coconut oil, melted
1/2 teaspoon baking powder
1/4 teaspoon ground star anise
A pinch of salt
1/4 cup coconut milk
4 tablespoons cinnamon sugar

Directions

Combine the flour, baking powder, brown sugar, nutmeg, star anise and salt.

In another bowl, whisk the eggs and milk until frothy. Add the wet mixture to the dry mixture and mix to combine well. Fold in the fresh blueberries.

Carefully place spoonfuls of batter into the Air Fryer cooking basket. Brush them with melted coconut oil.

Cook your fritters in the preheated Air Fryer at 370 degrees for 10 minutes, flipping them halfway through the cooking time. Repeat with the remaining batter.

Dust your fritters with the cinnamon sugar and serve at room temperature. Bon appétit!

Per serving: 218 Calories; 6.6g Fat; 35.6g Carbs; 4.7g Protein;

Cinnamon-Streusel Coffeecake

(**Ready in about** 30 minutes | **Servings** 4)

Ingredients

Cake:
1/4 cup yellow cornmeal
1 teaspoon baking powder
3 tablespoons white sugar
A pinch of kosher salt
1 egg Topping:
1/4 cup brown sugar
1/4 cup milk
2 tablespoons coconut oil
1/2 cup unbleached white flour
1 tablespoon unsweetened cocoa powder
3 tablespoons coconut oil
2 tablespoons polenta
1 teaspoon ground cinnamon
1/4 cup pecans, chopped

Directions

In a large bowl, combine together the cake Ingredients. Spoon the mixture into a lightly greased baking pan.

Then, in another bowl, combine the topping Ingredients. Spread the topping Ingredients over your cake.

Bake the cake at 330 degrees F for 12 to 15 minutes until a tester comes out dry and clean.

Allow your cake to cool for about 15 minutes before cutting and serving. Bon appétit!

Per serving: 364 Calories; 23.9g Fat; 35.1g Carbs; 5.1g Protein

Air Grilled Apricots with Mascarpone

(**Ready in about** 30 minutes | **Servings** 2)

Ingredients

6 apricots, halved and pitted
2 ounces mascarpone cheese
A pinch of sea salt
1 tablespoon confectioners' sugar
1 teaspoon coconut oil, melted
1/2 teaspoon vanilla extract

Directions

Place the apricots in the Air Fryer cooking basket. Drizzle the apricots with melted coconut oil.

Cook the apricots at 320 degrees F for about 25 minutes or until the top is golden.

In a bowl, whisk the mascarpone, vanilla extract, confectioners' sugar by hand until soft and creamy.

Remove the apricots from the cooking basket. Spoon the whipped mascarpone into the cavity of each apricot.

Sprinkle with coarse sea salt and enjoy!

Per serving: 244 Calories; 10.9g Fat; 30.1g Carbs; 7.5g Protein

Chocolate Chip Banana Crepes

(**Ready in about** 30 minutes | **Servings** 2)

Ingredients
1 small ripe banana
1 egg, whisked
1/8 teaspoon baking powder
1/4 cup chocolate chips

Directions
Mix all Ingredients until creamy and fluffy. Let it stand for about 20 minutes.

Spritz the Air Fryer baking pan with cooking spray. Pour 1/2 of the batter into the pan using a measuring cup.

Cook at 230 degrees F for 4 to 5 minutes or until golden brown. Repeat with another crepe. Bon appétit!

Per serving: 214 Calories; 5.4g Fat; 36.4g Carbs; 5.8g Protein;

Classic Flourless Cake

(**Ready in about** 2 hours | **Servings** 4)

Ingredients
Crust:
1 tablespoon flaxseed meal
1/3 cup almond meal
2 tablespoons powdered sugar
6 ounces cream cheese
1 teaspoon butter
1 teaspoon pumpkin pie spice
1 teaspoon caster sugar
Filling:
1 egg
1/2 teaspoon pure vanilla extract

Directions
Mix all the Ingredients for the crust and then, press the mixture into the bottom of a lightly greased baking pan.

Bake the crust at 350 degrees F for 18 minutes. Transfer the crust to the freezer for about 25 minutes.

Now, make the cheesecake topping by mixing the remaining Ingredients.

Spread the prepared topping over the cooled crust.

Bake your cheesecake in the preheated Air Fryer at 320 degrees F for about 30 minutes; leave it in the Air Fryer to keep warm for another 30 minutes.

Serve well chilled. Bon appétit!

Per serving: 254 Calories; 21.4g Fat; 9.4g Carbs; 6.1g Protein;

Old-Fashioned Baked Pears

(**Ready in about** 10 minutes | **Servings** 2)

Ingredients
2 large pears, halved and cored
1/2 cup rolled oats
1 teaspoon apple pie spice mix
2 teaspoons coconut oil
1 teaspoon lemon juice
1/4 cup walnuts, chopped
1/4 cup brown sugar

Directions
Drizzle the pear halves with lemon juice and coconut oil. In a mixing bowl, thoroughly combine the rolled oats, walnuts, brown sugar and apple pie spice mix.

Cook in the preheated Air Fryer at 360 degrees for 8 minutes, checking them halfway through the cooking time.

Dust with powdered sugar if desired. Bon appétit!

Per serving: 445 Calories; 14g Fat; 89g Carbs; 9g Protein;

Lemon-Glazed Crescent Ring

(**Ready in about** 25 minutes | **Servings** 6)

Ingredients
8 ounces refrigerated crescent dough
1 tablespoon coconut oil, at room temperature
1/3 cup powdered sugar
2 ounces caster sugar
1 tablespoon full-fat coconut milk
2 ounces mascarpone cheese, at room temperature
Glaze:
1/2 teaspoon vanilla paste
1 tablespoon fresh lemon juice

Directions
Separate the crescent dough sheet into 8 triangles. Then, arrange the triangles in a sunburst pattern so it should look like the sun.

Mix the mascarpone cheese, vanilla, coconut oil and caster sugar in a bowl.

Place the mixture on the bottom of each triangle; fold triangle tips over filling and tuck under base to secure.

Bake the ring at 360 degrees F for 20 minutes until dough is golden.

In small mixing dish, whisk the powdered sugar, lemon juice and coconut milk. Drizzle over warm crescent ring and garnish with grated lemon peel. Bon appétit!

Per serving: 227 Calories; 6.7g Fat; 35.4g Carbs; 5.3g Protein;

Fluffy Chocolate Chip Cookies

(**Ready in about** 20 minutes | **Servings** 6)

Ingredients

1/2 cup butter, softened
1/2 cup granulated sugar
1 cup quick-cooking oats
1 large egg
6 ounces dark chocolate chips
1/2 teaspoon coconut extract
1/2 teaspoon vanilla paste
1/2 cup all-purpose flour
1/2 teaspoon baking powder

Directions

Start by preheating your Air Fryer to 330 degrees F.

In a mixing bowl, beat the butter and sugar until fluffy. Beat in the egg, coconut extract and vanilla paste.

In a second mixing bowl, whisk the oats, flour and baking powder. Add the flour mixture to the egg mixture. Fold in the chocolate chips and gently stir to combine.

Drop 2-tablespoon scoops of the dough onto the parchment paper and transfer it to the Air Fryer cooking basket. Gently flatten each scoop to make a cookie shape.

Cook in the preheated Air Fryer for about 10 minutes. Work in batches. Bon appétit!

Per serving: 490 Calories; 30.1g Fat; 45.4g Carbs; 8.8g Protein

Authentic Spanish Churros

(**Ready in about** 20 minutes | **Servings** 4)

Ingredients

1/2 cup water
1 tablespoon granulated sugar
A pinch of ground cinnamon
1/2 teaspoon lemon zest
2 ounces dark chocolate
1/2 cup milk
1/4 cup butter, cut into cubes
A pinch of salt
1/2 cup plain flour
1 egg Chocolate Dip:
1 teaspoon ground cinnamon

Directions

Boil the water in a saucepan over medium-high heat; now, add the butter, sugar, cinnamon, salt and lemon zest; cook until the sugar has dissolved.

Next, remove the pan from the heat. Gradually stir in the flour, whisking continuously until the mixture forms a ball; let it cool slightly.

Fold in the egg and continue to beat using an electric mixer until everything comes together.

Pour the dough into a piping bag with a large star tip. Squeeze 4-inch strips of dough into the greased Air Fryer pan.

Cook your churros at 380 degrees F for about 10 minutes, shaking the basket halfway through the cooking time.

In the meantime, melt the chocolate and milk in a saucepan over low heat. Add in the cinnamon and cook on low heat for about 5 minutes. Serve the warm churros with the chocolate dip and enjoy!

Per serving: 287 Calories; 19.7g Fat; 22.5g Carbs; 5.2g Protein

Classic Brownie Cupcakes

(**Ready in about** 25 minutes | **Servings** 3)

Ingredients

1/3 cup all-purpose flour
1/4 teaspoon baking powder
3 tablespoons cocoa powder
1/2 teaspoon rum extract
1/3 cup caster sugar
2 ounces butter, room temperature
1 large egg
A pinch of ground cinnamon
A pinch of salt

Directions

In a mixing bowl, combine the dry ingredients. Combine the wet ingredients in a separate bowl. Stir in the wet ingredients gradually into the dry mixture.

Divide the batter evenly among the muffin cups and place them in the Air Fryer cooking basket.

Bake the cupcakes at 330°F for 15 minutes, or until a tester comes out dry and clean. Allow your cupcakes to cool for 10 minutes on a wire rack before unmolding. Good appetite!

Per serving: 264 Calories; 17.7g Fat; 24.4g Carbs; 4.6g Protein

Baked Fruit Salad

(**Ready in about** 15 minutes | **Servings** 2)

Ingredients

1 banana, peeled
1 tablespoon freshly squeezed lemon juice
1/2 teaspoon ground star anise
1/2 teaspoon granulated ginger 1
1 cooking pear, cored
1/4 teaspoon ground cinnamon
1 cooking apple, cored
/4 cup brown sugar
1 tablespoon coconut oil, melted

Directions

Toss your fruits with lemon juice, star anise, cinnamon, ginger, sugar and coconut oil.

Transfer the fruits to the Air Fryer cooking basket.

Bake the fruit salad in the preheated Air Fryer at 330 degrees F for 15 minutes.

Serve in individual bowls, garnished with vanilla ice cream. Bon appétit!

Per serving: 263 Calories; 7.3g Fat; 53.2g Carbs; 1.3g Protein;

Red Velvet Pancakes

(**Ready in about** 35 minutes | **Servings** 3)

Ingredients
1 cup all-purpose flour
1/8 teaspoon sea salt
1/2 teaspoon baking soda
1/2 cup powdered sugar
1 small-sized egg, beaten
1/2 cup milk
2 ounces cream cheese, softened
1 tablespoon butter, softened
1 teaspoon granulated sugar
1/8 teaspoon freshly grated nutmeg
2 tablespoons ghee, melted
1 teaspoon red paste food color

Directions
Thoroughly combine the flour, baking soda, granulated sugar, salt and nutmeg in a large bowl.

Gradually add in the melted ghee, egg, milk and red paste food color, stirring into the flour mixture until moistened. Allow your batter to rest for about 30 minutes.

Spritz the Air Fryer baking pan with cooking spray. Pour the batter into the pan using a measuring cup. Set the pan into the Air Fryer cooking basket.

Cook at 330 degrees F for about 5 minutes or until golden brown. Repeat with the other pancakes.

Meanwhile, mix the remaining Ingredients until creamy and fluffy. Decorate your pancakes with cream cheese topping. Bon appétit!

Per serving: 422 Calories; 19g Fat; 52.1g Carbs; 8.6g Protein;

Apricot and Almond Crumble

(**Ready in about** 35 minutes | **Servings** 3)

Ingredients
1 cup apricots, pitted and diced
4 tablespoons granulated sugar
1/2 teaspoon ground cinnamon
1 teaspoon crystallized ginger
1/3 cup self-raising flour
1/4 cup flaked almonds
2 tablespoons butter
1/2 teaspoon ground cardamom

Directions
Place the sliced apricots and almonds in a baking pan that is lightly greased with a nonstick cooking spray.

In a mixing bowl, thoroughly combine the remaining Ingredients. Sprinkle this topping over the apricot layer.

Bake your crumble in the preheated Air Fryer at 330 degrees F for 35 minutes. Bon appétit!

Per serving: 192 Calories; 7.9g Fat; 29.1g Carbs; 1.7g Protein;

Easy Monkey Rolls

(**Ready in about** 25 minutes | **Servings** 4)

Ingredients
8 ounces refrigerated buttermilk biscuit dough
1/4 teaspoon grated nutmeg
1/2 teaspoon ground cinnamon
4 ounces butter, melted
1/2 cup brown sugar
1/4 teaspoon ground cardamom

Directions
Spritz 4 standard-size muffin cups with a nonstick spray. Thoroughly combine the brown sugar with the melted butter, nutmeg, cinnamon and cardamom.

Spoon the butter mixture into muffins cups.

Separate the dough into biscuits and divide your biscuits between muffin cups.

Bake the Monkey rolls at 340 degrees F for about 15 minutes or until golden brown. Turn upside down just before serving. Bon appétit!

Per serving: 432 Calories; 29.3g Fat; 40.1g Carbs; 4.1g Protein

Sherry Roasted Sweet Cherries

(**Ready in about** 35 minutes | **Servings** 4)

Ingredients
2 cups dark cherries
3 tablespoons sherry
A pinch of sea salt
1/4 cup granulated sugar
A pinch of grated nutmeg
1 tablespoon honey

Directions
Arrange your cherries in the bottom of a lightly greased baking dish. Whisk the remaining Ingredients; spoon this mixture into the baking dish. Air fry your cherries at 370 degrees F for 35 minutes. Bon appétit!

Per serving: 53 Calories; 0.3g Fat; 11.1g Carbs; 0.1g Protein;

\

Greek Roasted Figs with Yiaourti me Meli

(**Ready in about** 20 minutes | **Servings** 3)

Ingredients

1 teaspoon coconut oil, melted
1/4 teaspoon ground cloves
1/4 teaspoon ground cinnamon
3 tablespoon honey
1/4 teaspoon ground cardamom
1/2 cup Greek yogurt
6 medium-sized figs

Directions

Drizzle the melted coconut oil all over your figs. Sprinkle cardamom, cloves and cinnamon over your figs.

Roast your figs in the preheated Air Fryer at 330 degrees F for 15 to 16

minutes, shaking the basket occasionally to promote even cooking.

In the meantime, thoroughly combine the honey with the Greek yogurt to make the yiaourti me meli.

Divide the roasted figs between 3 serving bowls and serve with a dollop of yiaourti me meli. Enjoy!

Per serving: 169 Calories; 1.9g Fat; 37.1g Carbs; 3.7g Protein;

Chocolate Lava Cake

(**Ready in about** 20 minutes | **Servings** 4)

Ingredients

4 ounces butter, melted
4 ounces dark chocolate
2 eggs, lightly whisked
1 teaspoon baking powder
4 tablespoons granulated sugar
2 tablespoons cake flour
1/2 teaspoon ground cinnamon
1/4 teaspoon ground star anise

Directions

Begin by preheating your Air Fryer to 370 degrees F. Spritz the sides and bottom of a baking pan with nonstick cooking spray.

Melt the butter and dark chocolate in a microwave-safe bowl. Mix the eggs and sugar until frothy.

Pour the butter/chocolate mixture into the egg mixture. Stir in the flour, baking powder, cinnamon, and star anise. Mix until everything is well incorporated.

Scrape the batter into the prepared pan. Bake in the preheated Air Fryer for 9 to 11 minutes.

Let stand for 2 minutes. Invert on a plate while warm and serve. Bon appétit!

Per serving: 450 Calories; 37.2g Fat; 24.2g Carbs; 5.6g Protein

Banana Chips with Chocolate Glaze

(**Ready in about** 20 minutes | **Servings** 2)

Ingredients

2 banana, cut into slices
1/4 teaspoon lemon zest
1 tablespoon coconut oil, melted
1 tablespoon cocoa powder
1 tablespoon agave syrup

Directions

Toss the bananas with the lemon zest and agave syrup. Transfer your bananas to the parchment-lined cooking basket.

Bake in the preheated Air Fryer at 370 degrees F for 12 minutes, turning them over halfway through the cooking time.

In the meantime, melt the coconut oil in your microwave; add the cocoa powder and whisk to combine well.

Serve the baked banana chips with a few drizzles of the chocolate glaze. Enjoy!

Per serving: 201 Calories; 7.5g Fat; 37.1g Carbs; 1.8g Protein;

Grandma's Butter Cookies

(**Ready in about** 25 minutes | **Servings** 4)

Ingredients

8 ounces all-purpose flour
A pinch of grated nutmeg
A pinch of coarse salt
1 stick butter, room temperature
1 teaspoon vanilla extract
1 teaspoon baking powder
1 large egg, room temperature.
2 ½ ounces sugar

Directions

Mix the flour, sugar, baking powder, grated nutmeg, and salt in a bowl. In a separate bowl, whisk the egg, butter, and vanilla extract.

Stir the egg mixture into the flour mixture; mix to combine well or until it forms a nice, soft dough.

Roll your dough out and cut out with a cookie cutter of your choice.

Bake in the preheated Air Fryer at 350 degrees F for 10 minutes. Decrease the temperature to 330 degrees F and cook for 10 minutes longer. Bon appétit!

Per serving: 492 Calories; 24.7g Fat; 61.1g Carbs; 6.7g Protein;

Cinnamon Dough Dippers

(**Ready in about** 20 minutes | **Servings** 6)

Ingredients

1/2 pound bread dough
1/2 cup caster sugar
1/2 cup cream cheese, softened
1 cup powdered sugar
1 tablespoon cinnamon
1/4 cup butter, melted
1/2 teaspoon vanilla
2 tablespoons milk

Directions

Roll the dough into a log; cut into 1-1/2 inch strips using a pizza cutter.

Mix the butter, sugar, and cinnamon in a small bowl. Use a rubber spatula to spread the butter mixture over the tops of the dough dippers.

Bake at 360 degrees F for 7 to 8 minutes, turning them over halfway through the cooking time. Work in batches.

Meanwhile, make the glaze dip by whisking the remaining Ingredients with a hand mixer. Beat until a smooth consistency is reached.

Serve at room temperature and enjoy!

Per serving: 332 Calories; 14.8g Fat; 45.6g Carbs; 5.1g Protei

Chocolate Apple Chips

(**Ready in about** 15 minutes | **Servings** 2)

Ingredients

1 large Pink Lady apple, cored and sliced
2 teaspoons cocoa powder
2 tablespoons lemon juice
A pinch of kosher salt
1 tablespoon light brown sugar

Directions

Toss the apple slices in with the remaining ingredients.

Bake at 350°F for 5 minutes, then shake the basket to ensure even cooking and cook for another 5 minutes.

Good appetite!

Per serving: 81 Calories; 0.5g Fat; 21.5g Carbs; 0.7g Protein;

Favorite Apple Crisp

(**Ready in about** 40 minutes | **Servings** 4)

Ingredients

4 cups apples, peeled, cored and sliced
1 tablespoon cornmeal
1/2 teaspoon ground cinnamon
1/2 cup quick-cooking oats
1/2 cup all-purpose flour
1 tablespoon honey
1/2 cup brown sugar
1/4 teaspoon ground cloves
1/4 cup water
1/2 cup caster sugar
1/2 teaspoon baking powder
1/3 cup coconut oil, melted

Directions

Toss the sliced apples with the brown sugar, honey, cornmeal, cloves, and cinnamon. Divide between four custard cups coated with cooking spray.

In a mixing dish, thoroughly combine the remaining Ingredients. Sprinkle

over the apple mixture.

Bake in the preheated Air Fryer at 330 degrees F for 35 minutes. Bon appétit!

Per serving: 403 Calories; 18.6g Fat; 61.5g Carbs; 2.9g Protein

Peppermint Chocolate Cheesecake

(**Ready in about** 40 minutes | **Servings** 6)

Ingredients

1 cup powdered sugar
1/2 cup all-purpose flour
1/2 cup butter
2 drops peppermint extract
1 teaspoon vanilla extract
1 cup mascarpone cheese, at room temperature
4 ounces semisweet chocolate, melted

Directions

In a mixing bowl, combine the sugar, flour, and butter. Press the mixture into the bottom of a baking pan that has been lightly greased.

Bake for 18 minutes at 350 degrees F. Set it in the freezer for 20 minutes. Then, combine the remaining ingredients to make the cheesecake topping.

Place this topping on top of the crust and place it in the freezer for another 15 minutes to cool. Chill before serving.

Per serving: 484 Calories; 36.7g Fat; 38.8g Carbs; 5g Protein

Baked Coconut Doughnuts

(**Ready in about** 20 minutes | **Servings** 6)

Ingredients

1 ½ cups all-purpose flour
1 teaspoon baking powder
A pinch of kosher salt
2 eggs
1/4 teaspoon ground cardamom
2 tbsp coconut oil, melted
1 teaspoon coconut essence
1 cup coconut flakes

A pinch of freshly grated nutmeg
1/2 cup white sugar
2 tablespoons full-fat coconut milk
1/4 teaspoon ground cinnamon
1/2 teaspoon vanilla essence

Directions

In a mixing bowl, thoroughly combine the all-purpose flour with the baking powder, salt, nutmeg, and sugar.

In a separate bowl, beat the eggs until frothy using a hand mixer; add the coconut milk and oil and beat again; lastly, stir in the spices and mix again until everything is well combined.

Then, stir the egg mixture into the flour mixture and continue mixing until a dough ball forms. Try not to over-mix your dough. Transfer to a lightly floured surface.

Roll out your dough to a 1/4-inch thickness using a rolling pin. Cut out the doughnuts using a 3-inch round cutter; now, use a 1-inch round cutter to remove the center.

Bake in the preheated Air Fryer at 340 degrees F approximately 5 minutes or until golden. Repeat with remaining doughnuts. Decorate with coconut flakes and serve.

Per serving: 305 Calories; 13.2g Fat; 40.1g Carbs; 6.7g Protein

Coconut Pancake Cups

(**Ready in about** 30 minutes | **Servings** 4)

Ingredients

1/2 cup flour
1 tablespoon coconut oil, melted
1/2 cup coconut chips

1/3 cup coconut milk
A pinch of ground cardamom
1 teaspoon vanilla
2 eggs

Directions

Mix the flour, coconut milk, eggs, coconut oil, vanilla, and cardamom in a large bowl.

Let it stand for 20 minutes. Spoon the batter into a greased muffin tin.

Cook at 230 degrees F for 4 to 5 minutes or until golden brown. Repeat with the remaining batter.

Decorate your pancakes with coconut chips. Bon appétit!

Per serving: 274 Calories; 17.3g Fat; 21.6g Carbs; 7.7g Protein

Classic Vanilla Mini Cheesecakes

(**Ready in about** 40 minutes + chilling time | **Servings** 6)

Ingredients

1/2 cup almond flour
1 tablespoon white sugar
1 (8-ounce) package cream cheese, softened
1 egg, at room temperature
Topping:
3 tablespoons white sugar

1 ½ tablespoons unsalted butter, melted
1/2 teaspoon vanilla paste
1/4 cup powdered sugar
1 ½ cups sour cream
1 teaspoon vanilla extract
1/4 cup maraschino cherries

Directions

Thoroughly combine the almond flour, butter, and sugar in a mixing bowl. Press the mixture into the bottom of lightly greased custard cups.

Then, mix the cream cheese, 1/4 cup of powdered sugar, vanilla, and egg using an electric mixer on low speed. Pour the batter into the pan, covering the crust.

Bake in the preheated Air Fryer at 330 degrees F for 35 minutes until edges are puffed and the surface is firm.

Mix the sour cream, 3 tablespoons of white sugar, and vanilla for the topping; spread over the crust and allow it to cool to room temperature.

Transfer to your refrigerator for 6 to 8 hours. Decorate with maraschino cherries and serve well chilled.

Per serving: 321 Calories; 25g Fat; 17.1g Carbs; 8.1g Protein

Bakery-Style Hazelnut Cookies

(**Ready in about** 20 minutes | **Servings** 6)

Ingredients

1 ½ cups all-purpose flour
1 stick butter
1 teaspoon baking soda
2 eggs, at room temperature

1 teaspoon fine sea salt
1 cup brown sugar
2 teaspoons vanilla
1 cup hazelnuts, coarsely chopped

Directions

Begin by preheating your Air Fryer to 350 degrees F. Mix the flour with the baking soda, and sea salt.

In the bowl of an electric mixer, beat the butter, brown sugar, and vanilla until creamy. Fold in the eggs, one at a time, and mix until well combined.

Slowly and gradually, stir in the flour mixture. Finally, fold in the coarsely chopped hazelnuts.

Divide the dough into small balls using a large cookie scoop; drop onto the prepared cookie sheets. Bake for 10 minutes or until golden brown, rotating

the pan once or twice through the cooking time.

Work in batches and cool for a couple of minutes before removing to wire racks. Enjoy!

Per serving: 450 Calories; 28.6g Fat; 43.9g Carbs; 8.1g Protein

Cocktail Party Fruit Kabobs

(**Ready in about** 10 minutes | **Servings** 6)

Ingredients

1 pears, diced into bite-sized chunks	2 mangos, diced into bite-sized chunks
2 apples, diced into bite-sized chunks	1 teaspoon vanilla essence
1 tablespoon fresh lemon juice	1/2 teaspoon ground cloves
1 teaspoon ground cinnamon	2 tablespoons maple syrup

Directions

Toss all Ingredients in a mixing dish. Tread the fruit pieces on skewers.

Cook at 350 degrees F for 5 minutes. Bon appétit!

Per serving: 165 Calories; 0.7g Fat; 41.8g Carbs; 1.6g Protein

Sunday Banana Chocolate Cookies

(**Ready in about** 20 minutes | **Servings** 8)

Ingredients

1 stick butter, at room temperature	2 ripe bananas, mashed
1 teaspoon vanilla paste	1 ¼ cups caster sugar
1 ½ teaspoons baking powder	1 2/3 cups all-purpose flour
1/4 teaspoon ground cinnamon	1/3 cup cocoa powder
1 ½ cups chocolate chips	1/4 teaspoon crystallized ginger

Directions

In a mixing dish, beat the butter and sugar until creamy and uniform. Stir in the mashed bananas and vanilla.

In another mixing dish, thoroughly combine the flour, cocoa powder, baking powder, cinnamon, and crystallized ginger.

Add the flour mixture to the banana mixture; mix to combine well. Afterwards, fold in the chocolate chips.

Drop by large spoonfuls onto a parchment-lined Air Fryer basket. Bake at 365 degrees F for 11 minutes or until golden brown on the top. Bon appétit!

Per serving: 298 Calories; 12.3g Fat; 45.9g Carbs; 3.8g Protein

Rustic Baked Apples

(**Ready in about** 25 minutes | **Servings** 4)

Ingredients

4 Gala apples	1/4 cup rolled oats
2 tablespoons honey	1/3 cup walnuts, chopped
1 teaspoon cinnamon powder	2/3 cup water
1/2 teaspoon ground cardamom	1/4 cup sugar
1/2 teaspoon ground cloves	

Directions

Use a paring knife to remove the stem and seeds from the apples, making deep holes.

In a mixing bowl, combine together the rolled oats, sugar, honey, walnuts, cinnamon, cardamom, and cloves.

Pour the water into an Air Fryer safe dish. Place the apples in the dish.

Bake at 340 degrees F for 17 minutes. Serve at room temperature. Bon appétit!

Per serving: 211 Calories; 5.1g Fat; 45.5g Carbs; 2.6g Protein;

The Ultimate Berry Crumble

(**Ready in about** 40 minutes | **Servings** 6)

Ingredients

18 ounces cherries	1/2 cup granulated sugar
1/4 teaspoon ground star anise	1 cup demerara sugar
1/2 teaspoon ground cinnamon	2 tablespoons cornmeal
1/2 teaspoon baking powder	2/3 cup all-purpose flour
	1/3 cup rolled oats
	1/2 stick butter, cut into small pieces

Directions

Combine the cherries, granulated sugar, cornmeal, star anise, and cinnamon in a mixing bowl. Divide the mixture among six custard cups that have been sprayed with cooking spray.

Combine the remaining ingredients in a mixing bowl. Sprinkle the berry mixture on top.

35 minutes in a preheated Air Fryer at 330 degrees F. Good appetite!

Per serving: 272 Calories; 8.3g Fat; 49.5g Carbs; 3.3g Protein;

Mocha Chocolate Espresso Cake

(**Ready in about** 40 minutes | **Servings** 8)

Ingredients

1 ½ cups flour	1 teaspoon baking powder
1/4 teaspoon salt	1 stick butter, melted
1/2 cup hot strongly brewed coffee	1 egg Topping:
1/4 cup flour	2/3 cup sugar
1/2 cup sugar	1/2 teaspoon ground cardamom
1 teaspoon ground cinnamon	1/2 teaspoon vanilla
3 tablespoons coconut oil	

Directions

Mix all dry Ingredients for your cake; then, mix in the wet Ingredients. Mix

until everything is well incorporated.

Spritz a baking pan with cooking spray. Scrape the batter into the baking pan. Then make the topping by mixing all Ingredients. Place on top of the cake.

Smooth the top with a spatula.

Bake at 330 degrees F for 30 minutes or until the top of the cake springs back when gently pressed with your fingers. Serve with your favorite hot beverage. Bon appétit!

Per serving: 320 Calories; 18.1g Fat; 35.9g Carbs; 4.1g Protein

Baked Peaches with Oatmeal Pecan Streusel

(**Ready in about** 20 minutes | **Servings** 3)

Ingredients

2 tablespoons old-fashioned rolled oats	1/2 teaspoon ground cinnamon
1 egg	2 tablespoons cold salted butter, cut into pieces
3 tablespoons golden caster sugar	3 tbsp pecans, chopped
3 large ripe freestone peaches, halved and pitted	

Directions

Mix the rolled oats, sugar, cinnamon, egg, and butter until well combined.

Add a big spoonful of prepared topping to the center of each peach. Pour 1/2 cup of water into an Air Fryer safe dish. Place the peaches in the dish.

Top the peaches with the roughly chopped pecans. Bake at 340 degrees F for 17 minutes. Serve at room temperature. Bon appétit!

Per serving: 247 Calories; 14.1g Fat; 28.8g Carbs; 5.9g Protein

Favorite New York Cheesecake

(**Ready in about** 40 minutes + chilling time | **Servings** 8)

Ingredients

1 ½ cups digestive biscuits crumbs	1 ounce demerara sugar
1/2 stick butter, melted	2 ounces white sugar
1/2 cup heavy cream	32 ounces full-fat cream cheese
1 ¼ cups caster sugar	3 eggs, at room temperature
1 tablespoon vanilla essence	1 teaspoon grated lemon zest

Directions

Coat the sides and bottom of a baking pan with a little flour.

In a mixing bowl, combine the digestive biscuits, white sugar, and demerara sugar. Add the melted butter and mix until your mixture looks like breadcrumbs.

Press the mixture into the bottom of the prepared pan to form an even layer. Bake at 330 degrees F for 7 minutes until golden brown. Allow it to cool completely on a wire rack. Meanwhile, in a mixer fitted with the paddle attachment, prepare the filling by mixing the soft cheese, heavy cream, and caster sugar; beat until creamy and fluffy.

Crack the eggs into the mixing bowl, one at a time; add the vanilla and lemon zest and continue to mix until fully combined. Pour the prepared topping over the cooled crust and spread evenly.

Bake in the preheated Air Fryer at 330 degrees F for 25 to 30 minutes; leave it in the Air Fryer to keep warm for another 30 minutes.

Cover your cheesecake with plastic wrap. Place in your refrigerator and allow it to cool at least 6 hours or overnight. Serve well chilled.

Per serving: 477 Calories; 30.2g Fat; 39.5g Carbs; 12.8g Protein

Authentic Indian Gulgulas

(**Ready in about** 20 minutes | **Servings** 3)

Ingredients

1 banana, mashed	1 egg
1/2 teaspoon vanilla essence	1/2 milk
1/4 teaspoon ground cardamom	1/4 cup sugar
3/4 cup all-purpose flour	1/4 teaspoon cinnamon
	1 teaspoon baking powder

Directions

In a mixing bowl, whisk the mashed banana with the sugar and egg; add the vanilla, cardamom, and cinnamon and mix to combine well. Gradually pour in the milk and mix again. Stir in the flour and baking powder. Mix until everything is well incorporated.

Drop a spoonful of batter onto the greased Air Fryer pan. Cook in the preheated Air Fryer at 360 degrees F for 5 minutes, flipping them halfway through the cooking time.

Repeat with the remaining batter and serve warm. Enjoy!

Per serving: 252 Calories; 4.9g Fat; 43.8g Carbs; 7.9g Protein;

English-Style Scones with Raisins

(**Ready in about** 20 minutes | **Servings** 6)

Ingredients

1 ½ cups all-purpose flour	1 teaspoon baking powder
1/4 cup brown sugar	1/2 cup double cream
1/4 teaspoon sea salt	1/4 teaspoon ground cloves
1/2 teaspoon ground cardamom	6 tablespoons butter, cooled and sliced
1 teaspoon ground cinnamon	1/2 cup raisins
2 eggs, lightly whisked	1/2 teaspoon vanilla essence

Directions

In a mixing bowl, thoroughly combine the flour, sugar, baking powder, salt, cloves, cardamom cinnamon, and raisins. Mix until everything is combined well.

Add the butter and mix again.

In another mixing bowl, combine the double cream with the eggs and vanilla; beat until creamy and smooth.

Stir the wet Ingredients into the dry mixture. Roll your dough out into a circle and cut into wedges.

Bake in the preheated Air Fryer at 360 degrees for 11 minutes, rotating the pan halfway through the cooking time. Bon appétit!

Per serving: 317 Calories; 18.9g Fat; 29.5g Carbs; 6.9g Protein

Red Velvet Pancakes

(**Ready in about** 35 minutes | **Servings** 3)

Ingredients

1/2 cup flour	1 teaspoon baking powder
2 tablespoons white sugar	1 teaspoon red paste food color
1/2 teaspoon cinnamon	
1 egg	1/2 cup milk
1 teaspoon vanilla Topping:	2 ounces cream cheese, softened
1/4 teaspoon salt	
3/4 cup powdered sugar	2 tablespoons butter, softened

Directions

In a large mixing bowl, combine the flour, baking powder, salt, sugar, cinnamon, and red paste food colour.

Add the egg and milk in a steady stream, whisking constantly, until well combined.

Allow it to stand for 20 minutes.

Coat the baking pan of the Air Fryer with cooking spray. Using a measuring cup, pour the batter into the pan.

Cook for 4 to 5 minutes, or until golden brown, at 230°F. Repeat with the rest of the batter.

Meanwhile, make your topping by combining all of the ingredients and mixing until creamy and fluffy. Make a topping for your pancakes. Good appetite!

Per serving: 392 Calories; 17.8g Fat; 50g Carbs; 7.8g Protein;

Salted Caramel Cheesecake

(**Ready in about** 1 hour + chilling time | **Servings** 10)

Ingredients

1 cup granulated sugar	3/4 cup heavy cream
2 tablespoons butter	1 teaspoon vanilla extract
1/3 cup water	1/2 teaspoon coarse sea salt
1/3 cup salted butter, melted	Crust:
1 ½ cups graham cracker crumbs	2 tablespoons brown sugar
	Topping:
20 ounces cream cheese, softened	1 cup sour cream
	3 eggs
1 cup granulated sugar	1 teaspoon vanilla essence
1/4 teaspoon ground star anise	

Directions

To make the caramel sauce, cook the sugar in a saucepan over medium heat; shake it to form a flat layer.

Add the water and cook until the sugar dissolves. Raise the heat to medium- high, and continue to cook your caramel for a further 10 minutes until it turns amber colored.

Turn the heat off; immediately stir in the heavy cream, butter, vanilla extract, and salt. Stir to combine well.

Let the salted caramel sauce cool to room temperature.

Beat all Ingredients for the crust in a mixing bowl. Press the mixture into the bottom of a lightly greased baking pan.

Bake at 350 degrees F for 18 minutes. Place it in your freezer for 20 minutes. Then, make the cheesecake topping by mixing the remaining Ingredients.

Pour the prepared topping over the cooled crust and spread evenly.

Bake in the preheated Air Fryer at 330 degrees F for 25 to 30 minutes; leave it in the Air Fryer to keep warm for another 30 minutes.

Refrigerate your cheesecake until completely cool and firm or overnight. Prior to serving, pour the salted caramel sauce over the cheesecake. Bon appétit!

Per serving: 501 Calories; 36.3g Fat; 35.6g Carbs; 9.1g Protein

Spanish-Style Doughnut Tejeringos

(**Ready in about** 20 minutes | **Servings** 4)

Ingredients

3/4 cup water
1/4 teaspoon grated nutmeg
1/4 teaspoon ground cloves
6 tablespoons butter

1 tablespoon sugar
3/4 cup all-purpose flour
2 eggs
1/4 teaspoon sea salt

Directions

To make the dough, boil the water in a pan over medium-high heat; now, add the sugar, salt, nutmeg, and cloves; cook until dissolved.

Add the butter and turn the heat to low. Gradually stir in the flour, whisking continuously, until the mixture forms a ball.

Remove from the heat; fold in the eggs one at a time, stirring to combine well.

Pour the mixture into a piping bag with a large star tip. Squeeze 4-inch strips of dough into the greased Air Fryer pan.

Cook at 410 degrees F for 6 minutes, working in batches. Bon appétit!

Per serving: 311 Calories; 22.3g Fat; 20.5g Carbs; 7.1g Protein

Banana Crepes with Apple Topping

(**Ready in about** 40 minutes | **Servings** 2)

Ingredients

Banana Crepes:
1/4 teaspoon baking powder
1 shot dark rum
1 teaspoon butter, melted
2 tablespoons brown sugar
Topping:
1/2 teaspoon cinnamon

1 large banana, mashed
1/2 teaspoon vanilla extract
2 eggs, beaten
2 apples, peeled, cored, and chopped
2 tablespoons sugar
3 tablespoons water

Directions

Mix all Ingredients for the banana crepes until creamy and fluffy. Let it stand for 15 to 20 minutes.

Spritz the Air Fryer baking pan with cooking spray. Pour the batter into the pan using a measuring cup.

Cook at 230 degrees F for 4 to 5 minutes or until golden brown. Repeat with the remaining batter.

To make the pancake topping, place all Ingredients in a heavy-bottomed skillet over medium heat. Cook for 10 minutes, stirring occasionally. Spoon on top of the banana crepes and enjoy!

Per serving: 367 Calories; 12.1g Fat; 57.7g Carbs; 10.2g Protein

Apricot and Walnut Crumble

(**Ready in about** 40 minutes | **Servings** 8)

Ingredients

2 pounds apricots, pitted and sliced
Topping:
1/2 cup brown sugar
2 tablespoons agave nectar
1/2 teaspoon ground cardamom
1 stick butter, cut into pieces
1/2 cup dried cranberries

2 tablespoons cornstarch
1 cup brown sugar
1 ½ cups old-fashioned rolled oats
1 teaspoon crystallized ginger
A pinch of salt
1/2 cup walnuts, chopped

Directions

Toss the sliced apricots with the brown sugar and cornstarch. Place in a baking pan lightly greased with nonstick cooking spray.

In a mixing dish, thoroughly combine all the topping Ingredients. Sprinkle the topping Ingredients over the apricot layer.

Bake in the preheated Air Fryer at 330 degrees F for 35 minutes. Bon appétit!

Per serving: 404 Calories; 16.4g Fat; 69.2g Carbs; 5.6g Protein

Pear Fritters with Cinnamon and Ginger

(**Ready in about** 20 minutes | **Servings** 4)

Ingredients

1 pears, peeled, cored and sliced
1 ½ cups all-purpose flour
A pinch of freshly grated nutmeg
2 eggs

1 teaspoon baking powder
A pinch of fine sea salt
1 tbsp coconut oil, melted
1/2 teaspoon ginger
1 teaspoon cinnamon
4 tablespoons milk

Directions

In a shallow bowl, combine all ingredients except the pears. Dip each pear slice in the batter until thoroughly coated.

Cook for 4 minutes at 360 degrees Fahrenheit in a preheated Air Fryer, flipping halfway through. Rep with the rest of the ingredients.

If desired, dust with powdered sugar. Good appetite!

Per serving: 333 Calories; 9.5g Fat; 52.2g Carbs; 10.5g Protein

Old-Fashioned Plum Dumplings

(**Ready in about** 40 minutes | **Servings** 4)

Ingredients

1 (14-ounce) box pie crusts
2 cups plums, pitted
2 tablespoons coconut oil
1/2 teaspoon ground cinnamon

2 tablespoons granulated sugar
1/4 teaspoon ground cardamom
1 egg white, slightly beaten

Directions

Place the pie crust on a work surface. Roll into a circle and cut into quarters.

Place 1 plum on each crust piece. Add the sugar, coconut oil, cardamom, and cinnamon. Roll up the sides into a circular shape around the plums.

Repeat with the remaining Ingredients. Brush the edges with the egg white. Place in the lightly greased Air Fryer basket.

Bake in the preheated Air Fryer at 360 degrees F for 20 minutes, flipping them halfway through the cooking time. Work in two batches, decorate and serve at room temperature. Bon appétit!

Per serving: 395 Calories; 19.2g Fat; 54.5g Carbs; 4.1g Protein

Almond Chocolate Cupcakes

(**Ready in about** 20 minutes | **Servings** 6)

Ingredients

3/4 cup self-raising flour
1 cup powdered sugar
1/4 teaspoon salt
2 ounces butter, softened
2 tablespoons almond milk
1/2 teaspoon vanilla extract

1/4 teaspoon nutmeg, preferably freshly grated
1 tablespoon cocoa powder
1 egg, whisked
1 ½ ounces dark chocolate chunks
1/2 cup almonds, chopped

Directions

In a mixing bowl, combine the flour, sugar, salt, nutmeg, and cocoa powder. Mix to combine well.

In another mixing bowl, whisk the butter, egg, almond milk, and vanilla.

Now, add the wet egg mixture to the dry Ingredients. Then, carefully fold in the chocolate chunks and almonds; gently stir to combine.

Scrape the batter mixture into muffin cups. Bake your cupcakes at 350 degrees F for 12 minutes until a toothpick comes out clean.

Decorate with chocolate sprinkles if desired. Serve and enjoy!

Per serving: 288 Calories; 14.7g Fat; 35.1g Carbs; 5.1g Protein

White Chocolate Rum Molten Cake

(**Ready in about** 20 minutes | **Servings** 4)

Ingredients

2 ½ ounces butter, at room temperature
1/2 cup powdered sugar
1/3 cup self-rising flour
1 teaspoon rum extract

2 eggs, beaten
3 ounces white chocolate
1 teaspoon vanilla extract

Directions

Begin by preheating your Air Fryer to 370 degrees F. Spritz the sides and bottom of four ramekins with cooking spray.

Melt the butter and white chocolate in a microwave-safe bowl. Mix the eggs and sugar until frothy.

Pour the butter/chocolate mixture into the egg mixture. Stir in the flour, rum extract, and vanilla extract. Mix until everything is well incorporated.

Scrape the batter into the prepared ramekins. Bake in the preheated Air Fryer for 9 to 11 minutes.

Let stand for 2 to 3 minutes. Invert on a plate while warm and serve. Bon appétit!

Per serving: 336 Calories; 19.5g Fat; 34.5g Carbs; 6.1g Protein

Summer Fruit Pie with Cinnamon Streusel

(**Ready in about** 40 minutes | **Servings** 4)

Ingredients

1 (14-ounce) box pie crusts
Filling:
1/3 cup all-purpose flour
1/2 teaspoon ground cinnamon
1/2 cup brown sugar
2 cups apricots, pitted and sliced peeled
2 cups peaches, pitted and sliced peeled Streusel:
1/3 cup cold salted butter

1/3 cup caster sugar
1/4 teaspoon ground cardamom
1 teaspoon pure vanilla extract
1 cup all-purpose flour
1 teaspoon ground cinnamon

Directions

Place the pie crust in a lightly greased pie plate.

In a mixing bowl, thoroughly combine the caster sugar, 1/3 cup of flour, cardamom, cinnamon, and vanilla extract. Add the apricots and peaches and mix until coated. Spoon into the prepared pie crust.

Make the streusel by mixing 1 cup of flour, brown sugar, and cinnamon. Cut in the cold butter and continue to mix until the mixture looks like coarse crumbs. Sprinkle over the filling.

Bake at 350 degrees F for 35 minutes or until topping is golden brown. Bon appétit!

Per serving: 582 Calories; 23.1g Fat; 86.5g Carbs; 8.5g Protein

RICE & GRAINS

Aromatic Seafood Pilaf

(**Ready in about** 45 minutes | **Servings** 2)

Ingredients

1 cup jasmine rice
1 small yellow onion, chopped
1 bay leaf
4 tablespoons cream of mushroom soup

Salt and black pepper, to taste
1 small garlic clove, finely chopped
1 teaspoon butter, melted
1/2 pound shrimp, divined and sliced

Directions

Bring 2 cups of a lightly salted water to a boil in a medium saucepan over medium-high heat. Add in the jasmine rice, turn to a simmer and cook, covered, for about 18 minutes until water is absorbed.

Let the jasmine rice stand covered for 5 to 6 minutes; fluff with a fork and transfer to a lightly greased Air Fryer safe pan.

Stir in the salt, black pepper, bay leaf, yellow onion, garlic, butter and cream of mushroom soup; stir until everything is well incorporated.

Cook the rice at 350 degrees F for about 13 minutes. Stir in the shrimp and continue to cook for a further 5 minutes.

Check the rice for softness. If necessary, cook for a few minutes more. Bon appétit!

Per serving: 481 Calories; 3.1g Fat; 81.5g Carbs; 29.9g Protein

Easy Pizza Margherita

(**Ready in about** 15 minutes | **Servings** 1)

Ingredients

6-inch dough
1 teaspoon extra-virgin olive oil Coarse
sea salt, to taste

2 tablespoons tomato sauce
2-3 fresh basil leaves
2 ounces mozzarella

Directions

Start by preheating your Air Fryer to 380 degrees F.

Stretch the dough on a pizza peel lightly dusted with flour. Spread with a layer of tomato sauce.

Add mozzarella to the crust and drizzle with olive oil. Salt to taste.

Bake in the preheated Air Fryer for 4 minutes. Rotate the baking tray and bake for a further 4 minutes. Garnish with fresh basil leaves and serve immediately. Bon appétit!

Per serving: 531 Calories; 24.1g Fat; 57.7g Carbs; 20.9g Protein

Famous Greek Tyrompiskota

(**Ready in about** 45 minutes | **Servings** 3)

Ingredients

1 cup all-purpose flour
1 teaspoon baking powder
1/2 cup halloumi cheese, grated
1 egg

1 tablespoon flaxseed meal
1/2 stick butter
1 teaspoon Greek spice blend
Salt to taste

Directions

Combine the flour, flaxseed meal, and baking powder in a mixing bowl. In a separate bowl, combine the butter, cheese, and egg. Incorporate the cheese mixture into the dry flour mixture.

Mix with your hands, then stir in the Greek spice blend; season with salt and stir again to combine thoroughly.

Form the batter into a log, wrap in cling film, and place in the refrigerator for about 30 minutes.

Using a sharp knife, cut the chilled log into thin slices. Cook your biscuits for 15 minutes in a preheated Air Fryer at 360 degrees F. Make use of batches.

Good appetite!

Per serving: 301 Calories; 18.9g Fat; 25.7g Carbs; 9.2g Protein

Bacon and Cheese Sandwich

(**Ready in about** 15 minutes | **Servings** 1)

Ingredients

2 slices whole-wheat bread
2 ounces bacon, sliced
1 tablespoon ketchup

1/2 teaspoon Dijon mustard
1 ounce cheddar cheese, sliced

Directions

Spread the ketchup and mustard on a slice of bread. Add the bacon and cheese and top with another slice of bread.

Place your sandwich in the lightly buttered Air Fryer cooking basket.

Now, bake your sandwich at 380 degrees F for 10 minutes or until the cheese has melted. Make sure to turn it over halfway through the cooking time.

Bon appétit!

Per serving: 406 Calories; 26.2g Fat; 27g Carbs; 14.2g Protein

Autumn Pear Beignets

(**Ready in about** 15 minutes | **Servings** 3)

Ingredients

1 medium-sized pear, peeled, cored and chopped
1/4 teaspoon ground cloves
1/2 teaspoon vanilla paste
5 ounces refrigerated buttermilk biscuits

2 tablespoons walnuts, ground
1/4 teaspoon ground cinnamon
2 tablespoons coconut oil, at room temperature
1/4 cup powdered sugar

Directions

In a mixing bowl, thoroughly combine the pear, sugar, walnuts, cloves, vanilla and cinnamon.

Separate the dough into 3 biscuits and then, divide each of them into 2 layers. Shape the biscuits into rounds.

Divide the pear mixture between the biscuits and roll them up. Brush the biscuits with coconut oil and transfer them to the Air Fryer cooking basket.

Cook your beignets at 330 degrees F for about 13 minutes, turning them over halfway through the cooking time. Serve with some extra powdered sugar if desired. Bon appétit!.

Per serving: 336 Calories; 17.5g Fat; 41.3g Carbs; 4.6g Protein

Festive Crescent Ring

(**Ready in about** 25 minutes | **Servings** 3)

Ingredients

1/2 (8-ounce) can crescent dough sheet
2 ounces capocollo, sliced
4 tablespoons tomato sauce
1 teaspoon dried oregano

1 ounces bacon, sliced
3 slices Colby cheese, cut half
1/3 teaspoon dried rosemary
1/2 teaspoon dried basil

Directions

Separate the crescent dough sheet into 8 triangles. Then, arrange the triangles in a sunburst pattern so it should look like the sun.

Place the cheese, bacon, capocollo and tomato sauce on the bottom of each triangle. Sprinkle with dried herbs.

Now, fold the triangle tips over the filling and tuck under the base to secure.

Bake the ring at 360 degrees F for 20 minutes until the dough is golden and the cheese has melted. Bon appétit!

Per serving: 370 Calories; 23.7g Fat; 23.6g Carbs; 15.1g Protein

Mediterranean Mini Monkey Bread

(**Ready in about** 15 minutes | **Servings** 3)

Ingredients

6 ounces refrigerated crescent rolls
1/2 cup provolone cheese, shredded
1/2 teaspoon dried basil

1/4 cup pesto sauce
1/4 cup ketchup
1/2 teaspoon dried oregano
2 cloves garlic, minced
1/2 teaspoon dried parsley flakes

Directions

Begin by preheating your Air Fryer to 350°F.

Make crescent rolls. Roll up the crescent rolls with the ingredients inside. Gently press the edges together with your fingertips to seal them.

Bake the mini monkey bread for 12 minutes, or until golden brown on top. Good appetite!

Per serving: 270 Calories; 9.5g Fat; 33.6g Carbs; 11.2g Protein

Oatmeal Pizza Cups

(**Ready in about** 25 minutes | **Servings** 3)

Ingredients

1 egg
1/2 teaspoon baking soda
1/4 teaspoon salt
2 tablespoons butter, melted
1 cup rolled oats
3 ounces mozzarella cheese, shredded

1/2 cup oat milk
1/8 teaspoon ground black pepper
3 ounces smoked ham, chopped
4 tablespoons ketchup

Directions

In a mixing bowl, beat the egg and milk until pale and frothy.

In a separate bowl, mix the rolled oats, baking soda, salt, pepper and butter; mix to combine well.

Fold in the smoked ham and mozzarella; gently stir to combine and top with ketchup.

Spoon the mixture into a lightly greased muffin tin.

Bake in the preheated Air Fryer at 330 degrees F for 20 minutes until a toothpick inserted comes out clean. Bon appétit!

Per serving: 305 Calories; 15.5g Fat; 30.6g Carbs; 21.2g Protein

Traditional Italian Arancini

(**Ready in about** 35 minutes | **Servings** 3)

Ingredients

3 cups vegetable broth
1 ounce Ricotta cheese, at room temperature
1 large egg
1 tablespoon fresh cilantro, chopped

2 ounces Colby cheese, grated
Sea salt and ground black pepper, to taste
1 cup white rice
1/2 cup Italian seasoned breadcrumbs

Directions

Bring the vegetable broth to a boil in a saucepan over medium-high heat. Stir in the rice and reduce the heat to simmer; cook about 20 minutes.

Add in the cheese and cilantro. Season with salt and pepper and shape the mixture into bite-sized balls.

Beat the egg in a shallow bowl; in another shallow bowl, place the seasoned breadcrumbs.

Dip each rice ball into the beaten egg, then, roll in the seasoned breadcrumbs, gently pressing to coat well.

Bake the rice balls in the preheated Air Fryer at 350 degrees F for about 10 minutes, shaking the basket halfway through the cooking time to ensure even browning. Bon appétit!

Per serving: 365 Calories; 9.5g Fat; 56g Carbs; 12.6g Protein

Basic Air Grilled Granola

(**Ready in about** 20 minutes | **Servings** 3)

Ingredients

1 cup rolled oats
1/4 teaspoon ground cinnamon
1/4 cup walnuts, chopped
1 tablespoon honey

A pinch of grated nutmeg
1 tablespoon coconut oil
A pinch of salt
1 tablespoon sunflower seeds
1 tablespoon pumpkin seeds

Directions

In a mixing bowl, thoroughly combine the rolled oats, salt, nutmeg, cinnamon, honey and coconut oil.

Spread the mixture into an Air Fryer baking pan and bake at 330 degrees F for about 15 minutes.

Stir in the walnuts, sunflower seeds and pumpkin seeds. Continue to cook for a further 5 minutes.

Store your granola in an airtight container for up to 2 weeks. Enjoy!

Per serving: 255 Calories; 14.3g Fat; 26.2g Carbs; 7.1g Protein

Fluffy Pancake Cups with Sultanas

(**Ready in about** 30 minutes | **Servings** 3)

Ingredients

1/2 cup all-purpose flour
1/2 cup coconut flour
1/3 cup coconut milk
1/2 teaspoon vanilla
1/4 teaspoon cardamom

1 tablespoon dark rum
2 eggs
1/3 cup carbonated water
1/2 cup Sultanas, soaked for 15 minutes

Directions

In a mixing bowl, thoroughly combine the dry Ingredients; in another bowl, mix the wet Ingredients.

Then, stir the wet mixture into the dry mixture and stir again to combine well. Let the batter sit for 20 minutes in your refrigerator. Spoon the batter into a greased muffin tin.

Bake the pancake cups in your Air Fryer at 330 degrees F for 6 to 7 minutes or until golden brown. Repeat with the remaining batter.

Bon appétit!

Per serving: 261 Calories; 7.7g Fat; 38g Carbs; 10g Protein

Apple Cinnamon Rolls

(**Ready in about** 20 minutes | **Servings** 4)

Ingredients

1 (10-ounces) can buttermilk biscuits
1 teaspoon cinnamon

1/4 cup powdered sugar
1 apple, cored and chopped
1 tablespoon coconut oil, melted

Directions

Line the bottom of the Air Fryer cooking basket with a parchment paper.

Separate the dough into biscuits and cut each of them into 2 layers. Mix the remaining Ingredients in a bowl.

Divide the apple/cinnamon mixture between biscuits and roll them up. Brush the biscuits with coconut oil and transfer them to the Air Fryer cooking basket.

Cook the rolls at 330 degrees F for about 13 minutes, turning them over halfway through the cooking time. Bon appétit!

Per serving: 268 Calories; 5.7g Fat; 50.1g Carbs; 5.2g Protein

Healthy Oatmeal Cups

(**Ready in about** 15 minutes | **Servings** 2)

Ingredients

1 large banana, mashed
1 tablespoon agave syrup
1 egg, well beaten
1 cup coconut milk
1 cup quick-cooking steel cut oats
3 ounces mixed berries

Directions

In a mixing bowl, thoroughly combine the banana, oats, agave syrup, beaten egg and coconut milk.

Spoon the mixture into an Air Fryer safe baking dish.

Bake in the preheated Air Fryer at 395 degrees F for about 7 minutes. Top with berries and continue to bake an additional 2 minutes.

Spoon into individual bowls and serve with a splash of coconut milk if desired. Bon appétit!

Per serving: 294 Calories; 8.5g Fat; 47.2g Carbs; 10.2g Protein

Traditional Japanese Onigiri

(**Ready in about** 30 minutes | **Servings** 3)

Ingredients

3 cups water
1 egg, beaten
1/2 cup cheddar cheese, grated
1/2 teaspoon coriander seeds
1/2 teaspoon cumin seeds
1 cup white Japanese rice
1 teaspoon dashi granules
1 tablespoon fish sauce
1/2 teaspoon kinako
1 teaspoon sesame oil
1/4 cup shallots, chopped
Sea salt, to taste

Directions

Bring the vegetable broth to a boil in a saucepan over medium-high heat. Stir in the rice and reduce the heat to simmer; cook about 20 minutes and fluff with a fork.

Mix the cooked rice with the remaining Ingredients and stir until everything is well incorporated.

Then, shape and press the mixture into triangle-shape cakes.

Bake the rice cakes in the preheated Air Fryer at 350 degrees F for about 10 minutes, turning them over halfway through the cooking time.

Serve with seasoned nori, if desired. Bon appétit!

Per serving: 374 Calories; 11.5g Fat; 53.2g Carbs; 12.2g Protein

Italian-Style Fried Polenta Slices

(**Ready in about** 35 minutes | **Servings** 3)

Ingredients

9 ounces pre-cooked polenta roll
1 teaspoon Italian seasoning blend
2 ounces prosciutto, chopped
1 teaspoon sesame oil

Directions

Cut the pre-cooked polenta roll into nine equal slices. Brush them with sesame oil on all sides. Then, transfer the polenta slices to the lightly oiled Air Fryer cooking basket.

Cook the polenta slices at 395 degrees F for about 30 minutes; then, top them with chopped prosciutto and Italian seasoning blend.

Continue to cook for another 5 minutes until cooked through. Serve with marinara sauce, if desired. Bon appétit!

Per serving: 451 Calories; 4.4g Fat; 91g Carbs; 11.2g Protein;

Last Minute German Franzbrötchen

(**Ready in about** 15 minutes | **Servings** 6)

Ingredients

6 slices white bread
1 tablespoon ground cinnamon Glaze:
1/2 teaspoon vanilla paste
1 tablespoon butter, melted
1/2 cup icing sugar
1/4 cup brown sugar
1 tablespoon milk

Directions

Flatten the bread slices to 1/4-inch thickness using a rolling pin. In a small mixing bowl, thoroughly combine the butter, brown sugar and ground cinnamon.

Spread the butter mixture on top of each slice of bread; roll them up.

Bake the rolls at 350 degrees F for 10 minutes, flipping them halfway through the cooking time.

Meanwhile, whisk the icing sugar, vanilla paste and milk until everything is well incorporated. Drizzle the glaze over the top of the slightly cooled rolls.

Let the glaze set before serving. Bon appétit!

Per serving: 157 Calories; 2.4g Fat; 30g Carbs; 3.1g Protein

Mexican-Style Bubble Loaf

(**Ready in about** 20 minutes | **Servings** 4)

Ingredients

1 (16-ounce) can flaky buttermilk biscuits

1/2 teaspoon granulated garlic
4 tablespoons olive oil, melted
1 teaspoon chili pepper flakes

1/2 cup Manchego cheese, grated

1 tablespoon fresh cilantro, chopped
1/2 teaspoon Mexican oregano
Kosher salt and ground black pepper, to taste

Directions

Open a can of biscuits and cut each biscuit into quarters. Brush each piece of biscuit with the olive oil and begin layering in a lightly greased Bundt pan.

Cover the bottom of the pan with one layer of biscuits.

Next, top the first layer with half of the cheese, spices and granulated garlic. Repeat for another layer.

Finish with a third layer of dough.

Cook your bubble loaf in the Air Fryer at 330 degrees for about 15 minutes until the cheese is bubbly. Bon appétit!

Per serving: 382 Calories; 17.5g Fat; 50.8g Carbs; 7.1g Protein

Mediterranean Monkey Bread

(**Ready in about** 20 minutes | **Servings** 6)

Ingredients

1 (16-ounce) can refrigerated buttermilk biscuits
1/4 cup black olives, pitted and chopped
4 tablespoons basil pesto
1 tablespoon Mediterranean herb mix

1 cup Provolone cheese, grated
1/4 cup pine nuts, chopped
3 tablespoons olive oil

Directions

Separate your dough into the biscuits and cut each of them in half; roll them into balls. Dip each ball into the olive oil and begin layering in a nonstick Bundt pan.

Cover the bottom of the pan with one layer of dough balls.

Prepare the coating mixtures. In a shallow bowl, place the provolone cheese and olives, add the basil pesto to a second bowl and add the pine nuts to a third bowl.

Roll the dough balls in the coating mixtures; then, arrange them in the Bundt pan so the various coatings are alternated. Top with Mediterranean herb mix

Cook the monkey bread in the Air Fryer at 320 degrees for 13 to 16 minutes. Bon appétit!

Per serving: 427 Calories; 25.4g Fat; 38.1g Carbs; 11.6g Protein

Cinnamon Breakfast Muffins

(**Ready in about** 20 minutes | **Servings** 4)

Ingredients

1 cup all-purpose flour
2 eggs
1 teaspoon cinnamon powder
1 teaspoon vanilla paste
4 tablespoons butter, melted

1 teaspoon baking powder
1 tablespoon brown sugar
1/4 cup milk

Directions

Start by preheating your Air Fryer to 330 degrees F. Now, spritz the silicone muffin tins with cooking spray.

Thoroughly combine all Ingredients in a mixing dish. Fill the muffin cups with batter.

Cook in the preheated Air Fryer approximately 13 minutes. Check with a toothpick; when the toothpick comes out clean, your muffins are done.

Place on a rack to cool slightly before removing from the muffin tins. Enjoy!

Per serving: 302 Calories; 17.1g Fat; 27.7g Carbs; 8.3g Protein

Hibachi-Style Fried Rice

(**Ready in about** 30 minutes | **Servings** 2)

Ingredients

1 ¾ cups leftover jasmine rice
2 teaspoons butter, melted
2 eggs, beaten
1 cup snow peas
1 tablespoon Shoyu sauce
1 tablespoon sake

Sea salt and freshly ground black pepper, to your liking
2 scallions, white and green parts separated, chopped
2 tablespoons Kewpie Japanese mayonnaise

Directions

Thoroughly combine the rice, butter, salt, and pepper in a baking dish.

Cook at 340 degrees F about 13 minutes, stirring halfway through the cooking time.

Pour the eggs over the rice and continue to cook about 5 minutes. Next, add the scallions and snow peas and stir to combine. Continue to cook 2 to 3 minutes longer or until everything is heated through.

Meanwhile, make the sauce by whisking the Shoyu sauce, sake, and Japanese mayonnaise in a mixing bowl.

Divide the fried rice between individual bowls and serve with the prepared sauce. Enjoy!

Per serving: 428 Calories; 13.4g Fat; 58.9g Carbs; 14.4g Protein

Basic Air Fryer Granola

(**Ready in about** 45 minutes | **Servings** 12)

Ingredients

1/2 cup rolled oats
3 tablespoons sunflower seeds
1 teaspoon coarse sea salt
1 cup walnuts, chopped
2 tablespoons honey
3 tablespoons pumpkin seeds

Directions

Combine all of the ingredients thoroughly and spread the mixture onto the Air Fryer trays. Spritz with nonstick cooking spray and set aside.

Bake at 230°F for 25 minutes, then rotate the trays and bake for another 10 to 15 minutes.

This granola will keep for up to 2 weeks in an airtight container. Enjoy

Per serving: 103 Calories; 6.8g Fat; 8.8g Carbs; 3.1g Protein;

Taco Stuffed Bread

(**Ready in about** 15 minutes | **Servings** 4)

Ingredients

1 loaf French bread
1/2 pound ground beef
1 ½ cups Queso Panela, sliced
1 onion, chopped
2 tablespoons fresh cilantro leaves, chopped
1 teaspoon garlic, minced
1 package taco seasoning
Salt and ground black pepper, to taste
3 tablespoons tomato paste

Directions

Cut the top off of the loaf of bread; remove some of the bread from the middle creating a well and reserve.

In a large skillet, cook the ground beef with the onion and garlic until the beef is no longer pink and the onion is translucent.

Add the taco seasoning, cheese, salt, black pepper, and tomato paste. Place the taco mixture into your bread.

Bake in the preheated Air Fryer at 380 degrees F for 5 minutes. Garnish with fresh cilantro leaves. Enjoy!

Per serving: 472 Calories; 21.9g Fat; 37.6g Carbs; 30.5g Protein

New York-Style Pizza

(**Ready in about** 15 minutes | **Servings** 4)

Ingredients

1 pizza dough
14 ounces mozzarella cheese, freshly grated
1 cup tomato sauce
2 ounces parmesan, freshly grated

Directions

Stretch your dough on a pizza peel lightly dusted with flour. Spread with a layer of tomato sauce.

Top with cheese. Place on the baking tray.

Bake in the preheated Air Fryer at 395 degrees F for 5 minutes. Rotate the baking tray and bake for a further 5 minutes. Serve immediately.

Per serving: 308 Calories; 4.1g Fat; 25.7g Carbs; 42.7g Protein

Favorite Cheese Biscuits

(**Ready in about** 30 minutes | **Servings** 4)

Ingredients

1 ½ cups all-purpose flour
1 teaspoon baking powder
1 teaspoon baking soda
1 cup Swiss cheese, shredded
1/3 cup butter, room temperature
1/2 cup buttermilk
2 eggs, beaten

Directions

In a mixing bowl, thoroughly combine the flour and butter. Gradually stir in the remaining Ingredients.

Divide the mixture into 12 balls.

Bake in the preheated Air Fryer at 360 degrees F for 15 minutes. Work in two batches.

Serve at room temperature. Bon appétit!

Per serving: 462 Calories; 25.8g Fat; 39.1g Carbs; 17.6g Protein

Pretzel Knots with Cumin Seeds

(**Ready in about** 25 minutes | **Servings** 6)

Ingredients

1 package crescent refrigerator rolls
2 eggs, whisked with 4 tablespoons of water
1 teaspoon cumin seeds

Directions

Roll the dough out into a rectangle. Slice the dough into 6 pieces.

Roll each piece into a log and tie each rope into a knot. Cover and let it rest for 10 minutes.

Brush the top of the pretzel knots with the egg wash; sprinkle with the cumin seeds. Arrange the pretzel knots in the lightly greased Air Fryer basket.

Bake in the preheated Air Fryer at 340 degrees for 7 minutes until golden brown. Bon appétit!

Per serving: 121 Calories; 6.5g Fat; 11.1g Carbs; 3.9g Protein

Ciabatta Bread Pudding with Walnuts

(**Ready in about** 45 minutes | **Servings** 4)

Ingredients
4 cups ciabatta bread cubes	1 cup milk
2 tablespoons butter	4 tablespoons honey
1 teaspoon vanilla extract	1/2 teaspoon ground
1/2 teaspoon ground cloves	cinnamon
2 eggs, slightly beaten	A pinch of salt
A pinch of grated nutmeg	
1/3 cup walnuts, chopped	

Directions

Place the ciabatta bread cubes in a lightly greased baking dish. In a mixing bowl, thoroughly combine the eggs, milk, butter, honey, vanilla, ground cloves, cinnamon, salt, and nutmeg.

Pour the custard over the bread cubes. Scatter the chopped walnuts over the top of your bread pudding.

Let stand for 30 minutes, occasionally pressing with a wide spatula to submerge.

Cook in the preheated Air Fryer at 370 degrees F degrees for 7 minutes; check to ensure even cooking and cook an additional 5 to 6 minutes. Bon appétit!

Per serving: 454 Calories; 18.2g Fat; 56.7g Carbs; 18.3g Protein

Sunday Glazed Cinnamon Rolls

(**Ready in about** 15 minutes | **Servings** 4)

Ingredients
1 can cinnamon rolls	1 cup powdered sugar
1 teaspoon vanilla extract	2 tablespoons butter
3 tablespoons hot water	

Directions

Place the cinnamon rolls in the Air Fryer basket.

Bake at 300 degrees F for 10 minutes, flipping them halfway through the cooking time.

Meanwhile, mix the butter, sugar, and vanilla. Pour in water, 1 tablespoon at a time, until the glaze reaches desired consistency.

Spread over the slightly cooled cinnamon rolls. Bon appétit!

Per serving: 313 Calories; 10.8g Fat; 52.9g Carbs; 2.1g Protein

Rich Couscous Salad with Goat Cheese

(**Ready in about** 45 minutes | **Servings** 4)

Ingredients
1/2 cup couscous	4 teaspoons olive oil
1/2 lemon, juiced, zested	Sea salt and freshly ground
1 tablespoon honey	black pepper, to your liking
1 red onion, thinly sliced	1/2 English cucumber, thinly
2 tomatoes, sliced	sliced
1 teaspoon ghee	2 tablespoons pine nuts
1/2 cup loosely packed Italian	2 ounces goat cheese,
parsley, finely chopped	crumbled

Directions

Put the couscous in a bowl; now, pour the boiling water over it. Cover and set aside for 5 to 8 minutes; fluff with a fork.

Place the couscous in a cake pan. Transfer the pan to the Air Fryer basket and cook at 360 digress F about 20 minutes. Make sure to stir every 5 minutes to ensure even cooking.

Meanwhile, in a small mixing bowl, whisk the olive oil, lemon juice and zest, honey, salt, and black pepper. Toss the couscous with this dressing.

Add the tomatoes, red onion, English cucumber, and goat cheese; gently stir to combine.

Rub the ghee in the pine nuts, using your hands and place them in the Air Fryer basket. Roast for 4 minutes; give the nuts a good toss. Put the cooking basket back again and roast for a further 3 to 4 minutes.

Scatter the toasted nuts over your salad and garnish with parsley. Enjoy!

Per serving: 258 Calories; 13g Fat; 28.3g Carbs; 8.8g Protein

Crème Brûlée French Toast

(**Ready in about** 10 minutes | **Servings** 2)

Ingredients
4 slices bread, about 1-inch thick	1 teaspoon ground cinnamon
A pinch of sea salt	2 tablespoons butter, softened
2 ounces brown sugar	1/2 teaspoon vanilla paste
2 ounces Neufchâtel cheese, softened	

Directions

In a mixing dish, combine the butter, cinnamon, brown sugar, vanilla, and salt. Spread the cinnamon butter on both sides of the bread slices.

Arrange in the cooking basket. Cook at 390 degrees F for 2 minutes; turn over and cook an additional 2 minutes.

Serve with softened Neufchâtel cheese on individual plates. Bon appétit!

Per serving: 407 Calories; 18.8g Fat; 51.7g Carbs; 8.3g Protein

The Best Fish Tacos Ever

(**Ready in about** 25 minutes | **Servings** 3)

Ingredients

1 tablespoon mayonnaise
1 teaspoon Dijon mustard
1 tablespoon sour cream
Sea salt, to taste
2 bell peppers, seeded and sliced
1 tablespoon water
1/4 cup parmesan cheese, grated
1 halibut fillets, cut into 1-inch strips
6 mini flour taco shells
1/2 teaspoon fresh garlic, minced
1/4 teaspoon red pepper flakes
1 egg
1 shallot, thinly sliced
1 tablespoon taco seasoning mix
1/3 cup tortilla chips, crushed
6 lime wedges, for serving

Directions

Thoroughly combine the mayonnaise, mustard, sour cream, garlic, red pepper flakes, and salt. Add the bell peppers and shallots; toss to coat well. Place in your refrigerator until ready to serve.
Line the Air Fryer basket with a piece of parchment paper.
In a shallow bowl, mix the egg, water, and taco seasoning mix.
In a separate shallow bowl, mix the crushed tortilla chips and parmesan.
Dip the fish into the egg mixture, then coat with the parmesan mixture, pressing to adhere.
Bake in the preheated Air Fryer at 380 degrees F for 13 minutes, flipping halfway through the cooking time.
Divide the creamed pepper mixture among the taco shells.
Top with the fish, and serve with lime wedges. Enjoy!

Per serving: 493 Calories; 19.2g Fat; 48.4g Carbs; 30.8g Protein

Savory Cheese and Herb Biscuits

(**Ready in about** 30 minutes | **Servings** 3)

Ingredients

1 cup self-rising flour
1/2 stick butter, melted
1/2 teaspoon honey
1/4 teaspoon kosher salt
1 teaspoon dried parsley
1/2 teaspoon baking powder
1/2 cup Colby cheese, grated
1/2 cup buttermilk
1 teaspoon dried rosemary

Directions

Preheat your Air Fryer to 360° F. Wrap a piece of parchment paper around the cooking basket.

Combine the flour, baking powder, honey, and butter in a mixing bowl. Stir in the remaining ingredients gradually.

Bake for 15 minutes in a preheated Air Fryer.

Working in batches is recommended. At room temperature, serve. Good appetite!

Per serving: 382 Calories; 22.1g Fat; 35.6g Carbs; 10.3g Protein

Puff Pastry Meat Strudel

(**Ready in about** 40 minutes | **Servings** 8)

Ingredients

1 tablespoon olive oil
1 small onion, chopped
2 garlic cloves, minced
Sea salt and ground black pepper, to taste
2 cans (8-ounces) refrigerated crescent rolls
1 egg, whisked with 1 tablespoon of water
2 tablespoons sesame seeds
2 tablespoons tomato puree
2 tablespoons matzo meal
1/3 pound ground beef
1/4 teaspoon dried marjoram
1/3 pound ground pork
1/2 cup marinara sauce
1 cup sour cream
1/2 teaspoon cayenne pepper

Directions

Heat the oil in a heavy skillet over medium flame. Sauté the onion just until soft and translucent. Add the garlic and sauté for 1 minute more.

Add the ground beef and pork and continue to cook for 3 minutes more or until the meat is no longer pink. Remove from the heat.

Add the tomato puree and matzo meal.

Roll out the puff pastry and spread the meat mixture lengthwise on the dough. Sprinkle with salt, black pepper, cayenne pepper, and marjoram.

Fold in the sides of the dough over the meat mixture. Pinch the edges to seal.

Place the strudel on the parchment lined Air Fryer basket. Brush the strudel with the egg wash; sprinkle with sesame seeds.

Bake in the preheated Air Fryer at 330 degrees F for 18 to 20 minutes or until the pastry is puffed and golden and the filling is thoroughly cooked.

Allow your strudel to rest for 5 to 10 minutes before cutting and serving. Serve with the marinara sauce and sour cream on the side. Bon appétit!

Per serving: 356 Calories; 16g Fat; 35.6g Carbs; 16.5g Protein

Paella-Style Spanish Rice

(**Ready in about** 35 minutes | **Servings** 2)

Ingredients

2 cups water
1 cube vegetable stock
1 chorizo, sliced
2 cloves garlic, finely chopped
1/2 teaspoon fresh ginger, ground
1/2 cup tomato sauce
Kosher salt and ground black pepper, to taste

1 cup white rice, rinsed and drained
2 cups brown mushrooms, cleaned and sliced
1/4 cup dry white wine
1 long red chili, minced
1 teaspoon smoked paprika
1 cup green beans

Directions

In a medium saucepan, bring the water to a boil. Add the rice and vegetable stock cube. Stir and reduce the heat. Cover and let it simmer for 20 minutes.

Then, place the chorizo, mushrooms, garlic, ginger, and red chili in the baking pan. Cook at 380 degrees F for 6 minutes, stirring periodically.

Add the prepared rice to the casserole dish. Add the remaining Ingredients and gently stir to combine.

Cook for 6 minutes, checking periodically to ensure even cooking. Serve in individual bowls and enjoy!

Per serving: 546 Calories; 12.4g Fat; 90.7g Carbs; 17.6g Protein

Beef and Wild Rice Casserole

(**Ready in about** 50 minutes | **Servings** 3)

Ingredients

3 cups beef stock
1/2 pound steak, cut into strips
1 carrot, chopped
2 garlic cloves, minced
1 chili pepper, minced

1 cup wild rice, rinsed well
1 medium-sized leek, chopped
1 tablespoon olive oil
Kosher salt and ground black pepper, to your liking

Directions

Place beef stock and rice in a saucepan over medium-high heat.

Cover and bring it to a boil. Reduce the heat and let it simmer about 40 minutes. Drain the excess liquid and reserve.

Heat the olive oil in a heavy skillet over moderate heat. Cook the steak until no longer pink; place in the lightly greased baking pan.

Add carrot, leek, garlic, chili pepper, salt, and black pepper. Stir in the reserved wild rice. Stir to combine well.

Cook in the preheated Air Fryer at 360 degrees for 9 to 10 minutes. Serve immediately and enjoy!

Per serving: 444 Calories; 13.1g Fat; 49.6g Carbs; 34.3g Protein

Baked Tortilla Chips

(**Ready in about** 15 minutes | **Servings** 3)

Ingredients

1/2 package corn tortillas
1 teaspoon salt

1/2 teaspoon chili powder
1 tablespoon canola oil

Directions

Using a cookie cutter, cut the tortillas into small rounds.

Canola oil should be applied to the rounds. Season with chilli powder and salt. Bake at 360°F for 5 minutes, shaking the basket halfway through, in a lightly greased Air Fryer basket. Working in batches, bake the chips until they are crisp.

Serve with salsa or guacamole if desired. Enjoy

Per serving: 167 Calories; 6.1g Fat; 26.4g Carbs; 3.2g Protein

Golden Cornbread Muffins

(**Ready in about** 30 minutes | **Servings** 4)

Ingredients

1/2 cup sorghum flour
1/2 cup yellow cornmeal
A pinch of grated nutmeg
1/4 cup white sugar
4 tablespoons butter, melted

2 teaspoons baking powder A
pinch of salt
2 eggs, beaten
1/2 cup milk
4 tablespoons honey

Directions

Start by preheating your Air Fryer to 370 degrees F. Then, line the muffin cups with the paper baking cups.

In a mixing bowl, combine the flour, cornmeal, sugar, baking powder, salt, and nutmeg. In a separate bowl, mix the eggs, milk, and butter.

Pour the egg mixture into the dry cornmeal mixture; mix to combine well. Pour the batter into the prepared muffin cups. Bake for 15 minutes. Rotate the pan and bake for 10 minutes more. Transfer to a wire rack to cool slightly before cutting and serving. Serve with honey and enjoy!

Per serving: 383 Calories; 18.3g Fat; 48.8g Carbs; 8.1g Protein

Cheese and Bacon Ciabatta Sandwich

(**Ready in about** 10 minutes | **Servings** 2)

Ingredients

2 ciabatta sandwich buns, split
4 slices Canadian bacon

2 teaspoons Dijon mustard
2 tablespoons butter
4 slices Monterey Jack cheese

Directions

Place the bottom halves of buns, cut sides up in the parchment lined Air Fryer basket.

Spread the butter and mustard on the buns. Top with the bacon and cheese Bake in the preheated Air Fryer at 400 degrees F for 3 minutes. Flip the sandwiches over and cook for 3 minutes longer or until the cheese has melted.

Serve with some extra ketchup or salsa sauce. Bon appétit!

Per serving: 504 Calories; 31.4g Fat; 28.5g Carbs; 26.8g Protein

Caprese Mac and Cheese

(**Ready in about** 25 minutes | **Servings** 3)

Ingredients

1/2 pound cavatappi
2 cups mozzarella cheese, grated
1/2 teaspoon Italian seasoning
2 tomatoes, sliced

1 cup cauliflower florets
Salt and ground black pepper, to taste
1 cup milk
1 tablespoon fresh basil leaves
1 cup Parmesan cheese, grated

Directions

Bring a pot of salted water to a boil over high heat; turn the heat down to medium and add the cavatappi and cauliflower.

Let it simmer about 8 minutes. Drain the cavatappi and cauliflower; place them in a lightly greased baking pan.

Add the milk and mozzarella cheese to the baking pan; gently stir to combine. Add the Italian seasoning, salt, and black pepper.

Top with the tomatoes and parmesan cheese.

Bake in the preheated Air Fryer at 360 degrees F for 15 minutes. Serve garnished with fresh basil leaves. Bon appétit!

Per serving: 587 Calories; 13.2g Fat; 69.7g Carbs; 46.5g Protein

Buckwheat and Potato Flat Bread

(**Ready in about** 20 minutes | **Servings** 4)

Ingredients

4 potatoes, medium-sized
1 cup buckwheat flour
1/2 teaspoon salt

1/2 teaspoon red chili powder
1/4 cup honey

Directions

Put the potatoes into a large saucepan; add water to cover by about 1 inch. Bring to a boil. Then, lower the heat, and let your potatoes simmer about 8 minutes until they are fork tender.

Mash the potatoes and add the flour, salt, and chili powder. Create 4 balls and flatten them with a rolling pin

Bake in the preheated Air Fryer at 390 degrees F for 6 minutes. Serve warm with honey.

Per serving: 334 Calories; 1.2g Fat; 77.3g Carbs; 8.4g Protein

Couscous and Black Bean Bowl

(**Ready in about** 35 minutes | **Servings** 4)

Ingredients

1 cup couscous
1 tablespoon fresh cilantro, chopped
1 bell pepper, sliced
1 red onion, sliced
1 teaspoon lemon juice
1 teaspoon lemon zest
4 tablespoons tahini

1 cup canned black beans, drained and rinsed
2 tomatoes, sliced
2 cups baby spinach
Sea salt and ground black pepper, to taste
1 tablespoon olive oil

Directions

Put the couscous in a bowl; pour the boiling water to cover by about 1 inch. Cover and set aside for 5 to 8 minutes; fluff with a fork.

Place the couscous in a lightly greased cake pan. Transfer the pan to the Air Fryer basket and cook at 360 digress F about 20 minutes. Make sure to stir

Per serving: 352 Calories; 12g Fat; 49.9g Carbs; 12.6g Protein;

Mediterranean Pita Pockets

(**Ready in about** 25 minutes | **Servings** 4)

Ingredients

1 teaspoon olive oil
1 onion
3/4 pound ground turkey
1 clove garlic, minced
4 small pitas Tzatziki
1/2 cucumber, peeled
1/4 teaspoon dried oregano
Sea salt, to taste

2 garlic cloves, minced
1/2 teaspoon mustard seeds
Salt and ground black pepper, to taste
1/2 cup Greek-style yogurt
2 tablespoons fresh lemon juice

Directions

Mix the olive oil, onion, garlic, turkey, salt, black pepper, and mustard seeds;

shape the mixture into four patties.

Cook in the preheated Air Fryer at 370 degrees F for 10 minutes, turning them over once or twice.

Meanwhile, mix all Ingredients for the tzatziki and place in the refrigerator until ready to use.

Warm the pita pockets in the preheated Air Fryer at 360 degrees F for 4 to 5 minutes or until thoroughly heated.

Spread the tzatziki in pita pockets and add the turkey patties. Enjoy!

Per serving: 350 Calories; 10.5g Fat; 42.1g Carbs; 24.9g Protein

Grilled Garlic and Avocado Toast

(**Ready in about** 15 minutes | **Servings** 2)

Ingredients

4 slices artisan bread
1 garlic clove, halved
2 tablespoons olive oil
1/4 teaspoon ground black pepper

1 avocado, seeded, peeled and mashed
1/2 teaspoon sea salt

Directions

Rub 1 side of each bread slice with garlic. Brush with olive oil.

Place the bread slices on the Air Fryer grill pan. Bake in the preheated Air Fryer at 400 degrees F for 3 to 4 minutes.

Slather the mashed avocado on top of the toast and season with salt and pepper. Enjoy!

Per serving: 389 Calories; 29.5g Fat; 28.8g Carbs; 5.6g Protein

Stuffed French Toast

(**Ready in about** 15 minutes | **Servings** 3)

Ingredients

6 slices of challah bread, without crusts
1 egg
1/2 teaspoon grated nutmeg
1 teaspoon ground cinnamon
1/4 cup butter, melted

3 tablespoons fig jam
1/4 cup Mascarpone cheese
4 tablespoons milk
1/2 cup brown sugar
1/2 teaspoon vanilla paste

Directions

Spread the three slices of bread with the mascarpone cheese, leaving 1/2-inch border at the edges.

Spread the three slices of bread with 1/2 tablespoon of fig jam; then, invert them onto the slices with the cheese in order to make sandwiches.

Mix the egg, milk, nutmeg, cinnamon, and vanilla in a shallow dish. Dip your sandwiches in the egg mixture.

Cook in the preheated Air Fryer at 340 degrees F for 4 minutes. Dip in the melted butter, then, roll in the brown sugar. Serve warm.

Per serving: 430 Calories; 24.1g Fat; 44.1g Carbs; 10.3g Protein

Almost Famous Four-Cheese Pizza

(**Ready in about** 15 minutes | **Servings** 4)

Ingredients

1 (11-ounce) can refrigerated thin pizza crust
1/2 cup tomato pasta sauce
1/4 cup Parmesan cheese, grated
1 cup mozzarella cheese. sliced

2 tablespoons scallions, chopped
1 tablespoon olive oil
4 slices cheddar cheese
1 cup provolone cheese, shredded

Directions

Stretch the dough on a work surface lightly dusted with flour. Spread with a layer of tomato pasta sauce.

Top with the scallions and cheese. Place on the baking tray that is previously greased with olive oil.

Bake in the preheated Air Fryer at 395 degrees F for 5 minutes. Rotate the baking tray and bake for a further 5 minutes. Serve immediately.

Per serving: 551 Calories; 34.3g Fat; 32.7g Carbs; 26.6g Protein

Crispy Pork Wontons

(**Ready in about** 20 minutes | **Servings** 3)

Ingredients

1 tablespoon olive oil
3/4 pound ground pork
1 green bell pepper, seeded and chopped
Salt and ground black pepper, to taste
6 wonton wrappers

1 red bell pepper, seeded and chopped
3 tablespoons onion, finely chopped
1 teaspoon dried thyme
1 habanero pepper, minced
1/2 teaspoon dried parsley flakes

Directions

Heat the olive oil in a heavy skillet over medium heat. Cook the ground pork, peppers, and onion until tender and fragrant or about 4 minutes.

Add the seasonings and stir to combine.

Lay a piece of the wonton wrapper on your palm; add the filling in the middle of the wrapper. Then, fold it up to form a triangle; pinch the edges to seal tight.

Place the folded wontons in the lightly greased cooking basket. Cook at 360 degrees F for 10 minutes. Work in batches and serve warm. Bon appétit!

Per serving: 296 Calories; 14.5g Fat; 21.8g Carbs; 18.3g Protein

Broccoli Bruschetta with Romano Cheese

(**Ready in about** 20 minutes | **Servings** 3)

Ingredients

6 slices of panini bread
1 teaspoon garlic puree
6 tablespoons passata di pomodoro (tomato passata)
1 cup small broccoli florets
3 tablespoons extra-virgin olive oil
1/2 cup Romano cheese, grated

Directions

Place the slices of panini bread on a flat surface.

In a small mixing bowl, combine together the garlic puree and extra-virgin olive oil. Brush one side of each bread slice with the garlic/oil mixture.

Place in the Air Fryer grill pan. Add the tomato passata, broccoli, and cheese. Cook in the preheated Air Fryer at 370 degrees F for 10 minutes. Bon appétit!

Per serving: 264 Calories; 14.2g Fat; 24.3g Carbs; 10.4g Protein

Polenta Bites with Wild Mushroom Ragout

(**Ready in about** 50 minutes | **Servings** 3)

Ingredients

2 cups water
2 tablespoons butter, melted
1 tablespoon olive oil
1/2 red onion, chopped
1/2 cup polenta
Sea salt and freshly ground black pepper, to taste
1 teaspoon cayenne pepper
1 teaspoon salt
6 ounces wild mushrooms, sliced
1/2 teaspoon fresh garlic, minced
1/2 cup dry white wine

Directions

Bring 2 cups of water and 1 teaspoon salt to a boil in a saucepan over medium-high heat. Slowly and gradually, stir in the polenta, whisking constantly.

Reduce the heat to medium-low and continue to cook for 5 to 6 minutes more. Stir in the butter and mix to combine. Pour the prepared polenta into a parchment-lined baking pan, cover and let stand for 15 to 20 minutes or until set.

In the meantime, preheat your Air Fryer to 360 degrees F. Heat the olive oil until sizzling. Then, add the mushrooms, onion, and garlic to the baking pan.

Cook for 5 minutes, stirring occasionally. Season with salt, black pepper, cayenne pepper, and wine; cook an additional 5 minutes and reserve.

Cut the polenta into 18 squares. Transfer to the lightly greased cooking basket. Cook in the preheated Air Fryer at 395 degrees F for about 8 minutes.

Top with the wild mushroom ragout and bake an additional 3 minutes. Serve warm.

Per serving: 220 Calories; 16.6g Fat; 12.4g Carbs; 6.8g Protein

Cornmeal Crusted Okra

(**Ready in about** 30 minutes | **Servings** 2)

Ingredients

3/4 cup cornmeal
1/2 teaspoon cumin seeds
Sea salt and ground black pepper, to taste
1 teaspoon cayenne pepper
1/2 pound of okra, cut into small chunks
1/4 cup parmesan cheese, grated
1 teaspoon garlic powder
2 teaspoons sesame oil

Directions

In a mixing bowl, thoroughly combine the cornmeal, parmesan, salt, black pepper, cayenne pepper, garlic powder, and cumin seeds. Stir well to combine.

Roll the okra pods over the cornmeal mixture, pressing to adhere. Drizzle with sesame oil.

Cook in the preheated Air Fryer at 370 digress F for 20 minutes, shaking the basket periodically to ensure even cooking. Bon appétit!

Per serving: 314 Calories; 10.1g Fat; 49.3g Carbs; 10.3g Protein

Tex Mex Pasta Bake

(**Ready in about** 40 minutes | **Servings** 4)

Ingredients

3/4 pound pasta noodles
1 tablespoon olive oil
3/4 pound ground beef
1 bell pepper, seeded and sliced
1 ½ cups enchilada sauce
Sea salt and cracked black pepper, to taste
1/2 teaspoon Mexican oregano
2 tablespoons fresh coriander, chopped

1 medium-sized onion, chopped
1 teaspoon fresh garlic, minced
1 jalapeno, seeded and minced
1 cup Mexican cheese blend, shredded
1/2 cup nacho chips
1/3 cup tomato paste

Directions

Boil the pasta noodles for 3 minutes less than mentioned on the package;

drain, rinse and place in the lightly greased casserole dish.

In a saucepan, heat the olive oil until sizzling. Add the ground beef and cook for 2 to 3 minutes or until slightly brown.

Now, add the onion, garlic, and peppers and continue to cook until tender and fragrant or about 2 minutes. Season with salt and black pepper.

Add the enchilada sauce to the casserole dish. Add the beef mixture and 1/2 cup of the Mexican cheese blend. Gently stir to combine.

Add the tomato paste, Mexican oregano, nacho chips, and the remaining 1/2 cup of cheese blend. Cover with foil.

Bake in the preheated Air Fryer at 350 degrees F for 20 minutes; remove the foil and bake for a further 10 to 12 minutes. Serve garnished with fresh coriander and enjoy!

Per serving: 666 Calories; 27.7g Fat; 72.2g Carbs; 42.3g Protein

Tyrolean Kaiserschmarrn (Austrian Pancakes)

(**Ready in about** 30 minutes | **Servings** 4)

Ingredients

1/2 cup flour A pinch of salt
1/2 cup whole milk
1 shot of rum
1/2 cup icing sugar

A pinch of sugar
3 eggs
4 tablespoons raisins
1/2 cup stewed plums

Directions

In a mixing bowl, combine the flour, salt, sugar, and milk until the batter is semi-solid.

Fold in the eggs, then add the rum and whisk to combine thoroughly. Allow it to stand for 20 minutes.

Coat the baking pan of the Air Fryer with cooking spray. Fill the bowl with the batter.

Using a measuring cup, pour the liquid into the pan. Sprinkle the raisins on top.

Cook for 4 to 5 minutes, or until golden brown, at 230°F. Repeat with the rest of the batter.

Cut the pancake into pieces, sprinkle with icing sugar, and serve alongside the stewed plums. Good appetite!

Per serving: 370 Calories; 5.8g Fat; 72.3g Carbs; 10.2g Protein

Alphabetical Index

Made in the USA
Monee, IL
13 May 2022